Authentic Personal Branding

A New Blueprint for Building and Aligning a Powerful Leadership Brand

Advance Praise for *Authentic Personal Branding*

"In *Authentic Personal Branding*, Hubert Rampersad has provided a sorely needed guidebook for knowledge workers. He shows us all how to build our own personal brand—and just as important—how to persuasively communicate this brand to the world. . . . I love his focus on authenticity. . . . My request to you, the reader, is—make this book part of your life. Don't just read this book for its "interesting" content. Don't be content with a few "aha" moments. Make it part of your life planning—and ultimately part of your life! If you do, you can become a more integrated and successful person—and better enable your company to help you make a positive difference in our world!"

— From the Foreword by Marshall Goldsmith

Author of *What Got You Here Won't Get You There,* a *New York Times* bestseller, *Wall Street Journal* #1 business book and the Harold Longman Award winner for Best Business Book of the Year for 2007. He is recognized by the American Management Association as one of 50 great thinkers and leaders who have impacted the field of management over the past 80 years.

"Hubert Rampersad has a knack for preparing comprehensive frameworks for analyzing important issues. . . . The four stage model that he suggests proposes an explicit way to turn a desired external identity into something concrete and actionable. . . . It's a wonderful step by step approach to making a desired brand explicit. . . . The mental models and their related investigative questions will help you know where you are today so you can get to where you want to be tomorrow. . . . This book offers an architecture to turn these ideas into action."

—From the Afterword by Dave Ulrich

Professor of Business, University of Michigan, and Partner, The RBL Group. Co-author of the bestselling book, *Leadership Brand* (Harvard Business Press, 2007). He was ranked as #1 management educator and guru by *Business Week*, #2 among management thinkers by Executive Excellence, and listed by *Forbes* as one of the "world's top five" business coaches.

"Personal Branding is not optional anymore. Your personal brand is your promise to the world. Hubert's book provides a systematic approach to enhance your personal brand and make it more powerful. Go ahead—make bigger PROMISES, fulfill them and get bigger REWARDS"

— **Rajesh Setty**, president of Foresight Plus, LLC
Author of *Beyond Code*

Authentic Personal Branding

A New Blueprint for Building and Aligning a Powerful Leadership Brand

Hubert K. Rampersad

With Foreword by Marshall Goldsmith and Afterword by Dave Ulrich

INFORMATION AGE PUBLISHING, INC.
Charlotte, NC • www.infoagepub.com

Library of Congress Cataloging-in-Publication Data

Rampersad, Hubert K.
Authentic personal branding : a new blueprint for building and aligning a powerful leadership brand / Hubert K. Rampersad ; with foreword by Marshall Goldsmith and afterword by Dave Ulrich.
p. cm.
Includes bibliographical references and index.
ISBN 978-1-60752-099-3 (pbk.) – ISBN 978-1-60752-100-6 (hardcover)
1. Branding (Marketing) 2. Identity (Philosophical concept) 3. Success in business. 4. Success. I. Title.
HF5415.1255.R36 2009
658.4'09–dc22

2009011493

Printed in the United States of America

To my wife Rita and my sons Rodney and Warren

Dream it, hope it, believe it, fix it in your mind, visualize it, accept it, respond to it with love, passion, and integrity, give your peak performance to it and you will achieve it
—Hubert Rampersad

Contents

PART 2
Authentic Company Branding

Foreword

I had the privilege of serving on the Board of the Peter Drucker Foundation (now the Leader to Leader Institute) for ten years. Peter was a pioneer in understanding the impact of *knowledge workers* in the new economy. He simply defined knowledge workers as *"people who know more about what they are doing than their boss does."* In a world where knowledge workers are the key to value in most corporations, personal brand management becomes critically important.

Professionals at all levels will need to be able to communicate their unique brand within and across organizations—and be able to communicate effectively to decision makers who may not have their level of technical expertise. One of the great ironies that I regularly encounter in the workforce, is the fact that many technically trained professionals have spent years "*honing their craft*" and developing their expertise—yet have spent almost no time in learning to communicate this expertise.

In *Authentic Personal Branding,* Dr. Hubert Rampersad has provided a sorely needed guidebook for knowledge workers. He shows us all how to build our own personal brand—and just as important—how to persuasively communicate this brand to the world.

In today's world of global competition, increasing pressure and constant communication, most professionals that I meet are working harder

---

Authentic Personal Branding, pages ix–x

than they have ever worked in their entire lives. If you are working 60–80 hours a week—not enjoying your work and not feeling psychologically connected with what you are doing—you are living in a very painful place called "*new age professional Hell.*" There are too many professionals living there today! Dr. Rampersad continually reinforces the connection between personal and professional well-being.

I love Hubert's focus on authenticity. Given the incredible expectations and demands faced by today's professionals, commitment has to be *real.* "*Faking it*" for that many hours is just too painful! Making an authentic connection between the values that we profess and the values that we live will not only make us better people, it will enable us to live happier and more productive lives.

Finally, professionals need to connect and integrate personal brand and company brand. Far too many companies have "*value statements*" on the walls that have nothing to do with the behavior of their leaders. Companies need to hire professionals whose values and behaviors are consistent with their desired brand. Professionals need to work in companies whose "lived" values and behaviors are consistent with their personal brand.

My request to you, the reader, is—make this book part of your life. Don't just read this book for its "interesting" content. Don't be content with a few "aha" moments. Make it part of your life planning—and ultimately part of your life! If you do, you can become a more integrated and successful person—and better enable your company to help you make a positive difference in our world!

Marshall Goldsmith

Author of *What Got You Here Won't Get You There,*
a *New York Times* bestseller, *Wall Street Journal* #1 business book
and the Harold Longman Award winner
for Best Business Book of the Year for 2007.

Preface

Create the highest, grandest vision possible for your life because you become what you believe.... Hold the highest vision possible for your life and it can come true... Go for your highest and greatest vision for your life and align your purpose with the flow of your life.... Follow your passion... Sooner or later, your passion is going to win out and nobody can stop you.

—Oprah Winfrey

Most buying decisions are based on trust, confidence, and the feeling of connection or emotions people have related to a product, service, or person. This is about branding. A brand is the expectations, image, and perceptions it creates in the minds of others, when they see or hear a name, product or logo. In life, as in business, branding is more effective, powerful, and sustainable than marketing and sales and an effective way to eliminate your competitors. It's about influencing others, by creating a brand identity that associates certain perceptions and feelings with that identity. Brands have become very important and powerful, which can be illustrated by the fact that we are exposed to thousands of brand messages each day and people are willing to pay much higher prices for a brand they know and trust compared to brands with which they are not familiar. So it's about time to focus on branding!

Branding isn't just for companies anymore. There is a new trend called Personal Branding. Personal Branding has become more important than Company/Corporate Branding, because we trust people more than companies and people are more accountable than companies, especially in this

Authentic Personal Branding, pages xi–xv

post-Enron era. Consequently, in this book I am focusing in more detail on Personal Branding than on Company Branding. Traditional Personal Branding works in the same way as Company Branding; communicating values, personality, and ability to its audience to produce a positive emotional response. Having a good professional reputation or brand seems to be a very important asset in today's online, virtual, and individual age. It is becoming increasingly essential and is the key to personal success. It is the positioning strategy behind the world's most successful people, like Oprah Winfrey, Tiger Woods, Michael Jordan, Donald Trump, Richard Branson and Bill Gates. It's therefore important to be your own brand and to become the CEO of your life.

Everyone has a Personal Brand but most people are not aware of this and do not manage this strategically, consistently, and effectively. You should take control of your brand and the message it sends and affect how others perceive you. This will help you to actively grow and distinguish yourself as an exceptional professional. Most traditional Personal Branding concepts focus mainly on personal marketing, image building, selling, packaging, outward appearances, promoting yourself, and becoming famous, which can turn into an ego trip and let you be perceived as egocentric and selfish. Your Personal Brand should be authentic, which means that it always should reflect your true character, and should be built on your dreams, life purpose, values, uniqueness, genius, passion, specialization, characteristics, and things what you love doing. If you are branded in this organic, authentic and holistic way your Personal Brand will be strong, distinctive, relevant, consistent, concise, meaningful, exciting, inspiring, compelling, enduring, crystal clear, persuasive and memorable. You will also create a life that is fulfilling, automatically attract the people and opportunities that are a perfect fit for you, and increase your ability to deliver peak performances.

In this book I introduce an organic, holistic and authentic Personal Branding model which will help you to unlock your potential and build a trusted image of yourself that you want to project in everything you do, which is about your true values, beliefs, dream, and genius. It will be combined with powerful tools to deliver peak performance and to create a stable basis for trustworthiness, credibility, and personal charisma. This new approach places more emphasis on understanding yourself and the needs of others, meet those needs while staying true to your values, improve yourself continuously, and realize growth in life based on this Personal Branding journey. This should be based on your life philosophy, dream, vision, mission, values, key roles, identity, self-knowledge, self-awareness, self-responsibility, positive attributes, and self-management, rather than inventing a brand that you would like to be perceived as and to sell this to others. With an authentic

Personal Brand, your strongest characteristics, attributes, and values can separate you from the crowd. Without this, you look just like everyone else.

The image of your brand is a perception held in someone else's mind. Successful Personal Branding entails managing this perception effectively and controlling and influencing how others perceive you and think of you. This book offers an advanced breakthrough formula and a new blueprint to build, implement, maintain, and cultivate an authentic, distinctive, relevant, consistent, concise, meaningful, crystal clear, and memorable Personal and Company Brand, which forms the key to enduring personal and business success. Part 1 of this book focuses on authentic Personal Branding and Part 2 on authentic Company Branding. Part 1 provides an excellent framework and roadmap for defining, formulating, implementing, maintaining, cultivating a well balanced and powerful authentic Personal Brand promise, which is in harmony with your dreams, life purpose, values, genius, passion, and with things what you love doing.

Building an authentic Personal Brand is an evolutionary and organic process and a journey towards a successful life. Your Personal Brand should emerge from your search for your identity and meaning in life, and it is about getting very clear on what you want, accepting it, fixing it in your mind, giving it all your positive energy, doing what you love and improve yourself continuously. This holistic process therefore starts with defining and formulating your Personal Ambition; it is about working out and influencing your destiny. By aligning your Personal Ambition with your Personal Brand you will fulfill your intense desires in a mystical way and will live effortlessly and become in flow. This branding framework will help you to create a brand that builds a trusted image of yourself and will help you enrich your relationships with others, master yourself, unlock your potential, and develop self-esteem. By aligning your Personal Brand with yourself you will create a stable basis for your trustworthiness, credibility, and personal charisma. Who you really are, what you care about, and were your passions lie should come out in your brand, and you should act and behave accordingly (you should be yourself) to build trust. Trust will be built faster when others believe you are real and when they witness you being true to your beliefs and aligned with who you really are. You will build trust when your values connect to your attitudes and actions and when you will be true to yourself. The result of this brand building process is a Personal Brand identity that is not fake, not cosmetic, not an ego trip, not selfish, not focused on just promoting yourself, and not a dirty business.

The proven authentic Personal Branding model entails a systematic and integrated voyage towards self-awareness, happiness, and enduring marketing success. A way of life in conformity with this system is a journey into the inner self, where your genius, values, hopes, dreams and aspirations lie quietly waiting to be discovered. The related practical tools will guide you to implement, maintain, and cultivate your brand effectively, articulate your brand with love and passion, improve your perceived value in the marketplace, become an expert in your field, and build credibility and a solid reputation within your industry. This innovative personal branding approach will allow you to view your life objectively and authentically and provides a roadmap to translate your genius, dreams and aspirations into manageable and measurable milestones and improvement actions.

This new approach has been proven in practice to produce sustainable results, not only for individuals but also for companies. In Part 2 of this book I introduce an authentic Company Branding model, which is similar to the authentic Personal Branding model, and which provides a new blueprint for

TURNING FINANCIAL CRISIS INTO OPPORTUNITY

Especially in times of financial crisis you need to be independent, become the CEO of your life and redefine yourself in order to create and attract new creative opportunities. This can be realized successfully according to the innovative four-stage authentic personal branding model introduced in this book. You can get yourself out of this crisis by rebrand and manage yourself effectively and by building, implementing and cultivating your authentic personal brand according to this model. If you are well branded according to this approach, you will master the financial crisis successfully, smartly save costs, generate new revenues, and attract the people and opportunities that are a perfect fit for you. Remember what Albert Einstein said: "In the middle of difficulty lies opportunity." Now is the best time to engage in a meaningful dialogue with yourself and build your personal brand in order to better master the financial crisis with your unique value proposition. This innovative personal branding approach will help you adjust your market offerings to the different crisis needs of various customer segments. During the crisis it is a great time to reposition yourself strongly in relation to your competitors, built a strong reputation, and become more creative and innovative. While some individuals fight for survival, this financial crisis is an excellent opportunity for visionary people who like to differentiate themselves and improve themselves continuously. They develop their own creative responses to this financial crisis instead of following the standard responses of individuals during a recession. They master the personal financial crisis because they have identified and leveraged their authentic dream, respond to it with passion and have faith in themselves and the courage to pursue their dream and personal brand.

formulating, implementing, and cultivating a sustainable, powerful, and authentic Company Brand. By aligning and synchronizing employee's authentic Personal Brand with their Company Brand you can realize the 'best fit' between employee and company. It's about aligning themselves with their company, which has an impact on the organizational bonding of employees. This book offers an effective tool to energize them and to give them the proud feeling that they count, that they are appreciated as human beings and that they make a useful and valuable contribution to the company. Employees are stimulated in this way to commit and focus on those activities which create value for clients. This approach will create a highly engaged and happy workforce and will build a strong foundation of peace and stability upon which creativity and growth can flourish, and life within the company will become a more harmonious experience. This alignment process is an opportunity to create warmth, pleasure, passion, heartfelt commitment, self-direction within the company, and motivation, which is often missed. Identification with the Company Ambition and Brand is the most important motive for employees to dedicate themselves actively to the company objectives and to maximize their potential. Doing work you love, related to your Personal and Company Brand that is interesting, exciting and provides learning opportunities has become a key performance driver. This book will guide you on this journey.

This book is also a synergistic product of the minds and efforts of many business writers and thinkers, from whom I have benefited. I am grateful for their inspiration. They deserve much of the credit here. I also would like to express my thanks to Dr. Regina Bowden who has given constructive feedback. Writing this book has been a challenge to me, as well as a learning process. A special word of thanks to my wife Rita and my sons Rodney and Warren, who inspired and stimulated me to take this challenge and to enjoy. I hope you enjoy this new authentic Personal and Company Branding concept as much as I love bringing it to you. I wish you lots of success on the road to a happier and more successful life, and on your voyage towards enhancing personal and company value. Feedback is welcome at *h.rampersad@tps-international.com*, *www.Total-Performance-Scorecard.com*, *www.personalbrandinguniversity.org*, and *www.rampersad.wordpress.com*. You may view my professional profile on LinkedIn, *www.linkedin.com/in/hubertrampersad*.

Hubert K. Rampersad
President, TPS International Inc.
Personal Branding University™, and
Personal Branding Group LLC
Miami Beach, April 2009

Author's Profile

Hubert K. Rampersad, B.S., M.Sc., Ph.D. is a leading expert on Personal and Corporate Branding, keynote speaker, and Personal Brand Coach. He is president of TPS International Inc., Personal Branding University, and Personal Branding Group (Florida, USA) and prominent author of the bestselling books *Total Performance Scorecard: Redefining Management to Achieve Performance with Integrity* (Butterworth-Heinemann Business Books, 2003) and *Personal Balanced Scorecard; The Way to Individual Happiness, Personal Integrity and Organizational Effectiveness* (Information Age Publishing Inc., 2006) which both has been translated in 20 languages. The title of his latest book is *TPS-Lean Six Sigma; Linking Human Capital to Lean Six Sigma—A New Blueprint for Creating High Performance Companies* (co-authored by Anwar El-Homsi, Information Age Publishing, 2007), translated in 15 languages. Dr. Rampersad is author of 10 other books and of more than 100 articles in leading journals. He is member of the Editorial Advisory Board of the journal *Training and Management Development Methods* (United Kingdom), member of the Editorial Advisory Board of the journal *Measuring Business Excellence* (United Kingdom), member of the Editorial Advisory Board of the *TQM Magazine* (United Kingdom), member of the Editorial Advisory Board of the *Journal of Knowledge Management Practice* in

Authentic Personal Branding, pages xvii–xix

Canada, and editorial advisor to *Singapore Management Review*. He is also a member of Marshall Goldsmith's prestigious Thought Leader Advisory Board (www.MarshallGoldsmithLibrary.com) and selected by The Marshall Goldsmith School of Management as one of the 35 distinguished thought leaders in the US in the field of leadership development. His views on happiness in life and work were published in *BusinessWeek* in June 2007. His unique Personal Balanced Scorecard coaching concept has been certified by the International Coach Federation (ICF), the world's largest coaching organization. His Total Performance Scorecard™, Personal Balanced Scorecard™, Authentic Personal Branding™, and TPS & Lean Six Sigma™ concepts are worldwide registered trademarks.

Dr. Rampersad is international crusader for individual's and company's happiness and empowerment. Energizing your personal brand is his passion. He has conducted presentations, workshops, and seminars for leading companies such as: Nokia, Philips Electronics, Lucent Technologies, and Shell Oil Company. Since 1987 he has been successful as an international management consultant guiding, coaching, and training leading organizations in the areas of his professional interest: personal & company branding, personal management, organizational behavior, organizational learning, performance management, Lean Six Sigma, organizational transformation, and leading complex change. The writing of this book has been a continuing learning process for him. If you would like to keep track of the latest developments in this field, please visit his blog *www.*rampersad.wordpress.com and his websites *www.Total-Performance-Scorecard.com* and *www.personalbrandinguniversity.org*. Dr. Rampersad can be reached at *h.rampersad@tps-international.com*. His professional profile can be viewed on LinkedIn, *www.linkedin.com/in/hubertrampersad*. For more information about his innovative management concepts, please write to:

TPS International Inc.
P.O. Box 601564
North Miami Beach
Florida 33160, USA
Phone: +1-786-537-7580
Fax: +1-714-464-4498
h.rampersad@tps-international.com
info@total-performance-scorecard.com
hubert@personalbrandinguniversity.org
www.total-performance-scorecard.com
www.rampersad.wordpress.com
www.linkedin.com/in/hubertrampersad
Skype: h.rampersad

Personal Branding University
P.O. Box 601564
North Miami Beach
Florida 33160, USA
Phone: +1-786-537-7580
Fax: +1-714-464-4498
h.rampersad@tps-international.com
www.pbuniversity.wordpress.com
www.personalbrandinguniversity.org

1

Introduction

Michael Jordan and Tiger Woods are really part of a very big advertising program, and the fact that they make so much money is because the markets have dictated that they get that money, and the fact that they endorse our products allows us to sell more products and create more jobs.

— Philip H. Knight, co-founder and former CEO of Nike

Most buying decisions are based on trust, confidence, and the feeling of connection people have related to a product, service, or person. It's the trusted relationship that counts, which often seems to be more important than performance. This is all about branding. A brand is the expectation, image, and perceptions it creates in the minds of others, when they see or hear a name, product or logo. Microsoft, Nike, Toyota, Volvo, and Coca-Cola tell us how they want others to perceive their products. These Company/Corporate Brands communicate what they want our perceptions and expectations of their products to be. Brands have become very important and powerful. This can be illustrated by the following data (McNally & Speak, 2003):

Authentic Personal Branding, pages 1–12

- The average person in North America is exposed to more than 3,000 brand messages each day.
- People are willing to pay nine to twelve percent higher prices for a brand they know and trust compared to brands with which they are not familiar.
- Coca-Cola's brand is to be worth about half the company's total market value.

Branding is more important than marketing and sales. In his book "*The Brand Called You*" (2005a) Peter Montoya points out that there is a difference between these three activities:

- *Marketing is presenting.* Creating a market by sending carefully crafted messages to the proper target audience through multiple channels creating awareness, affinity and understanding. It is planting the seed for sales by letting the customer know the product exists.
- *Sales is convincing.* Selling is using questioning tactics, listening skills, and persuasion skills to convince the audience that they can't do it without the product or service. It's how you close the deal, after your brand has done its work and branding has gotten past sales resistance.
- *Branding is influencing.* Creating a brand identity that associates certain perceptions, emotions, and feelings with that identity. Branding happens before marketing and sales. Without a strong brand, marketing is ineffective and selling is like beating your head against a wall of sales resistance.

Don't waste all the time and money you spend on marketing and sales by not maximizing your brand. It's about time to focus on branding. In life, as in business, branding is more effective, powerful, and sustainable than marketing and sales. According to Randall Hansen (2007), "Branding can be defined as a promise... a promise of the value of the product... a promise that the product is better than all the competing products... a promise that must be delivered to be successful." For example, Volvo is differentiated from other car companies by its promise of safety and security and IBM stands for dependability.

Branding isn't just for corporations anymore. There is a new trend called "Personal Branding." The reason for this is (Jane Tabachnick, 2007):

1. The technological revolution has changed the structure of careers today. It used to be that you went to work for one or two companies in your entire career. Today we will all have as many as four to eight jobs or careers in our lifetime. Personal Branding is essential to career development and an effective career tool because it helps define who you are, what do you stand for, what makes you unique, special, and different, how you are great, and why you should be sought out.
2. The change in the way we communicate. The Internet has elevated each of us to the position of publisher. Email, newsgroups, bulletin boards, blogs, and online network and discussion groups afford all of us the opportunity to learn, network and get exposure for our businesses and ourselves. People want to do business with people they know or people they feel they can trust, with whom they feel some sort of connection, and with whom they relate. If you are a familiar, friendly, and consistent presence and brand online, people will have the sense that they know you and be more receptive to doing business with you. So Personal Branding is also essential to business development.

Especially in this post-Enron era, when companies have become the symbol for greed, fraud and corruption, Personal Branding has become more important than Company Branding (Montoya, 2005b); *because we trust people more than companies, clients are looking for a personal and intimate experience with someone who will tailor service to them, people are more accountable than companies, people have more to lose than companies, and people care more than companies. So size doesn't matter.*

Being good and accomplished in your field is not enough. It's time to give serious effort to discovering your genius, passion, and your authentic dream, imagining and developing yourself as a powerful, consistent, and memorable personal with your own specific brand, as you do related work you love. Remember what Einstein said about genius: "*Intellectuals solve problems; geniuses prevent them... Any intelligent fool can make things bigger and more complex. It takes a touch of genius—and a lot of courage to move in the opposite direction.*" You can shape the market's perception of your Personal Brand by defining your unique strengths, values, and personality, sharing it with others in an exciting, persuasive manner, and cultivating your brand continuously. It's something that you can develop and manage, which is essential for future employability and success in life. Everyone has a chance and should take the responsibility to learn, improve, build up their skills and be a strong brand. It was branding guru Tom Peters (1997) who launched the Personal Branding movement with an essay published in *Fast Company* under the title "The Brand Called You." He wrote:

> Regardless of age, regardless of position, regardless of the business we happen to be in, all of us need to understand the importance of branding. We are the CEOs of our own companies: Me, Inc.... To be in business today, our most important job is to be the head marketer for the brand called "You." ... You are a brand. You are in charge of your brand... You need to think of yourself differently. You're not an "employee," you don't "belong to" any company for life, you're not defined by your job title and you're not confined by your job description.... Being CEO of Me Inc. requires you to grow yourself, to promote yourself, to get the market to reward yourself.

There is no job security. Be independent and (re)define yourself by building, implementing and cultivating your authentic Personal Brand. Become the CEO of your life as you attract and create new opportunities. According to branding guru Peter Montoya (2005b), there are three categories of business that need Personal Branding: (1) *Independent service professionals* (actors, agents, artists, athletes, authors, advisors, consultants, designers, dentists, caterers, chiropractors, real estate professionals, etc.) (2) *personal service business* (owners of gyms, auto shops, cleaners, bakeries, computer repair shops, print shops, child care, painters, gardeners, etc.) and (3) *value-adding product sellers* (auto dealers, bookstores, publishers, record stores, specialty retail, and so on.). They need a Personal Brand in order to influence key people in their domain.

Everyone has a Personal Brand but most people are not aware of this and do not manage this strategically and effectively. In Rajesh Setty's words (2006),

> Everyone has a Personal Brand, because very simply everyone makes a promise to the world—some explicitly but most implicitly... You are your biggest asset... Position yourself so that you can do things that you're passionate about. When you live your life, you live your brand. Your brand is who you really are.

You should take control of your brand and the message it sends and affect how others perceive you. This will help you to actively grow and distinguish yourself as an exceptional professional. Having a good professional reputation or brand seems to be a very important asset in today's online, virtual, and individual age. It is becoming increasingly essential and it's the key to success in life. It is the strategy behind the world's most successful people, like Oprah Winfrey, Tiger Woods, Michael Jordan, Donald Trump, Richard Branson and Bill Gates. It's therefore important to be your own brand in order to attract success just like they did.

There are many definitions of Personal Brand(ing) in the literature, such as (Peters, 1997; Hansen, 2007; Montoya, 2005a; McNally & Speak, 2003; Arruda, 2007):

- A perception or emotion maintained by somebody else about you.
- A reflection of who you are and what you believe, expressed by what you do and how you do it.
- Stimulating meaningful perceptions about the values and qualities that you stand for.
- Influencing how others perceive you.
- The value that others perceive you possess.
- The sum of the expectations and associations it creates in the minds of its target audience.
- An image of yourself that you want to project in everything you do.
- Eliminating the competition and making you unique and better than all your competition in the marketplace.

Having a strong Personal Brand has benefits. It:

- Stimulates meaningful perceptions about the values and qualities that you stand for.
- Tells others: who you are, what you do, what makes you different, how you create value for them, and what they can expect when they deal with you.
- Influences how others perceive you.
- Creates expectations in the mind of others of what they will get when they work with you.
- Creates an identity around you which makes it easier for people to remember who you are.
- Gets your prospects to see you as the only solution to their problem.
- Puts you above the competition and makes you unique and better than your competitors in the marketplace.

Most of the mentioned definitions of Personal Branding are from a personal marketing (selling) point of view and image building, which can turn into an ego trip. Personal Branding is more than just marketing and promoting yourself. The image of your Personal Brand is a perception held in someone else's mind. Successful Personal Branding entails managing this perception effectively. Your Personal Brand is the synthesis of all the expectations, images, and perceptions it creates in the minds of others, when they see or hear your name. Some examples below are related to this aspect of Personal Branding (see also Montoya, 2005a).

When we think Oprah Winfrey, we think warmth and women's empowerment.

Bill Gates brings to mind gadgets, geeks, and philanthropy.

Donald Trump is a successful real estate investor and associated with a massive ego.

JK Rowling is the professional writer behind the Harry Potter series.

Einstein is the great and gentle genius.

Mother Teresa brings to mind helping the poor and saintly behaviors.

Michael Jordan is the greatest basketball player today.

Tiger Woods is the greatest golfer in the world.

Peter Montoya (2005), author of *The Brand Called You*, believes the key to Personal Branding is knowing how you are perceived by others:

> A great Personal Brand is a Personal Brand identity that stimulates precise, meaningful perceptions in its audience about the values and qualities that a person stands for. It contains two important elements: emotional impact (your feeling about the person, confidence, trust, fascination) and consis-

tency (root the brand in the minds of the audience with repeated long-term exposure to the same brand message.

According to William Arruda, author of *Career Distinction: Stand Out by Building Your Brand* (2007):

> Personal Branding means identifying and communicating what makes you unique, relevant and compelling so that you can advance your career or business. It's a way of clarifying and communicating what makes you different and special and using those qualities to separate yourself from your peers so that you can greatly expand your success. It is about understanding your unique attributes—your strengths, skills, values, and passions—and using them to separate yourself from your competitors and guide your business decisions.

According to Thomas Gad, author of *4D Branding* (2001),

> Personal Branding is a fun and systematic way of becoming clearer and more defined as a person, not only in other people's eyes, but also in your own mind. To know "what you stand for" is not just about a philosophy of life and personal ethics, it's a practical decision tool for yourself, a way to promote your career and your potential.

Bill Lang's thinking about Personal Branding comes much closer to my authentic Personal Branding approach, namely:

> Personal branding is an image of yourself that you want to project in everything you do. It's not about being fake or superficial. If you are not authentic in what you do, that will come across. This must be about your true values, beliefs, and the service you provide to others.

I also agree with marketing consultant Kristie Tamsevicius, who stated that the underlying assumption of Personal-Branding philosophy is that each of us has unique gifts and a distinct purpose and dream in life. By connecting these gifts, purpose and dream, we open ourselves up to greater happiness and success in life (Frost, 2003). This fits very well to the holistic and authentic Personal Branding model, which I will introduce in the next Chapter. This new blueprint will help you to unlock your potential and build a trusted image of yourself that you want to project in everything you do. It is in harmony with your true values, beliefs, dreams, and genius. When your brand is combined with powerful tools, it will deliver peak performance and create a stable basis for trustworthiness, credibility, and personal charisma. This inside-out approach is durable and differs from traditional methods and is based on my passion for developing human potential. This new approach places more emphasis on understanding yourself and the needs of others. Meet those needs while staying true to your values, improve yourself continuously, and realize growth in life based on this Personal Branding journey. It focuses on the human side of branding, and includes your reputation, character and personality. If you are well branded according to this approach, you will find it easier to convince others and you will attract the people and opportunities that are a perfect fit for you.

In this book, the authentic Personal Branding process starts with determining who you are at your core authentic self. Rather than inventing a brand that you would like to be perceived as and to sell yourself to others, this one is based on your life philosophy, dreams, vision, mission, values, key roles, identity, self-knowledge, self-awareness, self-responsibility, positive attributes, and self-management. With an authentic Personal Brand, your strongest characteristics, attributes, and values can separate you from the crowd. Without this, you look just like everyone else. If you are not branded in an authentic, honest, and holistic way, if you don't deliver according to your brand promise, and if you focus mainly on selling, packaging, outward appearances, promoting yourself, and becoming famous, you will be perceived as egocentric and selfish. Remember what Albert Einstein said: *Try not to become a man of success but a man of value.*

The learning goals of this book are described in the following box.

LEARNING OBJECTIVES

After reading this book and applying its concepts, you will learn to:

- build, implement, maintain, and cultivate an authentic, distinctive, relevant, consistent, concise, meaningful, exciting, inspiring, compelling, enduring, crystal clear, ambitious, persuasive and memorable Personal Brand and Company Brand.
- create positive perceptions and emotions in the mind of your prospects (that you are different, special, unique, and authentic) based on your Personal Brand.
- build a truly lasting and trusted relationship with your clients, make an emotional connection with them, and managing their expectations and perception effectively.
- manage and influence how others perceive you and think of you.
- stimulate meaningful perceptions about the values and qualities you stand for.

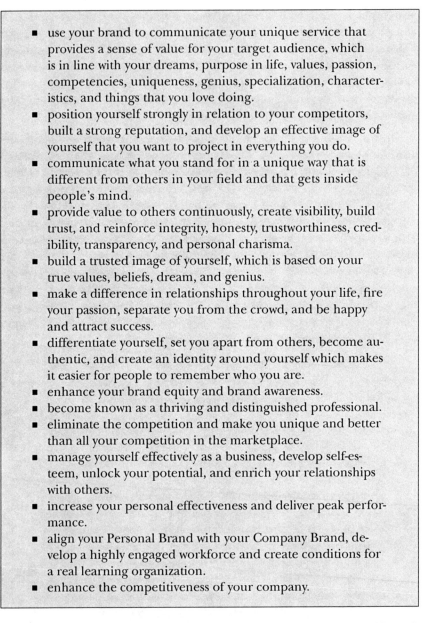

- use your brand to communicate your unique service that provides a sense of value for your target audience, which is in line with your dreams, purpose in life, values, passion, competencies, uniqueness, genius, specialization, characteristics, and things that you love doing.
- position yourself strongly in relation to your competitors, built a strong reputation, and develop an effective image of yourself that you want to project in everything you do.
- communicate what you stand for in a unique way that is different from others in your field and that gets inside people's mind.
- provide value to others continuously, create visibility, build trust, and reinforce integrity, honesty, trustworthiness, credibility, transparency, and personal charisma.
- build a trusted image of yourself, which is based on your true values, beliefs, dream, and genius.
- make a difference in relationships throughout your life, fire your passion, separate you from the crowd, and be happy and attract success.
- differentiate yourself, set you apart from others, become authentic, and create an identity around yourself which makes it easier for people to remember who you are.
- enhance your brand equity and brand awareness.
- become known as a thriving and distinguished professional.
- eliminate the competition and make you unique and better than all your competition in the marketplace.
- manage yourself effectively as a business, develop self-esteem, unlock your potential, and enrich your relationships with others.
- increase your personal effectiveness and deliver peak performance.
- align your Personal Brand with your Company Brand, develop a highly engaged workforce and create conditions for a real learning organization.
- enhance the competitiveness of your company.

This book consists of two parts. Part I focuses on authentic Personal Branding. This part is for everyone who wants to build, implement, maintain, and cultivate a strong authentic Personal Brand, separate themselves from the crowd and deliver peak performance. Part I is useful for everyone. Part II describes Company Branding and the alignment of the Personal and Company Brand. This part is for organizations that want to build, implement, maintain, and cultivate an effective authentic Company Brand and improve their competitiveness based on this. *Part I can be used separately from Part II.*

In Chapter 2, I introduce an organic, holistic and authentic Personal Branding model as start of Part I, which will help you unlock your potential and build a trusted image of yourself that you want to project in everything you do. Chapter 3 focuses on the definition and formulation of your Personal Ambition, which entails your personal vision, mission, and key roles. Without your Personal Ambition, your brand is not personal and not authentic. An integral breathing and silence exercise is introduced, which will assist you in formulating and implementing your Personal Ambition effectively and allow deep self-reflection. This chapter also explains the link to the Law of Attraction ("The Secret"). In Chapter 4, I discuss more closely, the definition and formulation of your Personal Brand. You are almost twice as likely to accomplish your brand if you write it down.

The formulation of your Personal Balanced Scorecard (PBSC) gets special attention in Chapter 5. The PBSC encompasses the related personal critical success factors, objectives, performance measures, targets, and improvement actions, which are divided into four different perspectives. Chapter 6 describes the implementation and cultivation of your Personal Ambition, Personal Brand and PBSC according to the Plan-Deploy-Act-Challenge (PDAC) cycle. This results in a step-by-step increase in happiness, enjoyment, learning, and marketing success. A way of life aligned with the PBSC and the PDAC cycle results in new challenges and the continuous development of related skills, whereby you will enjoy and love your work more and use your free time better. Your authentic Personal Branding should reflect your true self and must adhere to the moral and behavioral code set down by your Personal Ambition. In Chapter 7, I discuss the balance between your Personal Ambition/Brand and your personal behaviour and actions (alignment with yourself). It is necessary to bring both these elements in line to develop inner peace, personal charisma, and to improve personal integrity, trustworthiness and ethical behaviour.

Part II begins with Chapter 8, in which I introduce an organic, holistic and authentic Company Branding model, similar to the authentic Personal Branding model. Chapter 9 focuses on the definition and formulation of the Company Ambition, which entails the company vision, mission, and core values. In Chapter 10, I discuss the definition and formulation of the authentic Company Brand. The formulation of the Company Balanced Scorecard (CBSC) gets special attention in Chapter 11. The CBSC encompasses the related company critical success factors, objectives, performance measures, targets, and improvement actions, which are divided into four different perspectives. Chapter 12 describes the implementation and cultivation of the Company Ambition, Company Brand and Company Balanced Scorecard according to the Plan-Deploy-Act-Cultivate cycle. Chapter 13 is totally dedicated to the balance between your Personal Ambition/Brand and the Company Ambition/Brand (alignment with your company). It has to do with reaching a high degree of compatibility between personal and organization goals, and mutual value adding. To realize the 'best fit' between employee and organization, I introduce an ambition meeting between manager and employee. This will help companies to manage and use the talents within the organization effectively. The balance between Personal Ambition/Brand and Company Ambition/Brand stimulates engagement, commitment, trust, happiness, and motivation of the employees. After all, an organization is a living organism because of its people. People must be treated as people.

Appendix A includes the Personal Ambition, Personal Brand and PBSC forms needed for the exercises. In Appendix B, I introduce the Personal Brand Coaching framework and our related certification program, which is meant to be helpful for coaching yourself and others to develop and implement a sustainable and authentic Personal Brand. Appendix C describes the Personal BrandSoft. This is an on-line and interactive software system that will assist you with the formulation, implementation, and cultivation of your Personal Brand. It offers you the possibility to effectively build a sustainable, powerful, authentic, consistent, and memorable Personal Brand and manage and steer yourself on performance. Appendix D shows my strategic management system in which my Personal Ambition, Personal Brand, Personal Balanced Scorecard, and Strategic Map are included.

PART 1
Authentic Personal Branding

Customers must recognize that you stand for something.
—Howard Schultz, Chairman of Starbucks

2

An Authentic Personal Branding Model

I've come to believe that each of us has a personal calling that's as unique as a fingerprint—and that the best way to succeed is to discover what you love and then find a way to offer it to others in the form of service, working hard, and also allowing the energy of the universe to lead you.

—Oprah Winfrey

This chapter emphasizes the introduction of an organic, holistic and authentic Personal Branding model, which provides an excellent framework and roadmap to build, implement, maintain, and cultivate an authentic, distinctive, relevant, consistent, concise, meaningful, crystal clear, and memorable Personal Brand. One that is in harmony with your dreams, life purpose, values, passion, competencies, uniqueness, genius, specialization, characteristics, and things that you love doing. Authentic Personal Branding is a journey towards a happier and more successful life. Your Personal Brand should therefore emerge from your search for your identity, and

Authentic Personal Branding, pages 15–23

meaning in life, and it is about getting very clear on what you want, fixing it in your mind, giving it all your positive energy, doing what you love and develop yourself continuously. Your Personal Brand should always reflect your true character, and should be built on your values, strengths, uniqueness, and genius. If you are branded in this organic, authentic and holistic way your Personal Brand will be strong, clear, complete, and valuable to others. You will also create a life that is fulfilling and you will automatically attract the people and opportunities that are a perfect fit for you. If you are not branded in this unique way, if you don't deliver according to your brand promise, and if you focus mainly on selling and promoting yourself, you will be perceived egocentric, selfish and a unique jerk, and branding will be cosmetic and a dirty business. Remember:

no vision + no hope + no faith + no self-knowledge + no self-learning +
no thinking + no mindset change + no integrity + no happiness +
no passion + no sharing + no trust + no love
= no authentic Personal Branding

Love is an important element in this Personal Branding equation. It is about loving yourself (self-love), loving others, and loving what you do. You should love yourself in at least equal measure to others or things. This can be found in most religions: "to *love others as you love yourself*". Remember what Abraham Maslow said: "*We can only respect others when we respect ourselves. We can only give, when we give to ourselves. We can only love, when we love ourselves*". Loving yourself, others and the things you do are related to your Personal Ambition. Showing this love is related to your Personal Brand. Without knowing who you are (self-knowledge, that is part of your Personal Ambition), it's very difficult to love yourself and others. You need to make a positive emotional connection with yourself and find yourself interesting first, otherwise others will not make a positive emotional connection with you and will not find you interesting. So, first comes Personal Ambition, and then comes Personal Brand.

Sustainable, authentic, consistent, and memorable Personal Branding is related to some important criteria, which I have included in the Box 2.1. These criteria are partly based on Peter Montoya (2005a) and Rampersad (2006, 2007).

When you are branded according to these criteria and you commit yourself to act accordingly, your brand will be strong, you will distinguish yourself from the crowd, and your target audience will understand your brand much better. Building an authentic Personal Brand is a journey and an evolutionary and organic process. It starts with determining who you are at your core authentic self, which is based on your dream, vision, mission, life philosophy,

BOX 2.1
CRITERIA FOR EFFECTIVE AUTHENTIC PERSONAL BRANDING

1. *Authenticity*: be your own brand. You are the CEO of your life. Your brand must be built on your true personality. It should reflect your character, behavior, values, and vision. It should therefore be aligned with your Personal Ambition.
2. *Integrity*: you must adhere to the moral and behavioral code set down by your Personal Ambition (see Chapter 3).
3. *Consistency*: you need to be consistent in your behavior. This takes courage. Can others always depend and count on you? Are you doing relevant things again, and again, and again? For example McDonalds' hamburgers, cheeseburgers, and Big Macs are the same again, again, and again.
4. *Specialization*: focus on one area of specialization. Be precise, concentrated on a single core talent or unique skill. Being a generalist without any specialized skills, abilities, or talents will not make you unique, special, and different.
5. *Authority*: to be seen as a recognized expert in a certain field, extremely talented, highly experienced, and perceived as an effective leader.
6. *Distinctiveness*: distinguish yourself based on your brand. It needs to be expressed in a unique way that is different from the competition and needs to add value to others. It needs to be clearly defined that its audience can quickly grasp what it stands for.
7. *Relevant*: what you stand for should connect to what your target audience considers to be important.
8. *Visibility*: it must be broadcast over and over again, continuously, consistently and repeatedly, until it's embedded in the minds of the audience. It's about repetition and long term exposure.
9. *Persistence*: your brand needs time to grow. It should be developed organically. You've got to stick with it, don't give up, believe in yourself, and be patient. Great brands like Tiger Woods, Oprah Winfrey have taken years to become icons after a long period of dedicated work, sacrifice, courage, planning, and the patience to persist.
10. *Goodwill*: people do business with people they like. Your Personal Brand will produce better results and endure longer if you are perceived in a positive way. You must be associated with a value that is recognized as positive and

worthwhile. The goodwill of Bill Gates' brand is helping make the world a better place through the Bill & Melinda Gates Foundation, currently the largest transparently operated charitable foundation in the world.

11. *Performance*: performance is the most important element after your brand has become known. If you don't perform, and improve yourself continuously, Personal Branding will be a sham. Your Personal Brand should therefore be translated into your Personal Balanced Scorecard.

values, key roles, identity, self-knowledge, and self-awareness, rather than inventing a Personal Brand that doesn't reflect your true self. With an authentic Personal Brand, your strongest characteristics, attributes, and values can separate you from the crowd. Without this, you look just like everyone else.

I am including below a holistic blueprint and roadmap to help you formulating and implementing an authentic Personal Brand identity. This organic model consists of the following four phases (see Figure 2.1), which are the building blocks of a strong authentic Personal Brand:

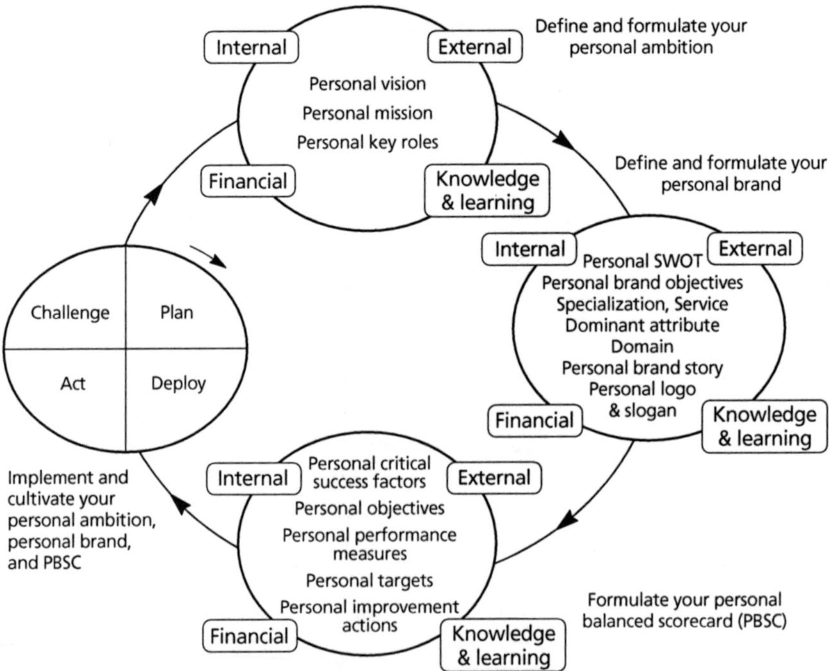

Figure 2.1 Authentic Personal Branding Model (© Hubert Rampersad).

1. Define and Formulate Your Personal Ambition

This phase involves defining and formulating your Personal Ambition in an exciting and persuasive manner and making it visible. Your Personal Ambition is the soul, starting point, core intention and the guiding principles of your Personal Brand. It's the fuel for your brand and encompasses your personal vision, mission, and key roles, related to four perspectives, that should be in balance: internal, external, knowledge & learning, and financial perspectives (see Figure 2.2). This will create balance in your brand and in your life. It is about identifying yourself and figuring out what your dreams are, who you are, what you stand for, what makes you unique and special, why you are different than anyone, what your values are, and identifying your genius, incorporating an introduced breathing and silence exercise. You are almost twice as likely to accomplish your brand if you write this down. Formulation is critical to building a strong brand. So take the time to think about your life and to write down your Personal Ambition state-

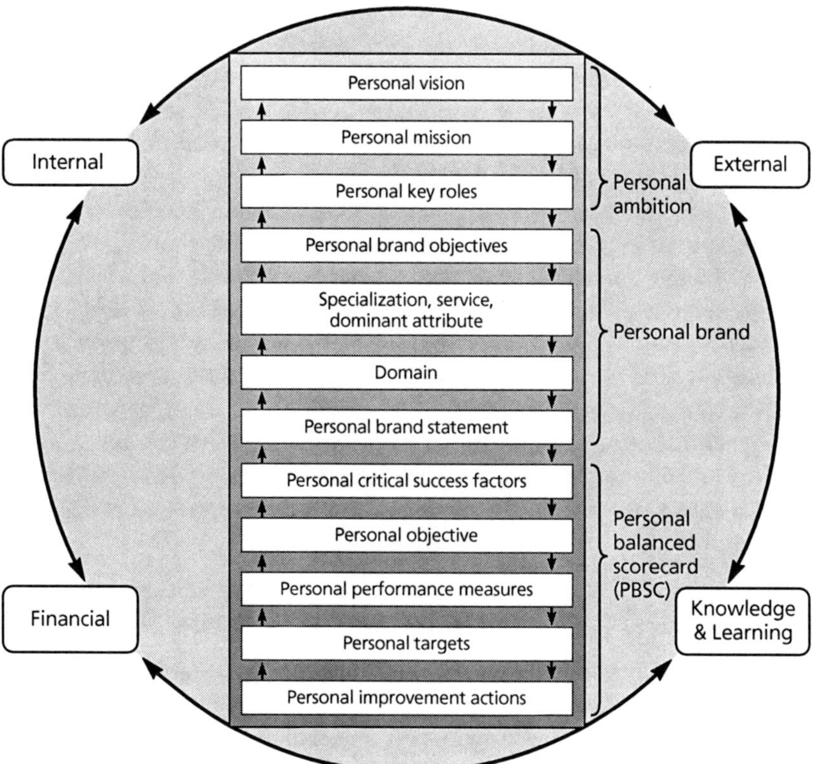

Figure 2.2 Authentic Personal Branding Framework (© Hubert Rampersad).

ment. The breathing and silence exercise that I will introduce in Chapter 3 will help you to think deeply during this soul searching process, to discover your genius, values and uniqueness, and to fix this in your mind. It will provide you life energy to translate the Personal Ambition into action. Your Personal Ambition makes your Personal Brand personal and links this to your values.

2. Define and Formulate Your Personal Brand

This phase involves defining and formulating an authentic, distinctive, relevant, consistent, concise, meaningful, exciting, inspiring, compelling, enduring, crystal clear, ambitious, persuasive and memorable Personal Brand promise, and use it as the focal point of your behavior and actions. Take the time to write down your Personal Brand statement, which is in harmony with your Personal Ambition, and create a related compelling brand story to promote the brand called You. First of all, perform a personal SWOT analysis (Strengths, Weaknesses, Opportunities and Threats) and evaluate yourself after using the breathing and silence exercise. The result of this analysis is the definition of your personal life style. This relates to your personal ambition and brand objectives. Your brand objectives entail what you want your Personal Brand to accomplish. These should also be related to the four mentioned perspectives: internal, external, knowledge & learning, and financial (see Figure 2.2). You also need to determine your specialization, concentrating on a single core talent. Define your main specific services, your key characteristics, your single leading and most powerful attribute. Finally, determine what your audience (domain) is and what their greatest needs are. Your Personal Brand Statement entails the total of your Personal Ambition, brand objectives, specialty, service dominant attribute, and domain. It also includes your Unique Value Proposition. The next step in this second stage is to define your Personal Brand Story (Elevator Pitch), which is the essence of what you want to say about your Personal Brand in order to produce a positive emotional reaction. Finally you should design your Personal Logo, which is a single graphical symbol that represents your Personal Brand.

3. Formulate Your Personal Balanced Scorecard (PBSC)

Personal Ambition and Personal Brand have no value unless you take action to make them a reality. Therefore the emphasis in this stage is developing an integrated and well balanced action plan based on your Personal Ambition and Personal Brand to reach your life and brand objectives and to eliminate any negative elements. It's about translating your Personal

Ambition and Personal Brand into your PBSC (action). Remember: vision without action is hallucination and a Personal Brand without continuous improvement of yourself based on your PBSC is merely cosmetic and will not lead to sustainable development of your potential and marketing success. Your PBSC entails your personal critical success factors that are related to your Personal Ambition and Brand and the corresponding objectives, performance measures, targets and improvement actions (see Figure 2.2). It is divided into the four perspectives: internal, external, knowledge & learning, and financial perspectives. Your PBSC translates your Personal Ambition and Personal Brand into manageable and measurable personal objectives, milestones and improvement actions in a holistic and balanced way. Your PBSC is needed to improve and manage yourself continuously based on your Personal Ambition and Brand. It's an effective tool that you can use to manage and master yourself and your brand. You can use it to develop improvement actions to achieve your objectives, keep track of your progress, record key brand information, explore your life and brand, define new career paths, build network of contacts, quantify and report your key accomplishments, etc. Your Personal Ambition and Personal Brand are related to your heart (emotions) and the right half of your brain. Your PBSC, however, is related to the left half of your brain. With the left half of your brain having mainly an analytical, logical and quantitative function. The right half of your brain has an intuitive, emotional, spiritual, and holistic function. One of the results of applying this holistic and authentic Personal Branding model along with the related introduced tools is the balance of the left and right side of your brain and the balance of your heart and head.

4. Implement and Cultivate Your Personal Ambition, Personal Brand, and Personal Balanced Scorecard

Personal Ambition, Personal Brand, and the PBSC have no value unless you implement them to make it a reality. Therefore the next step is to implement, maintain, and cultivate your ambition, brand and PBSC effectively. You have to articulate your Personal Brand with love and passion, be committed to change, and improve your perceived value in the marketplace and yourself continuously. In addition, try to build credibility and become an expert in your field. Get the word out through a variety of media channels, do work you love which is consistent with your Personal Brand and values, gain experience in areas of your brand in which you are weak, promote yourself, market your brand frequently and consistently, make conscious choices about the people you associate with, build a strong network, deliver on your brand promise, and in short live according to your brand promise. To guide you in this process I have introduced a unique learning cycle called the Plan-Deploy-Act-Challenge cycle (PDAC cycle), which should be followed continuously. This is necessary to let your brand awareness grow gradually. To live in accordance with your Personal Ambition, Personal Brand and related PBSC through its implementation using the PDAC cycle results in a journey towards self-awareness, joy, self-esteem, and happiness. Self-esteem is about how you perceive yourself and Personal Branding is about how others perceive you. Once you implement and launch your Personal Brand, remember to continue maintaining it. You need to refine your Personal Brand promise as you go along, figuring out which parts work and which don't, and make adjustments as necessary. You should continually refine your brand promise in the light of new insights, challenges, and experiences. There will always be competing brands ready to fill any gap you leave behind. The more you strengthen, maintain, protecting, and cultivate your brand, the more successful you'll be. It needs constant updating to reflect the new challenges you take, the lessons you have learned, and the growth of yourself and your brand. Repeat the PDAC cycle over and over again. If you are well branded according this authentic approach you will attract the people and opportunities that are a perfect fit for you and realize your brand and life objectives.

The effective combination of all these four tools and phases makes a strong, solid, and trusted authentic Personal Brand. This new model shows you how all Personal Branding elements fit together in a coherent and holistic whole, taking the following into account:

- Personal Ambition is the soul, starting point, core intention and the guiding principles of the Personal Brand.
- Personal Brand without Personal Ambition is not personal and not authentic.
- Personal Brand and Personal Ambition without Personal Balanced Scorecard is hallucination.
- Personal Brand, Personal Ambition, and Personal Balanced Scorecard without implementing these according to the Plan-Deploy-Act-Challenge cycle is a dirty business.
- Personal Brand, Personal Ambition, Personal Balanced Scorecard, and implementation according to the Plan-Deploy-Act-Challenge cycle is the Personal Brand Manifesto.

As we can see from Figure 2.1, the Personal Branding model consists of four wheels, which are interrelated and need to turn in the right direction in order to get the large Personal Branding wheel moving an evolving in the right direction successfully. The model gives us insight into both the way authentic Personal Branding can be developed effectively and the coherence between its different aspects. After the last phase is complete, the cycle is again followed in order to fine tune the Personal Ambition, Personal Brand, and PBSC with its surroundings on a continuous basis. By doing this you will constantly improve your brand and performance, and thus continuously satisfy yourself and others. Through this approach your customers, friends, colleagues, family and others will be satisfied continuously, and you will be able to make yourself and others happy on an ongoing basis. In the following chapters, each of the phases in the authentic Personal Branding model will be discussed in depth.

3

Define and Formulate Your Personal Ambition

The future belongs to those who believe in the beauty of their dreams.
— Eleanor Roosevelt

Everything starts with a dream. Before you can clearly define and describe an authentic Personal Brand, you need to look at the big picture. You need to start with the dream or vision of the person behind the brand. You need to define your purpose in life, values, roles in life, the meaning of your life, and what you want with your life. Remember what Washington Irving said: "Know what you want. Great minds have purposes; others have wishes." Everyone has a chance and should take the responsibility to define their dream, purpose in life, values, and key roles, build up their related brand and act accordingly. Being good and what you have accomplished is not enough. You should give serious effort to discovering your genius and authentic dream, imagining and developing yourself as a powerful, consistent, and memorable Personal Brand, and do related work you love. As stated before,

Authentic Personal Branding, pages 25–65

your Personal Ambition is the starting point, core intention and the guiding principles of your Personal Brand. It's the fuel for your brand. This soul searching process starts with defining and formulating your Personal Ambition and managing/mastering yourself first based on your dream. Without your ambition, your brand is not personal and not authentic. Defining and formulating your Personal Ambition is about working out your destiny. By accepting your destiny and aligning this with your brand you will fulfill your intense desires and become happy.

The first stage in the Personal Branding journey is primarily concerned with defining and formulating your Personal Ambition in an exciting and persuasive manner and make it visible (see Figure 3.1). Your Personal Ambition entails your dream (vision), your identity (mission) and key roles in life. Your dream is related to a *higher calling* and to your *genius*. Everyone has a higher calling, a so called *inner assignment*. We should be aware of this higher calling and must have the courage to follow it in order to be successful in life. One way to be aware of this higher calling is by listening to your inner voice through a breathing and silence exercise which I will discuss later in this chapter. Everyone has the responsibility to identify his/her own

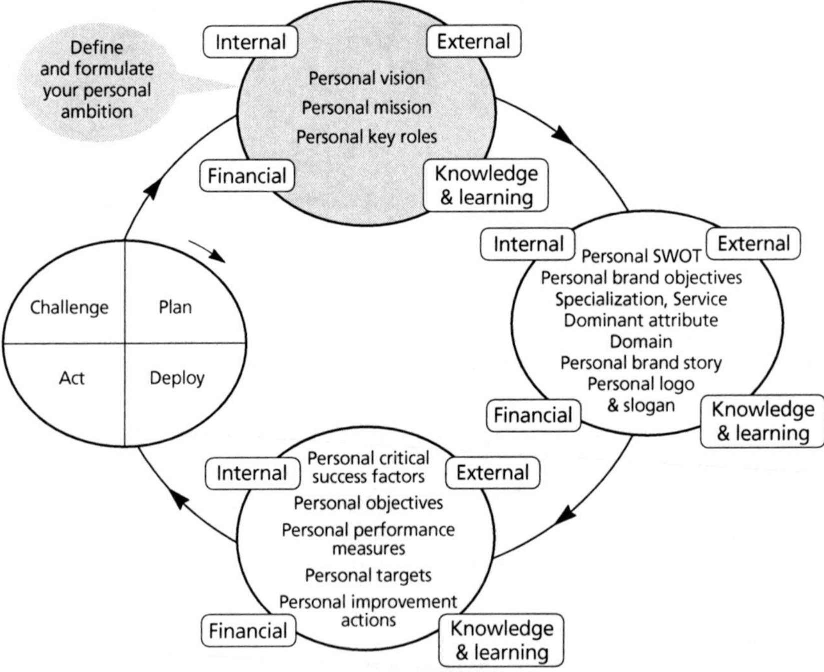

Figure 3.1 First stage in the Authentic Personal Branding Model.

dream, higher calling, and genius and to respond to it with love and passion. In this way you will become a visionary soul and will master yourself effectively. Visionary people are imaginative, idealists, innovators, and creators. They know their genius, dream, higher calling, and know what the meaning of life is. They make the world go 'round. Since everything starts with ideas, everything comes from them and begins there. Remember what George Bernard Shaw said: "*The people who get on in this world are the people who get up and look for the circumstances they want, and, if they can't find them, make them.*" You have to be able to dream outside the box. Remember what Walt Disney said: *"If you can dream it, you can do it."* Here are some individuals who defined and implemented their authentic dream successfully and whom I admire enormously.

Bill Gates's dream about 30 years ago was—A *PC on each desk in each house.* Recently he said,

> When I was 19, I saw the future and based my career on what I saw. I have been right... Personal computers have become the most empowering tool we have ever created. They are tools of communication, they are tools of creativity... and they can be shaped by their user.

One of the richest people in the world knew his genius at that time, namely developing and marketing PC software. Since then he is doing related work with love and passion. His Personal Brand started with his dream. Years ago he left Harvard, dropping out because he was too busy fulfilling his own dream to wait around for a Harvard degree. He is truly trying to make the world a better place, with his money, his brains, his Personal Brand and his connections. The Bill & Melinda Gates Foundation is currently the largest transparently operated charitable foundation in the world.

Oprah Winfrey's dream was/is—*Using television as a service to God.* This dream is the guiding principle of her brand, the emotional connection with her audience. *The* television talk-show host, born into poverty in Mississippi where she was sexually abused by a number of male relatives, is following her passion and genius that she defined about 30 years ago. Oprah has a reputation for doing good in the world and she walks her talk. She said:

> Create the highest, grandest vision possible for your life because you become what you believe.... Hold the highest vision possible for your life and it can come true... Go for your highest and greatest vision for your life and align

your purpose with the flow of your life.... Follow your passion... Sooner or later, your passion is going to win out and nobody can stop you."

JK Rowling's dream was—*To become a professional writer.* This dream was the starting point of her powerful Personal Brand. Once as a single mother living on welfare in a coldwater flat in Edinburgh, Scotland, she is the genius behind the *Harry Potter* series. As she later said: "I was very low, and I had to achieve something. Without the challenge, I would have gone stark raving mad." She is now one of the most famous writers in the world, and can financially take care of her family beyond her wildest dreams. JK is, just like Oprah, one of the richest women in the world and the only novelist among the world's wealthiest. Having reached her lifelong dream, she encourages children who want to write to read as much as they can.

Henry Ford's dream was—

> I will build a motor car for the great multitude... constructed of the best materials, by the best men to be hired, after the simplest designs that modern engineering can devise... so low in price that no man making a good salary will be unable to own one—and enjoy with his family the blessing of hours of pleasure in God's great open spaces.

This dream reflected his Personal Brand and the Ford Motor Company Brand. He was the first to introduce the assembly line in 1914, and to mass produce cars, which made them affordable for the general public. He was a technological genius who followed his passion and was the creative force behind an industry of unprecedented size and wealth that in only a few decades permanently changed the economic and social character of the United States. Henry Ford's and Oprah Winfrey's dream are good examples related to the question: "Where does God fit into this authentic Personal Branding process?"

Walt Disney's dream was—*Making life more enjoyable, and fun.* He pioneered the fields of animation, and found new ways to teach, and educate. His dream came from his unique ability (his genius) to see the entire picture and from the fond memory of the past and persistence for the future. He was a pioneer, innovator, creator, imaginative, and aesthetic person who followed his dream with passion; the possessor of one of the most fertile and unique imaginations the world has ever known. He built his brand by pursuing his dream with passion. He said: "I dream, I test my dreams against my beliefs, I dare to take risks, and I execute my vision to make those dreams come true."

Albert Einstein's dream 100 years ago was—*Understanding the universe.* His genius fundamentally changed the way we look at the universe. His dream was the guiding principle of his brand (the gentle genius). He saw the universe as a puzzle, and he delighted in trying to solve its mysteries. All he needed to contemplate the cosmos was his most valuable scientific tool—his imagination. He said: "Imagination is more important than knowledge." When somebody asked Einstein what question he would ask God if he could ask one, he replied, "Why was the universe created? Because then I would know the meaning of my own life."

Mahatma Gandhi's dream was—*Achieving freedom through the path of non-violence.* His Personal Brand reflected his life style and moral and behavioral code, set down by this dream. He was the man who played a significant role in achieving independence for India from the British Empire with his simplicity and strong willpower. Mohandas Karamchand Gandhi believed in living a simple life. He proved to the world that freedom can be achieved through the path of non-violence. Albert Einstein said of Gandhi: "Generations to come will scarcely believe that such a man in flesh and blood once trod upon this earth."

Martin Luther King, Jr.'s dream was—*Free at last.* Part of his "I Have a Dream" speech in 1964:

> I have a dream. It is a dream deeply rooted in the American dream. I have a dream that one day this nation will rise up and live out the true meaning of its creed; 'We hold these truths to be self-evident, that all men are created equal. I have a dream that one day on the red hills of Georgia, sons of former slaves and the sons of former slave-owners will be able to sit down together at the table of brotherhood . . . And so let freedom ring from the prodigious hilltops of New Hampshire . . . Let freedom ring from the mighty mountains of New York. . . . From every mountainside, let freedom ring . . . Free at last! Free at last!

His Personal Brand came from his relentless devotion to realize this dream. He once said: "Put yourself in a state of mind where you say to yourself,

'Here is an opportunity for me to celebrate like never before, my own power, my own ability to get myself to do whatever is necessary.'"

Nelson Mandela's dream was—*A free and just society in South Africa.* This dream and lifelong passion was the pillar of his Personal Brand. He made conscious choices based on what he truly stood for and got credit for his relentless commitment to his dream. Like Mahatma Gandhi and Martin Luther King, Jr., Nelson Mandela is a man of peace who is fighting against oppression. Nelson Mandela is a fighter. Instead of bowing down to the unjust Apartheid system of government, he became a lifelong warrior in the battle to free South Africa. Nelson Mandela's dream of transforming the racist society of South Africa into a multiracial democracy lasted more than 50 years. His determination to pursue that dream with passion and love, to keep fighting despite intense torments to both his people and himself, carried him to a day in May 1994 when he became the president of all South Africans.

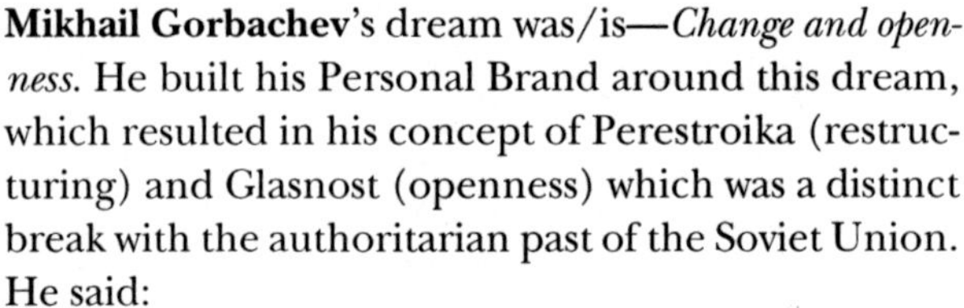

Mikhail Gorbachev's dream was/is—*Change and openness.* He built his Personal Brand around this dream, which resulted in his concept of Perestroika (restructuring) and Glasnost (openness) which was a distinct break with the authoritarian past of the Soviet Union. He said:

> We, our generation, were not associated with the repression. Moreover, we ourselves were aware of the repression, and that left its mark on us, because ours was an educated generation, a generation that knew its own value, and was capable of thinking for itself. When we found ourselves active participants in life, in work, and in politics, we began to see a great deal and see it clearly. Little by little there came the awareness that in this country, this society, this system, no matter how hard we tried, no matter how sincere our convictions were, very little good could be achieved. Therefore the system had to be changed.

Barack Obama's dream is—*Bring about real change, change that we can believe in.* His passion for change is the pillar of his Personal Brand. Parts of his speeches:

> America is a land of big dreamers and big hopes. It is this hope that has sustained us through revolution and civil war, depression and world war, a struggle for civil and social rights and the brink of nuclear crisis. And it is because our dreamers dreamed that we have emerged from each challenge more united, more prosperous, and more admired than

> before.... The true test of the American ideal is whether we're able to recognize our failings and then rise together to meet the challenges of our time. Whether we allow ourselves to be shaped by events and history, or whether we act to shape them. Whether chance of birth or circumstance decides life's big winners and losers, or whether we build a community where, at the very least, everyone has a chance to work hard, get ahead, and reach their dreams.... Change will not come if we wait for some other person or some other time. We are the ones we've been waiting for. We are the change that we seek.... I don't want to settle for anything less than real change, fundamental change—change we need—change that we can believe in. It's change that I've been fighting for over two decades ago. Because those dreams—American dreams—are worth fighting for.

They all (Bill Gates, Oprah Winfrey, JK Rowling, Henry Ford, Walt Disney, Albert Einstein, Mahatma Gandhi, Martin Luther King Jr., Nelson Mandela, Mikhail Gorbachev, and Barack Obama):

- identified and leveraged their authentic, relevant, meaningful, exciting, inspiring, enduring, ambitious dreams.
- responded to their dream with love and passion and added value to others.
- knew/know what made/make them unique, special, different and outstanding.
- recognized and identified their genius and expanded their limits based on this.
- succeeded by living according to their dream and doing related work they love(d).
- had/have faith in themselves and the courage to pursue their dream, and based on this delivered peak performances and were/are exceptional.

Dream it, hope it, believe it, fix it in your mind, visualize it, accept it, respond to it with love, passion, and integrity, give your peak performance to it and you will achieve it.

We admire these role models because of their genius, achievements, success, and added value to others. Anyone can deliver peak performances and be successful in life, because all of us have the genius within us to do so. Success is not something that will come automatically or something that the world will define for you. It's what you define in your ambitious dream and in the way you pursue this dream. Remember what Marva Collins said:

"Success doesn't come to you . . . you go to it." You must have a dream in life, follow your heart and love what you do, if you expect exceptional success. You will surely have it, since people who ask for it, wish it, dream it, fix it in their mind, visualize it, feel it, allow it, give your peak performance to it, respond to it with love, passion and integrity, attract success. The discussed role models have proven that if someone has a clear authentic dream, responds to it with love and passion, has the courage to pursue this dream, has faith in him/herself, and lives according to their dream, this dream will guide that person's life and will result in purposeful and resolute actions. Our heroes took the responsibility to identify their authentic dreams and to respond to them with love and passion. Stop complaining and do not blame others for your failures. Take the initiative and the responsibility to develop, implement, and cultivate your authentic dream as well, and keep it at the forefront of your mind each day. You should have faith in yourself. Norman Vincent Peale said: "Believe in yourself! Have faith in your abilities! Without a humble but reasonable confidence in your own powers you cannot be successful or happy."

You should conquer and engage yourself with the framework, models and tools which I provide in this book. Remember what Buddha said: "Whoever won a thousand times from thousand armies, is nothing compared to someone who conquers himself." According to Lao-tzu, effective leadership comes from self-awareness and self-conquest. He said: "He who knows other men is discerning; he who knows himself is intelligent. He who overcomes others is strong; he who overcomes himself is mighty."

Almost anyone can deliver peak performances, even people who were traumatized in their youth—like Thomas Edison, a sickly child, who was considered mentally challenged by his teacher; Eleanor Roosevelt, who was considered a lonely, neurotic girl; and Albert Einstein, whose early years were marked with fear and disappointment. All these people have left a great mark on the world. As Eleanor Roosevelt said: "We gain strength, and courage, and confidence by each experience in which we really stop to look fear in the face . . . we must do that which we think we cannot."

Once you discover the core of your nature, your higher self, and know who you really are (which I call your personal mission), you will find that it is possible to make every dream come true. In Walt Disney's words, "All our dreams can come true, if we have the courage to pursue them." Henry David Thoreau said:

> If a man advances confidently in the direction of his dreams to live the life he has imagined, he will meet with a success unexpected in common hours . . . Go confidently in the direction of your dreams. Live the life you have imagined.

Ralph Waldo Emerson believed that: "Your dream is the germ from which all growth of nobleness proceeds." By discovering and formulating your higher self, you will become visionary and will find out that you have something unique to offer. Your work is to find out what that is, and to work at it with passion and love. Once you better understand who you are, what your genius and unique talents are, what you stand for, what your long-term intentions are, and what type of relationship you would like to have with others, it will be much easier to channel your energy in the right direction, to achieve a dream which is worthy of your effort.

Your dream can be thought of as a synonym for your personal vision. Personal mission is aimed at the *being (is* an articulation of what you're all about*),* and personal vision at *becoming.* Your personal vision motivates you, your personal mission inspires you and personal key roles guide your relationships with others. Your values are included in all these three elements. Personal Ambition is here defined as personal vision, mission, and key roles, which are divided into four perspectives: internal, external, knowledge & learning, and financial. A personal vision and mission statement is a bit different from a company vision/mission statement, but the fundamental principles are the same (see Rampersad, 2003, 2007). Your Personal Ambition is your personal lighthouse keeping you steadily on the course of your dream. You should formulate your Personal Ambition in an exciting and persuasive manner and make it visible. The biggest problem most people face is writing this down. You are almost twice as likely to accomplish your ambition and brand if you write it down. So formulation is critical to building a strong Personal Brand. Take the time to write it down based on your answer to some questions which I will ask you later. Before providing you the tools to define and formulate your own authentic Personal Ambition successfully, I will first discuss the importance of this first element in the Personal Branding model.

According to Stephen Covey (1993, 2004), your Personal Ambition is an individualized constitution on which your life and behaviour are based. This in turn forms the basis for determining your decisions about what you want to achieve and what the meaning of your life is. Formulating your Personal Ambition is a spiritual search for your identity and a voyage towards realizing your related dream. It includes a collection of challenges and ethical starting points that form the context for your actions. And the key to action is understanding yourself. Through your Personal Ambition and your related Personal Brand and PBSC, you can master yourself and become more proactive, more disciplined, more effective and more responsible for yourself. Your Personal Ambition and your Personal Brand allows you to express your genius, dream, intentions, identity, ideals, values, and driving force, as well as to gain more insight about yourself. This self-knowledge influences your attitude towards others as well as your emotional intelligence.

By focusing inward and thinking about our actions—as undertaken through self-examination, we learn more and more about ourselves and therefore are able to function better. We learn not only more, but also the truth about ourselves. As Thomas Huxley has said, *"Learn what is true in order to do what is right."* By formulating your Personal Ambition based on this holistic approach, you raise a mirror to yourself and strike a personal note in terms of self-examination. The changes in the thinking process and mindset which form its foundation are meant to prepare you for action, to set you in motion, and to create inner involvement for work you love. On the basis of insights acquired through this process, you become more proactive, self-assured, and you will work smarter through self-learning and self-knowledge. We become more creative as we grow more conscious of ourselves—our real character, inner processes and driving forces. The words of Galileo Galilei may also be recalled here—*"You cannot teach a man anything; you can only help him discover it in himself."* To fathom your life, or to get a better self-image and greater self-knowledge, together with challenges, your learning ability gets greater. This leads to inner harmony. The more innovative an individual wants to be, the more he/she should develop self-knowledge.

According to the holy Hindu scriptures known as the *Vedas*, personal vision is related to self-knowledge. A visionary is a person who sees or knows what others do not see or know. The Buddhist concept of vision defines *wisdom*. Wisdom signifies that one clearly sees the nature of existence and the human situation in that existence. The opposite of wisdom is *ignorance*. The Sanskrit word for ignorance is *avidya*, which means blindness. The Tibetan word for ignorance is *marig-pa*, meaning unintelligence. According to Eastern philosophy visionary people are wise (knowledgeable) and people without a personal vision are blind and ignorant (unintelligent). Such ignorance also applies to people with wrong personal visions that result in preposterous and useless deeds that create misery for themselves and others, and destroy their Personal Brand.

Self-knowledge or self-image includes self-awareness *and self-regulation*. Self-awareness is the ability to recognize and understand your strengths, weaknesses, needs, values, ambition, moods, emotions, and drives, as well as their effect on others. Self-regulation is the ability to control or redirect disruptive impulses, feelings, and moods. Self-awareness and self-regulation have an impact on self-confidence, trustworthiness, integrity, and openness to learn. It is an inner, spiritual learning process, which is related to both emotional and spiritual intelligence. This inner process starts with self-knowledge, or *knowing*. By routine application of your Personal Ambition, Personal Brand, and PBSC, self-knowledge will lead to *wisdom*. Between knowing and wisdom lies an enormous distance which can be reduced by systematic application of the authentic Personal Brand system. This will also help you to use of and balance between the left and right sides of your brain. Balance is one of the results of applying the authentic Personal Branding method along with the breathing and silence exercise and the Plan-Deploy-Act-Challenge cycle (see Chapter 6). The left half of your brain has mainly an analytical, logical and quantitative function, while the right half of your brain has an intuitive and holistic function. Many people do not have a proper balance between the left and right sides of their brain. Most people only use the left side of their brain; because of this, they miss opportunities that allow them to become more adept at using the right hemisphere of the brain and to deal with complex problems in an integrated way. Your Personal Ambition and Personal Brand relates specifically to the right side of the brain, while your Personal Balanced Scorecard has to do with the left side of your brain. Defining your Personal Ambition encourages you to start acting intuitively thus making more effective use of the right side of your brain. Research has shown that top managers who believe in their intuition and make decisions intuitively are usually the most successful. I am referring to Weston Agor (1998):

> Fully developed intuition is highly efficient—a way of knowing immediately. It is fast and accurate. Intuitive abilities will become more and more valuable during the coming period of surprises, complexities, and rapid changes. The organizations of tomorrow will require a breed of executives trained in these decision-making techniques. Successful executives tend to rely less on the fact-gathering and more on their instincts. Any time decisions must be made quickly or an issue is so complex that complete information is not available, the manager who has developed his intuition will have an advantage over those who have not. And in the rapidly changing, complex world of the future, these situations will be more and more common.

In recent years I have applied the Personal Ambition approach in various companies in many countries, and have observed that this system also has a very positive effect on the self-awareness and self-regulation of people. People with a high degree of self-awareness recognize how their feelings effect them, others, and their performance, they understand their clients, are honest, proactive, innovative, and goal oriented, speak openly, have self-confidence, and take calculated risks. People with a high degree of self-regulation are able to create an environment of trust and fairness, can master their emotions, and are action oriented, trustworthy, and very effective in leading change.

Your Personal Ambition and Personal Brand allow you to formulate your dream, key roles, purpose in life, uniqueness, and values honestly and make these available to you. Once completed, your Personal Ambition and Personal Brand impact your personal well being, and success at work and in the rest of life. It enables you to distance yourself from your mindset and to listen attentively to your inner voice. It also allows you to unlock your potential, change your behaviour, to unlearn bad habits, to let go of things, and change your future course.

I will now describe the way to define and formulate your own authentic Personal Ambition. *Your* Personal Ambition encompasses your personal vision, mission, and key roles, divided among four perspectives, see Figure 3.2. These perspectives should be in balance and are of essential importance to your self-development, personal well-being, and marketing success of your brand. They are, namely,

1. *Internal*: your physical health and mental state. How can you control these in order to create value for yourself and others?
2. *External*: relations with your customers, spouse, children, friends, manager, colleagues, and others. How do they see you?
3. *Knowledge and learning*: your skills and learning ability. How do you learn, and how can you remain successful in the future?
4. *Financial*: financial stability. To what degree are you able to fulfil your financial needs?

These four basic perspectives form an integral part of your Personal Ambition, Personal Brand and PBSC. Figure 3.2 shows the Personal Ambition framework, including the related ambition questions. Ask yourself these questions and answer them honestly.

Personal Ambition is a set of guiding principles which clearly state what your dream is, where you are going, who you are, what you stand for, what makes you unique, which key roles are you fulfilling in life, etc. and which also embodies your values. Your Personal Ambition makes your Personal Brand personal. It can be defined by the following formula:

> Personal Ambition =
> personal vision + mission + key roles (divided along the four perspectives: internal, external, knowledge & learning, and financial).

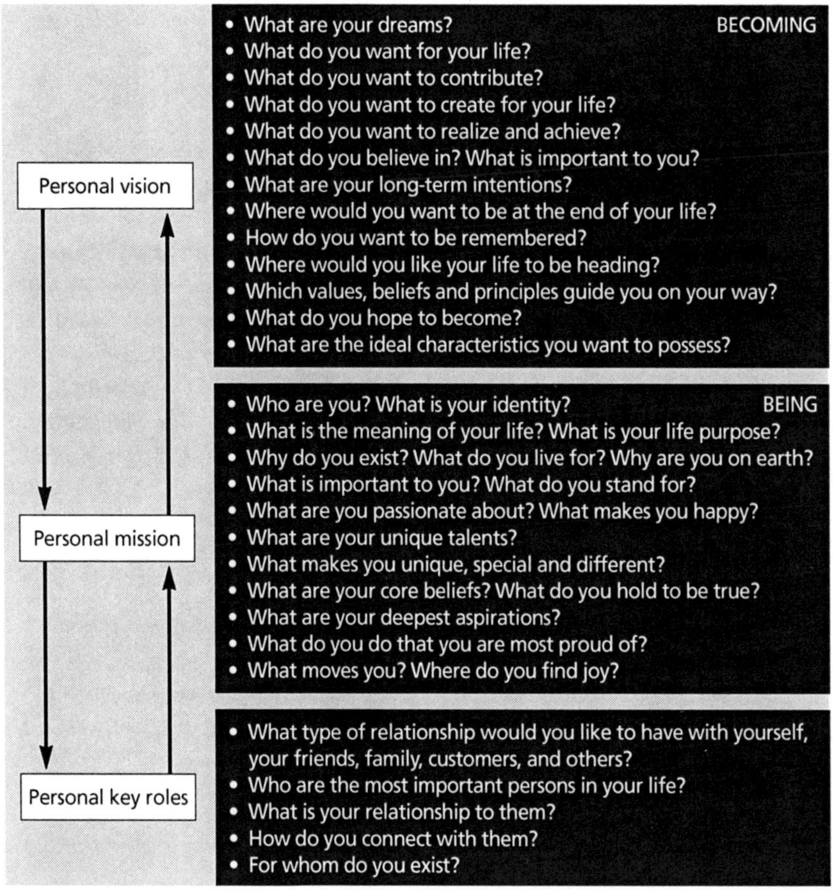

Personal vision

BECOMING

- What are your dreams?
- What do you want for your life?
- What do you want to contribute?
- What do you want to create for your life?
- What do you want to realize and achieve?
- What do you believe in? What is important to you?
- What are your long-term intentions?
- Where would you want to be at the end of your life?
- How do you want to be remembered?
- Where would you like your life to be heading?
- Which values, beliefs and principles guide you on your way?
- What do you hope to become?
- What are the ideal characteristics you want to possess?

Personal mission

BEING

- Who are you? What is your identity?
- What is the meaning of your life? What is your life purpose?
- Why do you exist? What do you live for? Why are you on earth?
- What is important to you? What do you stand for?
- What are you passionate about? What makes you happy?
- What are your unique talents?
- What makes you unique, special and different?
- What are your core beliefs? What do you hold to be true?
- What are your deepest aspirations?
- What do you do that you are most proud of?
- What moves you? Where do you find joy?

Personal key roles

- What type of relationship would you like to have with yourself, your friends, family, customers, and others?
- Who are the most important persons in your life?
- What is your relationship to them?
- How do you connect with them?
- For whom do you exist?

Figure 3.2 Personal Ambition Framework (© Hubert Rampersad).

Every element in this formula will be explained in detail below. The formulation of your Personal Ambition is most effective when it complies with the following criteria:

- Your personal vision motivates you, your personal mission inspires you, and your key roles guide your relationships.
- Your personal vision is about becoming and your personal mission about being.
- The four perspectives—financial, external, internal, and knowledge and learning—are a part of it.
- The emphasis is on unselfishness *and* authenticity.

- Your values should explicitly be included in your personal vision, mission, and key roles.
- Your Personal Ambition statement should differentiate you and direct the way you think and behave.
- Is specific to each person and includes ethical starting points, with an emphasis on your dream, uniqueness, genius, skills, principles, and values.
- Personal mission is short, clear, simple, and formulated in the present tense; it is concrete and may be used as a guideline. Keep your mission statement limited to one sentence and no more than twenty five words.
- Is unique for each person and recognizable as such to others.
- Is formulated positively, in an arresting manner, and is durable. The mission is not time-bound, while the vision is (approx. ten years).
- Personal vision is ambitious and should give direction to personal initiative and creativity, and combines personal power and energy.
- Personal mission indicates how a person wants to distinguish himself or herself in society.
- Is based on self-image, self-knowledge, self-acceptance, and self-development; it requires a positive image of ourselves and of others.
- Is based on a breathing and silence exercise.
- Is formulated and visualized as a metaphor.

The importance of this Personal Ambition development process can be illustrated by the following statement of David McNally and Karl Speak (2003):

> When someone's life is purposeless, when they exist with no vision for the future, there is no grounding for their values, no motivation to act, and nothing that inspires the desire to enrich their own lives and the lives of those who surround them. Any effort to be authentic in these circumstances, therefore, is a meaningless endeavour. On the other hand, if you belief there is a purpose to your life, that what you envision yourself contributing to the world is important, that your values have depth and substance and merit, then it's much easier to feel inspired to discover ways to become more effective. When your purpose, vision, and values are expressed as a brand people find distinctive, relevant, and consistent, you've got something the world shows no signs of ever getting enough of... Rediscovering what lights you up internally is an important part of the personal-brand-building process. It reignites your passion and makes you come alive.... Many people are born, but few people truly

live . . . Envision, work for, and fight for the freedom to choose a future that reflects the way you want to live and the life you truly want to lead. Life is never more rich, more full, or more rewarding than when you are moving faithfully and persistently toward a compelling vision. When you are purposefully creating, you become fully alive. That vitality imbues your Personal Brand with an essential energy that can make it even more viable and attractive."

In the following sections, each of the phases in the Personal Ambition framework will be discussed in depth.

Personal Vision

Your personal vision statement is a description of the way in which you want to realize your dream in the long term. It indicates where you are going, which values, beliefs and principles guide you on your way, what you want to achieve, what you want for your life, what your long-term intentions are, what talents, skills and experiences you need to add value to others, where you want to be at the end of your life, what you hope to become, where you would like your life to be headed, the ideal characteristics you want to possess, your ideal job situation, and what you want to be. Ask yourself these questions and answer them honestly. Also identify the attitudes you need to change and understand how to make your values relevant to others. Your personal vision takes care of inner guidance and determines today's actions in order to reach the most desired future. It functions as an ethical compass, which gives meaning to your life. It is a concrete translation of your inner longings, and keeps in mind the four aforementioned perspectives.

Your personal vision must result in purposeful long term actions and efforts to realize your dreams. It gives direction to your mission and efforts. A possible way to formulate your Personal Ambition is by identifying some examples where you have had personal success in recent years (in your work and private life). Ask yourself where you have added value to others, and made a difference. Write them down and identify common themes. Also develop a list of values that you believe identify who you are, and narrow these to a few of the most important values. Your values are the principles by which you live your life, which affect the way you think, feel, behave, and make decisions. It's about what you believe, what you are willing to do to achieve your brand and life objectives, what is important to you, what you hold to be true, and what you respect. Your values must be included in your personal vision, mission, and key roles. Table 3.1 shows a list of values and the related perspectives, which is adjusted from McNally & Speak (2003). According to them, there is a strong connection between understanding your most important values and making better decisions—the kind of deci-

TABLE 3.1 Identify Your Personal Values

Value Description	Not important	Very important	Internal	External	Knowledge & Learning	Financial
Achievement (results, tasks completed)				X		
Adventure (new experiences, challenge, excitement)			X		X	
Contribution (desire to make a difference, to give)				X		
Compassion (understanding of the emotional state of another)				X		
Cooperation (teamwork)				X		
Creativity (new ideas, innovation, experimenting)					X	
Economic security (freedom from financial worries)						X
Empathy (recognize, perceive and feel the emotion of another)				X		
Fairness (equal chance, equal hearing for all)				X		
Fame (desire to be well-known, recognized)				X		
Family happiness (desire to get along, harmony)			X	X		
Friendship (intimacy, caring, support)				X		
Generosity (desire to give time or money readily)				X		
Health (physical and mental fitness, energy, no disease			X			
Independence (self-reliance, freedom from controls)			X			
Influence (desire to shape ideas, people)				X		
Inner harmony (desire to be at peach with oneself)			X			
Integrity (honesty, sincerity, consistent demonstration of your values)			X			
Learning (growth, knowledge, understanding)					X	
Loyalty (duty, respect, allegiance)				X		

Nature (care for and appreciation of the environment)		X		
Personal development (improvement, reach potential)			X	
Pleasure (enjoyment, fun, happiness)	X			
Power (authority, influence over people and/or situations)		X		
Prestige (visible success, rank, status)		X		
Quality (excellence, high standards, minimal errors)		X		
Recognition (respect, acknowledgement)		X		
Responsibility (desire to be accountable, trustworthy, mature)	X			
Security (desire to feel safe about things)	X			
Service (desire to assist others, to improve society)		X		
Self respect (pride in self, feeling worthy)	X			
Spirituality (belief in a higher power or God)	X			
Stability (continuity, predictability)	X			
Sympathy (closely understanding feelings of others)	X			
Tolerance (openness to others, their views and values)		X		
Tradition (treasuring the past, customs)	X		X	
Variety (diversity of activities and experiences)			X	
Wealth (material prosperity)				X
Wisdom (desire to understand life, to exercise sound judgment)			X	
•				
•				
•				
•				

sions that help you develop more effective relationships with others. The list of values entails your Personal Code of Ethics.

I have selected the following values out of this list, which I have embedded in my Personal Ambition statement: *creativity, integrity, learning, pleasure, health, compassion, contribution, and economic security* (they are related to the four perspectives). Take a look at my Personal Vision statement below, I hope it will inspire you.

MY PERSONAL VISION

To live life completely, honestly, and compassionately and to serve the needs of mankind to the best of my ability. I want to realize this in the following way:

- Enjoy physical and mental health.
- Passionate and compassionate to inspire others, earn their respect, and always serve out of love.
- Energize innovative organizations where human spirit thrives and which model the best practices in business performance and personal integrity.
- Experience enjoyment in my work by being full of initiative, accepting challenges continuously, and to keep on learning.
- Achieve financial security.

My values and the four basic perspectives—internal, external, knowledge & learning, and financial—are clearly recognizable in my ambition statement. These perspectives must be an integral part of personal ambition in order to be able to formulate your Personal Ambition and your PBSC completely, and in order to improve yourself continuously based on your PBSC (to live a balanced life). They are identified as critical success factors and translated in my PBSC into personal objectives, performance measures, targets and improvement actions (see Chapter 5).

Personal Mission

Your personal mission is about being and giving meaning to your life. It encompasses your philosophy of life and your overall objectives, indicating who you are, the reason for your existence, why are you on earth, what you stand for, what makes you unique, special and different, what is decisive for your success, what are your unique talents, what are your overall life objectives, what is your life purpose, what do you live for, what are your core beliefs, what are your deepest aspirations, what makes you happy, how do others see you, what do you do that you are most proud of. Reflect on these questions and answer them honestly:

- What moves you?
- Where do you find joy?
- What words would others use to describe you?
- What can others depend on you for?
- Are you seen as, someone who is reliable? Or, are you seen as someone who is self-serving?
- Do you stand out among your competitors and colleagues? You need to identify what makes you unique, then stick with it, not lose sight of it, and maintain your focus.

To get an accurate picture about your mission, find out how you are introduced to others, and what your friends, families and colleagues say about you when you are not around. Define what you stand for within your chosen field, and define in your vision where you want to go and how you want to get there. Define what is unique about you, what your purpose in life and main objectives are and what makes you different. How do others perceive your values? What do others gladly pay you to do? This takes a bit of thinking and self-knowledge. To help you do that, I am including the breathing and silence exercise in this Chapter to help you think deeply and to get energy to formulate and implement your Personal Brand successfully. Reflect on how to distinguish yourself from others and figure out what it takes to create a distinctive role for yourself. Identify the characteristics that make you distinctive from others. According to Tom Peters (1997):

> Forget your job title. Ask yourself: What do I do that adds remarkable, measurable, distinguished, distinctive value? Forget your job description. Ask yourself: What do I do that I am most proud of? Ask yourself: What have I accomplished that I can unabashedly brag about? If you're going to be a brand, you've got to become relentlessly focused on what you do that adds value, that you're proud of, and most important, that you can shamelessly take credit for. Ask yourself: What turns me on? Learning something new? Gaining recognition for my skills? What's my personal definition of success? Money? Power? Fame? Or doing what you love?

These questions seem easy, but are are difficult to answer and yet are central to your sense of self. Imagine stepping outside of your physical body, taking a look at the real you, and asking yourself some of the above mentioned questions. Listen carefully to the answers of your inner voice. "Who am I?" is an identity question. It initiates a self-examination of your *personal identity* (the unique position you find yourself in) and a voyage of discovery. As Socrates, said—"The unstudied life is not worth to be lived," and "If you live without studying life, it is not worth calling it life."

This process is closely related to *spirituality*. Spirituality is the manifestation of the perfection that is already present in you. It means realizing your inner essence. Religion is something external to you, whereas spirituality is something that is within you. Spirituality is needed in the modern world of business because it provides greater intuition in making tough decisions. One of Deepak Chopra's (1995) spiritual laws of success is the law of the *Dharma*. Dharma is a Sanskrit word, which can be translated as "goal in life". This law has the following three components:

- You are on this earth to discover your real "me," to find out that your real "me" is spiritual. This lies beyond your ego. Go look for it.
- You possess unique talents, which no one else has. Discover them.
- Use these talents to serve mankind.

Bill George (Medtronic Inc.) has this to say about ego:

> One of the things you have to do is to find a way to get egos out of the way, and it has to start with the CEO. People at the top of every large organization have strong egos. That's not just true of business. It exists in Congress, medicine, law.

According to Gary Jacobs (1998):

> There is a direct correspondence between man's inner life of thoughts, feelings and impulses—his consciousness—and the circumstances and events in this outer environment. The external situation is an extension of his inner consciousness expressed in outer life... Man's ego acts as a knot dividing the individual from the world around, the inner from the outer... The higher, less selfish, personal and egoistic one's motivation, the more he grows, and the more he receives.

Mahatma Gandhi once said that the ego should be at zero to be able to find inner freedom.

Your personal vision and mission have to do with your inner freedom, need and motives, as well as your self-awareness, imagination, conscience, and your priorities in life. Through your conscience you realize what your principles are, which can be effectively rendered through your talents.

Thus, you will be able to give direction to your life and create your future through your vision and mission. Remember what Peter Drucker said: "The best way to predict the future is to create it." Your Personal Ambition needs to be formulated in such a way that you will be stimulated to reflect on your life and on everything you undertake. Take a look at my Personal Mission statement below; it differentiates me. The more unique I can make myself based on this, the stronger my Personal Brand will be (see Chapter 4).

MY PERSONAL MISSION

Enjoy the freedom to develop and share knowledge, especially if this can mean something in the lives of others.

OTHER EXAMPLES OF PERSONAL MISSION STATEMENTS

- To create a world of love and empowerment, by loving and empowering others and myself.
- To be authentic and gracious, creating joy and deeper meaning in others' lives based on my uniqueness.
- To serve mankind as an ambassador of God by demonstrating how to perpetuate goodness and elevate the souls of all with whom I might interact.
- To serve the needs of mankind to the best of my ability by helping to build strong, viable organizations and guiding people to healthful and joyful living.

Personal Key Roles

In order to build a strong Personal Ambition and Personal Brand you should identify the key relationships you plan to have with people who truly matter to you. These relationships are related to the essential roles in your life that you want to fulfil. The key roles indicate what type of trustworthy relationships you would like to have with your life companion, children, friends, customers, employer, co-workers, and others. They identify the most important people in your life, your relationship to them, how you connect with them, and how you want them to truly understand and acknowledge who you are and what you do. This relationship evolves and grows; the deeper the relationship, the better the mutual understanding. The most intimate relationship you have is with yourself. This is covered in your authentic personal vision and mission, which is based on self-awareness. You will strengthen the relationship with yourself and build personal integrity by aligning your Personal Ambition and Personal Brand (authentic you; your personality, spirit, character) with your behaviour and actions—with who and what you really are. This is alignment with yourself, see Chapter 7. As you will discover in Chapter 5, by integrating your key roles in the external perspective of your Personal Balanced Scorecard you will create *work/life balance*; for example by spending more quality time with your spouse and children. Consequently, you will be valued for a strong Personal Brand at home. With this in mind, reflect on the following questions formulated by McNally & Speak (2003) that can help you define some important key roles:

- Regarding your *spouse or life partner*: What attracts me to this person? What are the affinities between us? What does he/she expect of me? What attitudes and behaviour does he/she want from me? How am I relevant to her/him? How can I strengthen this relationship?
- Regarding your *children*: Where in childhood are they now, and what stage are they moving to? What in particular do they expect of me? How can I remain both distinctive and relevant in these relationships?
- Regarding your *friends*: Whom do I regard as my closest friends? What do they expect of me? How can I remain both distinctive and relevant in these relationships?

Make a list of key roles that you are fulfilling in life with your family, friends and important others, and select your top four or five key roles from this list, which fit your personal vision and mission. Take a look at my Personal Key Roles below. My first key roles in life are spouse and father. My wife's name is Rita (49) and my son's names are Rodney (23) and Warren (18).

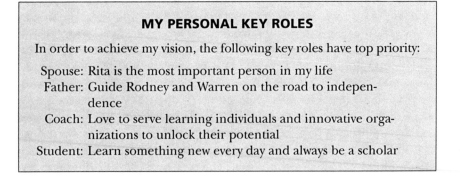

MY PERSONAL KEY ROLES

In order to achieve my vision, the following key roles have top priority:

Spouse: Rita is the most important person in my life
Father: Guide Rodney and Warren on the road to independence
Coach: Love to serve learning individuals and innovative organizations to unlock their potential
Student: Learn something new every day and always be a scholar

My personal vision, mission, and key roles will be aligned with my Personal Brand in Chapter 4 and translated into actions (my PBSC) in Chapter 5.

OTHER EXAMPLES OF PERSONAL KEY ROLES

- Husband: To be happy together, to do fun things, to stimulate each other and enjoy it. To build a future together, in which I give and receive love, show respect and give trust.
- Mother: A support for my children on which they can fall back, and to be there while they strive towards a happy life. To help them get the most out of the possibilities which their body and soul have to offer.
- Daughter: To give and receive love from my parents and to learn from their wisdom in life.
- Sister: To share and do things together.
- Friend: To trust that which will never be damaged. My friends can always count on me, I will never disappoint them.
- Colleague: To work for successes with my colleagues, to share knowledge and to ensure that there is an open and harmonious working atmosphere. I will make sure that my colleagues see me as a trustworthy and knowledgeable person.
- Manager: To help make the organization for which I work successful and through this, serve the community.
- Advisor: To help my customers attain their goals. To assist organizations in achieving top performance.

My Personal Ambition as a Metaphor

My Personal Ambition is visualized as a metaphor. It's a stylized form of a surfer on a surfboard (see Figure 3.3). This is related to my life & work style, which is: *enthusiastic, energetic, creative, passionate, collaborative, compassionate, love sharing, learning,* and *surfing on the Internet.*

The dynamic sport of surfing involves riding challenging waves while standing up on my surfboard. I paddle my surfboard from the beach out behind the waves and then paddle back towards the shore in an attempt to "catch the wave." Once the wave has picked me up, I get on the board in various ways and surf towards shore, continuously challenged by the waves.

Figure 3.3 My Personal Ambition is visualized as a metaphor.

To achieve this successfully I need to surf with love and passion, to be skilled, energetic and creative, knowledgeable about the surfing sport, enjoy physical and mental health, share the waves with other surfers (collaborate and compassionate in order not to collide with them), and be in harmony with the waves. The beautiful thing about surfing is that I have great fun and enjoyment, even when the waves are small and calm. The waves are never still. My Personal Brand similarly helps me ride the waves of life, balancing and sharing who I am and what I do.

My Life Story

I wish to share my personal life story in detail with you , which will let me better explain my Personal Ambition and Personal Brand. It entails how I grew up, my Personal Ambition, profession, educational background, life lessons and experiences, exciting achievements, and my passions. It's an essential part of my personal brochure. My personal life story will help you to understand me much better and to learn about the things that shaped me as a person. Telling detailed stories about your life is a powerful Personal Branding tool because people love to learn about others. By sharing your Personal Ambition statement and your life story with others in a compelling, passionate and engaging way, you will make your Personal Brand more personal and effective, and will make your prospects trust you and feel connected to you. By providing you this information you will probably develop an affinity with me. By expressing my Personal Ambition and life story consistently over time, my Personal Brand will grow stronger and stronger. Aspects of my life story and my Personal Ambition will be integrated in my Personal Brand statement in the next chapter.

MY LIFE STORY

I was born in Suriname (a former Dutch Colony in South America) in 1957. My father worked as a policeman and had little money to raise

10 children (I am number 7). We were living in a very old house in Paramaribo, almost in poverty. Life was quite hard and we lived from week to week. So my parents decided to migrate to the Netherlands in 1971 in order to create better learning opportunities for us. They used all their savings to finance this migration. I was 12 years old when we moved to the Netherlands. At that time, I had a dream to make people happy, serve the needs of mankind, and help create a better world. This was my higher calling, my inner assignment. I remember this. I looked up at factories and buildings and said, "*I want to make the people that go to those factories and buildings live a happy life.*" I was also very eager to learn and I knew that life is short, so I chose to work hard and to grasp every opportunity to educate myself and to make my parents proud of me and not to disappoint them.

I decided to study Mechanical Engineering at Enschede Polytechnic Institute, where I got my Bachelor of Science degree. After this, I received a Masters of Science in Robotics from Delft University of Technology, and a Ph.D. in Management from Eindhoven University of Technology. I was the first person at this university who got his doctorate within 2 years. My dissertation was published by John Wiley, Inc. in the United States. I was also the first person among my family, friends and relatives to receive these advanced degrees.

During this time, I married and had two sons. In order to support my growing family and to pay for tuition, I worked in the evenings and during the weekends as a labourer in factories. While doing this, I noticed that many employees were unhappy. I also noticed that executives contributed to this unhappiness by their disrespectful and often unethical behavior towards their employees. These practices certainly harmed the productivity of their organization. In 1987, I had my first consulting job in the high-tech industry and taught part-time at the Rotterdam School of Management, focusing on developing innovative personal and business management techniques. After 5 years, I started my own consulting firm serving industrial companies. I also became author of 4 four Dutch books and 50 articles in the field of technology and reengineering business processes within factories.

In 2001, I started thinking about people in a more holistic way; about what would make them engaged and more happy at work, as well as, in their private life and spare time, about how to create work-life balance, how to reduce the gap between company life and private life, how to create more enjoyment, love, happiness, and passion at work, how to help executives act in a more ethical manner, how to create a climate of trust and real learning, and how to eliminate fear and distrust. I wanted to turn my experience and passion into something greater—to humanize companies and to stimulate love, passion, and happiness in organizations. In doing all of this, I knew that greater productivity would then emerge. During this time of inner reflection, I developed my own spirituality—something had changed within me. I discovered that my higher calling was to help people live a higher quality of life by developing their knowledge of themselves and sharing this with others.

During this time, I reformulated my dream into this vision: "To live life completely, honestly, and compassionately and to serve the needs of mankind to the best of my ability" and this related mission "Enjoy the freedom to develop and share knowledge, especially if this can mean something in the life of others." Based on my vision and mission, I wrote 12 books that are translated in various languages in the mean time, and more than 100 articles in leading journals and magazines. My book, *Total Performance Scorecard (TPS): Redefining Management to Achieve Performance with Integrity* was published by Butterworth-Heinemann in the U.S. in 2003. I realized that I wrote the book in order to help humanize companies, to stimulate personal integrity, to enable greater enjoyment and happiness at work, to tackle lack of employee engagement, to develop a happy workforce of committed employees and managers, and to reinforce honesty and trustworthiness in the workplace. My TPS book received praise from professors at top universities, such as Harvard Business School, Yale School of Management, MIT, University of Michigan, INSEAD, ESADE, IMD, and London Business School

TPS became my first internationally best selling book and was translated in 22 languages, which changed my life forever. Based on this success, I began to build an international Total Performance Scorecard movement/network in 2004, which has resulted in strategic alliances in many countries. Padmakumar Nair (professor in Organization, Strategy and International Management at the University of Texas *School* of Management) said the following about this in 2004:

> I am amazed with the fact that the *Total Performance Scorecard* concept is spreading like gospel. Dr. Hubert Rampersad's innovative and pragmatic approach to combine organizational and personal performance agendas into one line of thinking helps organizational participants to come up with tangible solutions to current performance and leadership issues.

I started to conduct workshops, seminars, and presentations based on TPS for leading companies such as Nokia, Philips Electronics,

Lucent Technologies, and Shell Oil Company and became keynote speaker at numerous conferences.

Feeling the desire to introduce the TPS process into the United States, in 2006, I decided to move with my family to America in order to establish TPS International Inc. and to launch my new business management concept globally. In the same period I published *Managing Total Quality: Enhancing Personal and Company Value* (Tata McGraw-Hill). I also published, *Personal Balanced Scorecard: The Way to Individual Happiness, Personal Integrity, and Organizational Effectiveness* (Information Age, 2006) which now has been translated in 20 languages. My related article was awarded in the UK with "*The most outstanding paper.*" Our related *Personal Balanced Scorecard* Certified Coaching program has been certified by the International Coach Federation (ICF), the world's largest coaching organization.

The title of my latest book is *TPS–Lean Six Sigma: Linking Human Capital to Lean Six Sigma* (Information Age, 2007, co-authored by Anwar El-Homsi), and also this book has already been translated in 15 languages. Based on this book and the new TPS–Lean Six Sigma brand we have established a new company called TPS–Lean Six Sigma LLC. I am also a member of the Editorial Advisory Board of the journal *Training and Management Development Methods* (UK), member of the Editorial Advisory Board of the journal *Measuring Business Excellence* (UK), member of the Editorial Advisory Board of the *TQM Magazine* (UK), member of the Editorial Advisory Board of the *Journal of Knowledge Management Practice* in Canada, and editorial advisor to *Singapore Management Review* and also a member of Marshall Goldsmith's prestigious Thought Leader Advisory Board (www.MarshallGoldsmithLibrary.com) and selected by The Marshall Goldsmith School of Management as one of the 35 distinguished thought leaders in the United States in the field of leadership development. My views on happiness in life & work and on a new blueprint for creating high performance companies were published in *Business Week* in June 2007.

BusinessWe
A Balancing Act for Life
Author Hubert Rampersad talks about his personal balanced scorecard coaching framework and his views on happiness in life and work
by Marshall Goldsmith
Read the rest of the story

> Most of my publications are related to employee engagement and how to create love, passion, and happiness within companies. *Total Performance Scorecard, Personal Balanced Scorecard, Authentic Personal Branding, and TPS–Lean Six Sigma* are now worldwide registered trademarks. Due to this, I have established a global business, with strategic alliances in more than 80 countries, conducting keynote speeches and seminars almost bi-weekly somewhere in the world, and coaching executives in many countries about how to master themselves and to become more ethical and effective. I am also hon. professor at Ural State University in Russia. My Personal Brand evolved organically into something I had not anticipated, namely a crusader for employee's and company's happiness and empowerment.
>
> I am living happily with my wife and my two sons in Miami, Florida. My success is based on my higher calling, and my authentic dream in life. I was aware of my Personal Ambition and my Personal Brand and responded to these with love and passion. I had the courage to pursue my dream, have faith in myself, and live according to this dream and my higher calling. I took responsibility for identifying my authentic dream, genius, and brand, and to keep it at the forefront of my mind each day. I knew very clearly what I wanted, asked for it, wished it, dreamed it, formulated it in my Personal Ambition, Personal Brand, and PBSC, fixed it in my mind, visualized it, felt it, allowed it, enjoyed it, accepted my responsibility for everything in my life, determined what to give in return, and gave it all my positive energy. I hope you will do the same.

So now you know why I wrote this book. It's based on my own life. I want to share my life with you. I wrote this book because I am a crusader for individual's and company's happiness and empowerment; I want to help you to become successful and add value to others as well. You also have the ability to deliver peak performances, because you have the genius within you to do so and you have a higher calling as well. The only thing you need to do is to discover this and to respond to it with love, passion, faith and courage. It's your ethical duty to do so. It's also my ethical duty to help you with this. By way of this book, I will provide you some new insights, models, and tools, tested in practice, so that you can create a stable basis for your growth and influence your own future and destiny. Your Personal Ambition is strongly related to your destiny. When your brand is in line with your destiny you and when you accept this, you will live effortlessly and will become in flow. This will create a stable basis for your happiness and your intense desires will be fulfilled in a mystical way.

Listening to Your Inner Voice

The biggest hindrance in creating our Personal Ambition is our own thinking. Most people don't spend much time thinking about their life. Consequently their Personal Brands don't reflect distinctiveness, relevance, and consistency. Henry Ford said, "Thinking is the hardest work there is, which is probably the reason why so few engage in it." How much time do you commit each day—each week—to *really* think about your life? If you're like most people, your answer is not much time at all. We are too preoccupied and do not really create an atmosphere of silence for just a few minutes everyday to think about ourselves and to listen to our inner voice. Although this voice is present in all of us, it cannot always be heard because: (1) most of us are not capable of hearing this voice because we are too focused on the outside world; and (2) the inner voice is drowned out by the noise around us. To hear your inner voice you must tune into the same wavelength in which your spirit communicates with yourself. Abraham Maslow expressed himself in this manner:

> There exists a personal "I" that which I sometimes call "listening to your intuitions." This means: letting your own I emerge. Most of us do not listen to ourselves but to the interrupting voice of others. You will discover that all knowledge is contained in life itself.

Ophray Winfrey advises people in her talk show:

> Take five minutes every day in the morning to listen to your inner voice directing your life.... Be silent enough to hear this voice, be quiet, part of your responsibility is to honor the quiet inside yourself so you can hear the call. People are too busy... you haven't even given yourself five minutes to hear... take five minutes to center yourself in the morning... set your intention every day... if you don't have five minutes, you don't deserve to have the life of your dreams.

Vivekananda said: "The greatest force is derived from the power of thought. Thought makes our body. Whatever we think we become. Pure and elevated thought makes us pure." In Buddha's words, "We are what we think with our thoughts. We make the world." It is therefore important to listen to your inner voice—it tells you what is best for you and how you can control your inner processes. An important rule here is: listen effectively to yourself, trust your inner voice, and obey it. You will then act with conviction. This process is related to the *Secret (Law of Attraction)* which will be discussed at the end of this chapter.

I will introduce an integrated breathing and silence exercise in the next section, which will assist you in turning your attention inward, to give you control over your awareness, to let you think deeply and to create an atmosphere in which you can listen attentively to your inner voice. You have the responsibility to respond to this voice and you must have the courage to follow through. By formulating your Personal Ambition and through reflection on it through the breathing and silence exercises, you will discover your genius and get a better hold on your life as your self-awareness increases. Awareness is your inner voice that selectively chooses internal and external events for processing. Awareness consists of energy and information in the form of thoughts. As Abraham Maslow once said, "What is necessary to change a person is to change his awareness of himself."

Formulating your Personal Ambition is primarily done by transcribing your inner voice after contemplating a couple of probing Personal Ambition questions, which will be discussed in the next section.

An Integrated Breathing and Silence Exercise

By paying attention to your own thoughts by way of a breathing and silence exercise, you can discover your identity and you will be able to distance yourself from your mindset. Through this exercise, you learn to look at life with new eyes, and can perceive what goes on within you. Because of this, you will know where you stand in life. Formulating your Personal Ambition can serve as a crowbar to pry off your rusty prejudices which block your creativity. You will be better equipped to create your future and discover a destination for yourself. After all, only if you know yourself will you be able to discover your talents and develop your Personal Brand and personal goals. Then you can put them to the service of yourself and others.

Breathing and silence exercises will assist you in turning your attention inward and in gaining control over your awareness. They help in bringing the left and the right side of your brain in balance. Breathing and thinking ability arise from the same center. Once breathing control is achieved, thought control follows and vice versa. The mind is intimately connected with breathing. When your mind is agitated, your breathing becomes quick and shallow. When you are relaxed and focused, your breathing is deep and calm. Breathing unites body and soul. According to Sri Sri Ravi Shankar, breathing is the link between body, thinking and emotions. Every emotion results in a certain breathing pattern. When you pay attention to your breathing, you will find that your thoughts and emotions relax. Breathing plays an important role also by removing anger from your thoughts and body. Because of the breathing exercise, your breathing becomes deeper, more regular and slower resulting in a restful effect on you.

Breathing and relaxation are inextricably connected. Proper breathing creates a good basis for physical and mental health. After all, when we breathe, we take in oxygen. Most people breathe quickly, superficially and uneasily, only using one-third of their lung capacity. A life energy deficiency results in a low energy level, coupled with stuffiness and listlessness. A surplus of life energy makes you cheerful and strong, lets you relax and results in a positive attitude, free from stress. You need life energy to set your Personal Ambition and Personal Brand in action. A nice Personal Ambition and Brand without the energy to act is meaningless. The breathing exercise below will assist you in developing energy. It will result in purposeful effort and action to make your dream come true and to launch your brand successfully.

Silence can be thought of as a synonym for meditation. It is the most effective way of communication. Meditation is a state that creates clarity and gives you a direct experience of your spirit. The spirit, according to Buddha, is a combination of feelings, observations, thoughts and sensory awareness. During meditation, your spirit has a chance to settle down and relax, to develop awareness and to aid in acting more effectively. Your spirit decides, for the most part, about how you act and in what state of mind you are. Meditation includes the re-discovery of a natural state of awareness and forms an effective basis for your self-knowledge. Meditation does not mean concentration, but a deep state of relaxation, letting go, calmness, a high state of awareness, mental strength, inner peace, enjoyment and satisfaction. Concentration is the result of meditation. This happens through your enhanced mental power and awareness and a calmer spirit. A calmer state of mind leads to clear thinking, which results in more creativity, less waste of energy and a holistic view of reality. This is really necessary in order to formulate and implement your Personal Ambition and Personal Brand effectively. There are other advantages of meditation—because of a calmer spirit, one has lower blood pressure and heart beat, the ability to better deal with stress, and controlling of pain, etc. All of us have human values; because of stress and tension they are not visible. Meditation makes them visible. There is evidence that people who meditate regularly live longer than those who do not.

Meditation makes it possible to look at the world through the eyeglasses of our thoughts. It assists you in observing and accepting your thoughts and feelings. During meditation, let your thoughts come and go; this includes the thoughts in regard to your Personal Ambition, such as who you are, what you stand for, what makes you unique, where you are going, which values and principles guide you on your way, what type of relationship you would like to have with others, etc. This silent process makes it easy to answer these questions, and because of it, your Personal Ambition and Personal Brand statement become more effective and authentic. These questions are connected to your inner voice and enable you to discover the truth about yourself and your life. Your thoughts should be positive. Positive thoughts will help you to reach your life and brand objectives; negative thoughts will prevent you reaching these objectives and will make you feel bad.

There are several forms of breathing and silence exercises. In the following boxed text, I introduce a simple integrated breathing and silence exercise, which has proven to be very effective. The breathing part of this exercise is adjusted from Sri Sri Ravi Shankar. Performing this breathing and silence exercise for 20–30 minutes early in the morning and 20–30 minutes in the evening will give exceptional results if regularly practiced. It is very important that you breathe through your nose. Because of this, your breath will be preheated and deeper, and you will be energized.

AN INTEGRATED BREATHING AND SILENCE EXERCISE (Rampersad, 2006)

Step 1: Breathing Exercise

1. Look for a quiet spot with fresh air and make sure that you will not be disrupted.
2. Sit in a comfortable chair with an upright back, and keep your back straight, and your shoulders and neck relaxed.
3. Gently rest your hands on your knees, with your palms upward and close your eyes.
4. Breath deeply through your nose according to the following rhythm: inhale deeply during a count to four (your stomach fills like a balloon), hold your breath during four counts, and exhale fully and slowly during a count of six (your stomach flattens again) and stop for two counts. Focus on the rhythm of breathing in and out.
5. Focus your attention entirely on your breathing during this process and observe how your life energy flows through your body. During the breathing you will become more relaxed. Concentrate on the feeling of relaxation in your whole body (face, shoulders, hands, feet, etc.).
6. Repeat this process during 10–15 minutes.

Step 2: Silence Exercise

1. After finishing the breathing exercise, remain in your sitting position with your back straight, relax your arms, keep your eyes closed and breath normally through your nose.
2. Focus entirely on your thoughts; do not concentrate on anything else. If thoughts do enter, do not force them out but simply let them pass like clouds making way for the beautiful blue sky.
3. Allow your thoughts to come and go, including the thoughts related to the Personal Brand questions.
4. Be open to all images that come up in your mind. Imagine that you are in a garden and that a wise man approaches you who, after introducing himself, asks you some of the Personal Brand questions mentioned below. Listen carefully to the answers of your inner voice and write these down immediately after this exercise.
5. Open your eyes slowly after 10–15 minutes and write the answers of your inner voice in your Personal Ambition statement and your Personal Brand diary. The purpose of this diary is to be able to use this information to update your Personal Ambition and Personal Brand and keep record of your experiences and progress in each session.

Personal Ambition Questions

You should reflect during the breathing and silence exercise on some of the following questions:

- Where am I going? Where would I like my life to be headed?
- What do I want to be? What do I hope to become? What do I want to achieve with my life?
- What future would I like to have? Where would I want to be at the end of my life? What is my main purpose in life?
- Who am I? What is my identity? Why am I on this earth? Why am I here? What is my self-image? How do I see myself? What kind of person am I? What do I believe in?
- What do I stand for? What do I live for? What are my core beliefs?
- What makes me unique, special, different, and outstanding?
- How do others see me? What do they say about me? What attracts them to me?

- What do others think of me? What can they depend on me for? How do they perceive my values?
- What do others value about my work?
- What is decisive for my success? What are my unique talents?
- What do I get consistent recognition for? What do I do that I am most proud of?
- What talents, skills and experience do I need to add value to others? What do I do that adds remarkable, distinguished, distinctive value? How do others perceive my values?
- What do I do best and effortlessly? What creates flow in my mind and body?
- What gives me satisfaction? What am I passionate about?
- What makes me happy or sad? When I was happy, what made me so happy?
- What do I enjoy the most? Will I enjoy this in the future as well? What moves me? Where do I find joy? What turns me on?
- Which values and principles are closest to my heart, are sacred to me, and are rooted most deeply in my life?
- Which of these values clash with each other and with my strong sides?
- How do I create meaning in my life and see to it that everything is not about earning money?
- To what extent is material wealth important to me?
- How do I want to know myself and be known to others?
- What would I like to have engraved on my tombstone?
- Which memories would I like to leave behind after my death?
- What do I want to be remembered for?
- If I die, what legacy would I like to leave behind, and what would I like to have meant to others?
- What difference will it have made that I existed?
- What constraints stand in the way of realizing that future? What weaknesses do I have to deal with those constraints?
- What prevents me from being who I want to be and what I want to be?
- Who will find me and my unique strengths valuable in the marketplace?
- What do I think about others?
- How much do I know about my audience?

- What are my ambitions and deepest aspirations about the community in which I want to live? What do I want to help realize?
- What is good and what is bad?
- What do I most want to learn? Which habits would I like to unlearn? What do I very much like to do? What do I think is very important? What do I find nice and attractive? What am I willing to sacrifice to realize my objectives? What do I really want?
- What do I want to invest in life and what do I want to gain from it?
- How would I prefer my daily life to be?
- In which kind of environment do I prefer to be?
- How is my mental and physical health?
- What are the five best qualities of individuals who I admire?
- To what extent are spiritual values important to me? What do I think of religion?
- Who are the most important persons in my life? What is my relationship to them?
- How do I connect with my life companion, friends, family, colleagues, and others?
- What type of relationship would I like to have with my friends, family, customers, and others?
- Why do I do what I do? What is the importance of what I do?
- What am I good at and what not? In what did I fail? What are my biggest failures?
- What are my problems? What are the effects of my problems on my relationships with others? What effects have the problems on my physical health?
- Why did I go to work for my present employer?
- How am I at work?
- What have I done up till now, and what have I achieved?
- What is difficult for me to give up in my private, social, and business life?
- Which social questions intrigue me? Which social contributions would I like to make?
- What do I want to be in my organization? What am I trying to achieve? What is keeping me back?
- How can I serve mankind?

- Which contribution am I trying to make to the realization of my organizational ambition?
- What are the most important motivators in my job?
- To which job do I aspire? What are my wishes? What do I strive for? What are my concerns?
- What is happening to my profession, material possessions, family, life companion, friends, and others?
- Why am I active in a certain club?
- Will the things mentioned above still be important to me ten years from now?

If you are being coached during this process, allow this person to help you with the breathing and silence exercise by:

- Counting softly.
- Reminding you to allow your thoughts to come and go.
- Asking you several of the Personal Ambition questions that are appropriate for you, and to pause between the questions to allow time for thought. Answer the questions honestly.
- Helping you with the selection of these questions.
- Helping you to keep record of your experiences and progress during the exercise.

All the seemingly simple Personal Ambition questions are difficult to answer, when people are not open, or do not want to make an effort to find out what they want from their life and are blind to it. The breathing and silence exercise is meant to create an atmosphere of silence and inner peace, so that you will be able to answer these questions. By doing these exercises daily, you will be able to achieve a lot of things on your own. This exercise allows you to think deeply about yourself and makes you aware of yourself and your core beliefs. By questioning yourself and listening intently to your inner voice, which systematically answers the above questions for you, you will be able to discover and change your obstructive beliefs. By doing this, you will gain more insight into the workings of your mind and the influence this has on your brand, behaviour, thought, and learning ability. Through this you can also accomplish the following:

- Build, implement, maintain, and cultivate your Personal Brand, Personal Ambition, and PBSC effectively.

- Enable you to get in touch with yourself, and clarify your Personal Ambition, and the human values within you.
- Reach a mental state where you can forget about you and feel happy.
- Increase your personal effectiveness and deliver mind-expanding performances.
- Discover your subconscious motives and through this get more out of yourself and coach yourself effectively.
- Understand your thoughts better and thus control your inner conflicts better (between feelings and reason), and come in contact with your inner truth.
- Deal with your environment with greater inner peace, harmony, self-confidence, and involvement.
- Create positive energy and utilize this effectively for the sake of yourself and others.
- Make optimum use of your Personal Brand, abilities and capabilities, and eliminate annoying behaviour.
- Think and act more proactively, deal with your attitude in a more conscious way, and create a positive atmosphere.
- Deal better with emotions, stress, and burnout.
- Divide your attention more satisfactorily between work, hobbies, and family.
- Improve your personal learning style, as well as your self-awareness, self-discipline and consciousness and about self-responsibility.
- Develop self-knowledge.
- Turn your ambition, brand, and PBSC into action effectively.

  To turn your ambition and brand into action, you need energy. Energy is increased by habitually practicing the breathing and silence exercise.

Brainwaves during Breathing and Silence Exercise

During the breathing and silence exercise, you produce brainwaves. These are like small electric currents in your head, which are of different measurable frequencies. The lower the frequency, the more inwardly directed your attention is. This is related to increased relaxation and inner peace. Anna Wise (1995) distinguishes the following four brainwave areas (see Figure 3.4):

- *Beta waves*: these waves have a frequency of 14–38 Hz (frequency in Hertz = number of vibrations per second). You are actively aware of the outside world. You are unable to concentrate during this stage of the exercise. Relaxation exercises calm the beta waves.

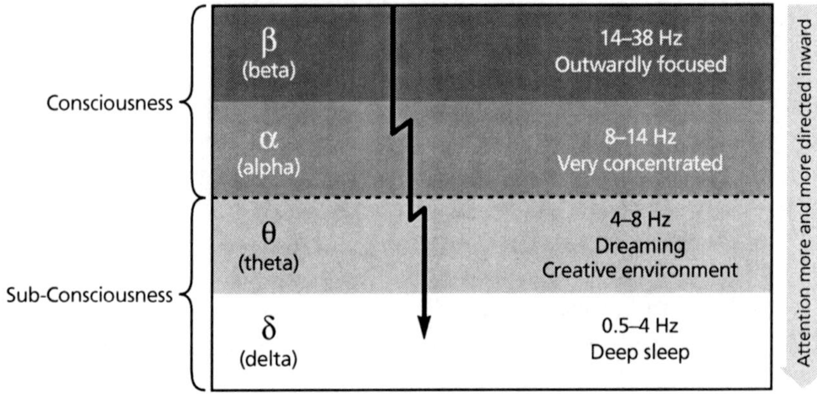

Figure 3.4 Brain waves during breathing and silence exercise.

- *Alpha waves*: these waves have a frequency of 8–14 Hz. They are associated with relaxation and increase as you turn your attention more inward.
- *Theta waves*: these waves have a frequency of 4–8 Hz. These brainwaves are related to creativity, inspiration, dreams, and storage of memories in the long-term memory.
- *Delta waves*: these waves have a frequency of 0.5–4 Hz. These waves are produced primarily during deep sleep. These waves are related to empathy and intuition.

Beyond the Secret (Law of Attraction)

The introduced Personal Ambition system is partly related to the Law of Attraction, which is explained in the movie/book *The Secret* (Byrne, 2006). The Law of Attraction says that thoughts have an energy that attracts like energy and you attract into your life whatever you think about. This tool refers to what Buddha said: "What you have become is the result of what you have thought." It suggests the following:

> your dominant thoughts will find a way to manifest. . . . Whatever you focus on the most is what will be most attracted to your life. . . . Once you are aware of this law and how it works, you can start to use it to deliberately attract what you want into your life . . . Like attracts like . . . You get what you think about, whether wanted or unwanted . . . You are a living magnet . . . You get what you put your energy and focus on . . . Energy attracts like energy . . . it has it roots in Quantum Physics.

Just focusing on your dominant thoughts, wishful thinking about what you want to achieve, and trying to become rich quickly can lead to an ad-hoc, short term, and cosmetic success, and on the other hand it can affect your Personal Brand negatively and can ruin your reputation. The Secret is an unstructured process. It can be a selfish and a greedy business and can make you a big looser if you don't reflect your true character, don't work hard, don't deliver and perform continuously, and don't live and act according to your authentic self. Remember also what Gandhi said: "To believe in something, and not to live it, is dishonest." Who you really are, what your dreams are, what you care about, what you are passionate about, what you want with your life, etc. should come out and be embedded in your ambition, brand, and PBSC You should act, behave, perform, and deliver accordingly in order to get what you want in a more enduring and sustainable way. If you are holistically branded according the introduced authentic Personal Branding model and if you implement, maintain, and cultivate your brand according to the Plan-Deploy-Act-Challenge cycle, your brand will get energy from likeminded brands and will attract success, people with similar beliefs, and opportunities that are a perfect fit for you, much more effectively, than just focusing on your *dominant* thoughts only. As a result of this, attracting success will be much easier and sustainable. By aligning your Personal Ambition and destiny with your Personal Brand you will fulfill your intense desires in a mystical way and will live effortlessly and become happy. This is no secret. In the boxed text below I introduce "Beyond the Secret," which will help you realize your dreams and brand desires in a more sustainable, enduring, and harmonious way.

BEYOND THE SECRET
(© Hubert Rampersad)

1. *Get very clear on what you want with your life and formulate your Personal Ambition and Personal Brand statement based on this.* Ask for it, wish it, dream it, formulate it, and fix it in your mind by using the breathing and silence exercise. This exercise will assist you to fix it in your mind. List in your Personal Ambition statement what you want to achieve. You must accept personal responsibility for everything in your life. Determine what you intend to give in return for what you desire and give it all your positive energy.
2. *Visualize your Personal Ambition and Personal Brand.* Visualize the end results in your mind during the breathing and silence exercise and visualize it after this exercise as a metaphor (drawing, paint or logo).

3. *Formulate your Personal Balanced Scorecard (PBSC) for carrying out your desire and to make it a reality.* Translate your Personal Ambition and Personal Brand into your Personal Branding strategy and an execution plan in order to make it a reality. List what you must do to achieve your brand and personal objectives. Specify how you are going to measure success at each step along the way. Based on the PBSC you will be accountable for your results.
4. *Feel it, allow it, believe it, accept it, be open to receiving it, and enjoy it by implementing, maintaining, and cultivating your Personal Ambition, Personal Brand, and PBSC according to the Plan-Deploy-Act-Challenge (PDAC) cycle.* Live according to the PDAC cycle and focus your thoughts upon the things you desire which are related to your Personal Ambition and Personal Brand, with great feeling such as love, passion, enthusiasm, and gratitude. Feel and behave as if your desire is on its way. Feel yourself already in possession of your desire. The feeling, love, passion, and courage related to your Personal Ambition and Personal Brand will create the power of attraction. Read your Personal Ambition and Personal Brand statement every day. Follow your heart (your Personal Ambition and Personal Brand), your head (your PBSC), and be passionate about and love what you do. Accept a larger challenge which is in line with your improved talents and skills and get on with it. Enjoy the experience and document what you have learned and celebrate the successes.

Assignment

- Draft a statement of your personal vision.
- Draft a related statement of your personal mission.
- Formulate your personal key roles.
- Choose 5–6 values in Table 3.1 that are most important to you and energize your relationships and integrate these in your Personal Ambition statement.
- Visualize your Personal Ambition statement.
- Formulate your life story.

Perform the breathing and silence exercise and listen to your inner voice, in order to formulate your Personal Ambition effectively. Use the standard form in Appendix A to formulate your Personal Ambition statement.

Ask for guidance if you need support in defining and formulating your Personal Ambition effectively. In Appendix B you will find the Personal Brand Coaching framework and our related certification program, which is meant to be helpful to guide you in this process. The related Personal Branding Soft, described in Appendix C, will assist you to execute this process efficiently.

The more clarity you have about your Personal Ambition, the greater the chance of achieving your Personal Brand objectives. Your Personal Ambition is the soul of your Personal Brand and provides the starting point for this. In the next chapter, I will show you how to successfully connect your Personal Ambition to your Personal Brand in a way that can have a profound impact on your life.

4

Define and Formulate Your Personal Brand

A great brand taps into emotions... Emotions drive most, if not all, of our decisions. A brand reaches out with a powerful connecting experience. It's an emotional connecting point that transcends the product... A great brand is a story that's never completely told. A brand is a metaphorical story that's evolving all the time... Stories create the emotional context people need to locate themselves in a larger experience.

— Scott Bedbury

The second stage in the Personal Branding journey is primarily concerned with defining and formulating a sustainable, strong, authentic, consistent, and memorable Personal Brand identity, which is in harmony with your Personal Ambition (see Figure 4.1).

Figure 4.2 shows the framework and the building blocks for defining and formulating your authentic Personal Brand. First of all, perform a personal SWOT analysis and evaluate yourself honestly—calling to mind the

Authentic Personal Branding, pages 67–86

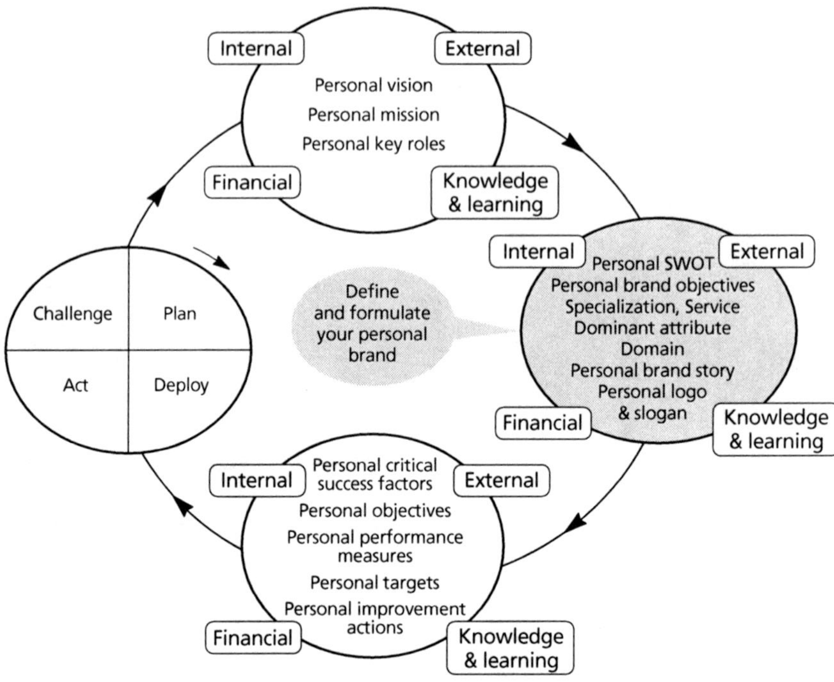

Figure 4.1 Second stage in the Authentic Personal Branding model.

results of the breathing and silence exercise. The result of this analysis and evaluation is the definition of your personal life style. This relates to your Personal Brand objectives, to what results you want to achieve with your Personal Brand. These should be related to the four perspectives: internal, external, knowledge & learning, and financial. Determine your specialization, concentrating on a single core talent, what your main specific services are, what your key characteristics are, what your single leading and most powerful attribute is, who your audience (domain) is, and what their greatest needs are. Your Personal Brand Statement entails the total of your Personal Ambition, brand objectives, specialty, service, dominant attribute, and domain. Your Unique Value Proposition (UVP) is part of this. The next step is to define your Personal Brand Story (Elevator Pitch), which is the essence of what you want to say about your Personal Brand in order to produce a positive emotional reaction. Finally, you should design your Personal Logo, which is a single graphical symbol that represents your Personal Brand.

In the following sections, each of the phases in the Personal Branding framework will be discussed in depth.

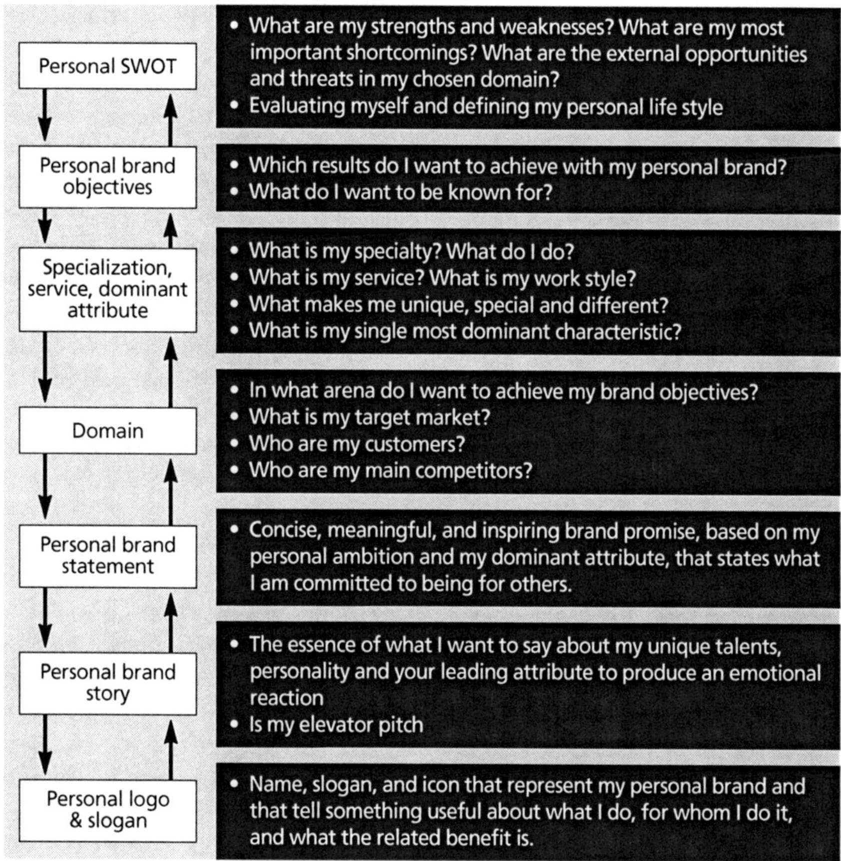

Personal SWOT
• What are my strengths and weaknesses? What are my most important shortcomings? What are the external opportunities and threats in my chosen domain?
• Evaluating myself and defining my personal life style
Personal brand objectives
• Which results do I want to achieve with my personal brand?
• What do I want to be known for?
Specialization, service, dominant attribute
• What is my specialty? What do I do?
• What is my service? What is my work style?
• What makes me unique, special and different?
• What is my single most dominant characteristic?
Domain
• In what arena do I want to achieve my brand objectives?
• What is my target market?
• Who are my customers?
• Who are my main competitors?
Personal brand statement
• Concise, meaningful, and inspiring brand promise, based on my personal ambition and my dominant attribute, that states what I am committed to being for others.
Personal brand story
• The essence of what I want to say about my unique talents, personality and your leading attribute to produce an emotional reaction
• Is my elevator pitch
Personal logo & slogan
• Name, slogan, and icon that represent my personal brand and that tell something useful about what I do, for whom I do it, and what the related benefit is.

Figure 4.2 Framework for defining and formulating your Authentic Personal Brand. (© Hubert Rampersad)

Personal SWOT Analysis

A personal SWOT analysis forms the basis of your brand and personal objectives, by examining your strengths and weaknesses in the internal environment and opportunities and threats in the external environment. This self-assessment will also help you to identify areas where you may need to improve. The confrontation matrix (see Chapter 5, Table 5.2) will be helpful at this time. The breathing and silence exercise forms a reflective environment in preparation for the SWOT analysis. To execute the SWOT analysis you should examine your current situation, by asking yourself some of the following questions and answering them honestly: What are my strengths and weaknesses? How can I capitalize on my strengths and overcome my weaknesses? What are the external opportunities and threats in my chosen field and domain? Do I deliver my work on time, every time? Do I anticipate and solve problems before they become crises? Do I always complete my projects within the budget? What am I passionate about? What do people think of me? What would my colleagues or my customers say is my greatest and clearest strength? What would they say is my greatest weakness? Am I achieving my goals? What are some of the strengths that have contributed to my success up to the present? How might these create problems for me in the future? Which problems would I like to solve first? You also have to acknowledge things, which you want to improve. Weaknesses include habits that restrict you, have an unfavourable influence on your life and deliver poor results. If you identify a skill that you know is important in your chosen field, but you are weak in that skill area, include this in your PBSC so you can take steps to improve that skill. It is also important to focus in your PBSC on things in which you are good, to make your performance even better. While analyzing your shortcomings, reflect on the following questions—what do I think are my biggest shortcomings? Has anyone ever mentioned any of these shortcomings to me? Can I describe a situation where any of these shortcomings would be a serious handicap? You could also ask yourself this question—what is the most important challenge I face regarding my work and career? Factors that may be related to these questions are, for example, talent, ability, intelligence, goal-orientation, perseverance, self-control, health, integrity, creativity, tolerance, enthusiasm, the home and work environments, responsibility, job prestige, status, power, freedom, having more free time, and so on. Talk to others about how they see you and ask referral clients what the person who referred them said about you. To illustrate what has been said about the personal SWOT analysis, I will share my own SWOT with you, see Table 4.1. I have included some improvement actions in my PBSC (see Chapter 5) and implemented this according to the PDAC cycle (see Chapter 6) to turn my weaknesses into strengths.

Evaluation of Yourself

Based on the list you made of all your strengths and weaknesses and opportunities and threats, you need to evaluate yourself honestly and define your personal life style, which is in harmony with your Personal Ambition and life story. This stage in the branding process entails aligning your Personal Ambition with your Personal Brand. Analyze the gap between your current situation and what you want to realize with your brand. Tracking your past accomplishments will also help to evaluate yourself. While evaluating yourself, you should reflect on the following questions:

TABLE 4.1 My SWOT

	Positive aspects	Negative aspects	
Internal environment	**My strengths (S)** Internal positive aspects that are under control and upon which I will capitalize in my PBSC S1: Creative and holistic insight S2: Work Experience S3: Good communicative skills S4: Enthusiastic, energetic, creative, open-minded, passionate (I love the work I do) and compassionate S5: Self-knowledge; I am aware of my personal ambition, interests, skills, personality, learning style, and values S6: Good education	**My weaknesses (W)** Internal negative aspects that are under my control and that I will plan to improve (my objectives and related improvement actions in my PBSC) W1: Impatient W2: Weak language skills W3: Diabetic W4: Weak work/life Balance	**Aspects that are under my control**
External environment	**Opportunities (O) in My Field and Domain** Positive external conditions that I do not completely control but of which I will plan to take advantage (my objectives and related improvement actions in my PBSC) O1: Great network in Asia O2: Positive trends in outplacement field that will create more jobs O3: Organizations are investing more in human capital and employee engagement O4: Individuals are becoming aware about the importance of authentic personal branding, sustainable performance management O5: My domain is particularly in need of my set of skills O6: Opportunities for professional development in my field O7: Internet	**Threats (T) in my Field and Domain** Negative external conditions that I do not completely control but the effect of which I will be able to lessen (my objectives and related improvement actions in my PBSC) T1: Weak network in North America T2: Copying behavior of competitors T3: Competitors with stronger marketing/sales force (more money) T4: Competitors who went to Harvard Business School, MIT, Yale, and Stanford (schools with better reputation). T5: Negative trends in the US industry that diminish jobs T6: Many managers are not aware of the importance of a good work-life balance	**Aspects that are not completely under my control**

- How do I relate to others?
- What are my most important values?
- What are my strongest areas? Do they add value to my domain?
- What is the strongest personality characteristic I project to others?

- For what ability, talent or skill am I best known?
- What is the value that others associate with me most?
- What moral principle or value do I associate with myself?
- What do others say about me?
- How do others, who have never met me, describe me?
- How am I perceived?

The answers to these questions are also used to formulate your Personal Ambition effectively. Through this process you will improve your self-knowledge or self-image, which includes self-awareness. Self-awareness is the ability to recognize and understand your strengths, weaknesses, needs, values, emotions, and drives, as well as their effect on others.

Take a look at my personal life style below. It includes aspects of my Personal Ambition. It entails my personality regarding my life, which personalizes my brand and reflects my values. I spend much time thinking about my life, by performing the breathing and silence exercises regularly. Consequently my Personal Brand reflects distinctiveness, relevancy, and consistency.

MY PERSONAL LIFE STYLE

Enthusiastic, energetic, creative, passionate and compassionate to inspire, collaborative, holistic insight, open-minded, and love learning

Personal Brand Objectives

After you have analyzed your strengths, weaknesses, and related threats and opportunities, performed the breathing and silence exercise, evaluated yourself, and defined your personal style, you should use that information to define your Personal Brand objectives. List the brand objectives to bridge the gap. For this, you should reflect on the following questions:

- What do I want my Personal Brand to accomplish? Is this: Increased business? Recognition? Satisfaction?
- What do I want to be known for in my profession and domain?
- What emotions would I like my brand to produce in others?
- What do I want others to think about me?

The Personal Brand objectives should be realistic and related to the four perspectives: internal, external, knowledge & learning, and financial. Take a look at my Personal Brand objectives.

MY PERSONAL BRAND OBJECTIVES

Be of additional value to individuals and organizations, high Personal Brand awareness, financially and physically healthy, be innovative and creative, and satisfaction.

Specialization

After you have defined your Personal Brand objectives, you should determine your specialization, your expertise. You should know your niche, domain and specialty, and focus on your area of specialization. You should be precise and concentrated on a single core talent or unique skill. In this authentic Personal Branding concept, specialization is based on the Personal Ambition, which means that the Personal Brand is built around the person's dream, values, key roles, and purpose in life.

Remember: Being a generalist without any specialized skills, abilities, or talents will not make you unique, special, and different. Michael Jordan has been a baseball player, golfer, and spokesman, but his main focus was basketball. Oprah Winfrey differentiated herself with an honest desire to build a legacy as crusader for women's empowerment. Walt Disney focused on family entertainment.

Take a look at my specialization below; I have narrowed down the scope of what I do, which is in line with my strengths. I am a specialist, not a generalist. I don't want to be all things to everybody. I am not doing everything like most professionals in my field. As a result of my specialization, I am different from them, and I am setting myself apart from them, by doing a few things that I enjoy most very good for a specific target market. This is my niche that I love, that I am passionate about, and which is related to my Personal Ambition:

MY SPECIALIZATION

Integrated and sustainable personal and business performance management with an authentic human focus

Service

Once you have defined your specialization, you should determine your service and tailor this to your target market (domain). Reflect on the following questions:

- What do I do?
- What are my primary services?
- What is my related work style?
- How do I want prospects in my target market to view my service?

Take a look at my service, my related work style and what I do.

MY SERVICE

Personal and business performance management consulting, training, coaching, and certification, based on the holistic and authentic Total Performance Scorecard (TPS) principles.

I launched the Total Performance Scorecard (TPS) concept in 2003, with the book *Total Performance Scorecard: Redefining Management to Achieve Performance with Integrity,* which has been translated into 22 languages. It's a new holistic performance management approach, which leads to the maximum personal development of all corporate associates and the optimal use of their capabilities for the realization of the highest performance (Rampersad, 2003). It focuses on a sustainable increase of personal and organizational performances in an integrated way. I customized my service to my target market by launching the Personal Balanced Scorecard as well in 2006. The PBSC process impacts your personal well being and allows you to express your intentions, identity, ideals, values, and driving force, as well as, to gain more insight in yourself.

Your work style is related to your specialization. My work style and what I do are strongly related to my work (job related). My discussed personal life style is related to my life, which is included in my Personal Ambition and life story. Take a look at my work style below. As you can see, there is some overlap between my life style and my work style because there is no large gap between my work life and private life.

MY WORK STYLE

Enthusiastic, energetic, creative, enjoy and love what I do, devoted to serve and share, passionate and compassionate to inspire, love learning by surfing on the Internet, human focus, and holistic insight to guide effectively related to personal and business management.

What I do is also related to my specialization. When people ask me "what do you do?" I used to say, *I'm a consultant, trainer and coach in the performance management business.* This is not enough because there are many consultants, trainers and coaches in this area. Now I tell them what I really do, what I enjoy the most, at which I am best, and what my value is to my target market:

WHAT I DO

Passionate and compassionate to inspire others, love to serve learning individuals to unlock their potential, and dedicated to energize innovative organizations.

Dominant Attribute

After you've defined your service, determine your main attribute. Define what makes you unique, special and different and know how others see you and what attracts them to you. You have to be unique and fill a special niche to be successful in the marketplace. For this, you should reflect on the following questions:

- What are my key characteristics that are very clear to anyone and which add value to others?
- What unique parts of my personal life style and my work style make an impact on others when I am on top of my performance?
- What are the top five characteristics that reflect my brand?
- What is the single leading and most powerful attribute of my Personal Ambition?
- What are my unique and natural talents?
- What separates me from the masses?
- What are my personal core competencies?

- How do I want prospects and key influencers to think about me and describe me to others?
- How am I introduced to others? How do my friends describe me to others?
- What makes me distinctive, related to my most prized personal value?
- What is the strongest personality characteristic I project to others?
- What do others say about me when I am not around?
- How do others react when they first meet me?

Michael Jordan's top five key characteristics are: *skilled basketball player, charismatic, team leader, athletic, positive outlook.* His single dominant attribute is: *Skilled basketball player.* Albert Einstein's dominant attribute is: *Genius.* Take a look at my top five key characteristics and my dominant attribute.

MY TOP FIVE KEY CHARACTERISTICS

Passionate, compassionate, creative, enthusiasm, energetic

These characteristics are the foundations of my brand. My single most dominant characteristic, called dominant attribute, is *passion.* I have chosen this characteristic because this is who I am, what makes me distinctive, what correlates to my most prized value, and it appeals to and is valued by my target market. I have the courage to consistently display this with everyone. I have therefore included this attribute in my Personal Brand statement and my brand story. This is what makes my brand unique.

MY DOMINANT ATTRIBUTE

Passionate

Passion is always the first idea that enters others' minds when they hear or read about me. This is also what my target market needs, and what creates value to others.

Domain

Once you have defined your dominant attribute, the next step is to choose and define your audience (which is in harmony with your Personal Ambition, brand objectives, specialty, service, and dominant attribute) and to know your audience and their greatest needs. In this inside-out approach, you should reflect on the following questions:

- In what arena do I want to achieve my Personal Brand objectives?
- What is my target market? Does it have the potential to make money? Do I enjoy working in this target market?
- Who are my customers?
- What are their greatest needs? What do they want? What do they value? What do they expect? What are they worried about?
- What do they expect from me?
- What are the values of my domain?
- Who will find me and my unique strengths valuable in the marketplace?
- What original knowledge or skills do I bring to my clients, industry or company?
- What experience will be valuable to my domain? What qualities does it value most?
- Is my personality suited to my domain's culture?
- What communication channels dominate in my domain?
- How are people promoting themselves?
- Who are my main competitors?
- What makes me different from my competitors?

Take a look at my domain, the greatest needs of my customers, and my key competitors.

MY DOMAIN

Learning individuals and innovative organizations within the service and manufacturing industry.

I am focusing on people and companies that are willing to learn and improve consciously. I don't want to waste my time and energy trying to help people and companies who are not committed to change and learning. I have selected the service and manufacturing industry because of the growth potential of this target market, its wealth, size, and need for my services. I enjoy working in this industry, learning a lot about it, I understand it much better, and I am aware of the value this industry sees in my brand.

GREATEST NEEDS OF MY CUSTOMERS

Sustainable employee engagement, happy and passionate workforce, personal effectiveness & growth, high labor productivity, awareness for personal integrity

My Personal Brand must be relevant to my domain, which means that I must understand and care about what's important to my customers. Employee engagement, a happy and passionate workforce, personal effectiveness & growth, high labour productivity, and awareness for integrity are very important to them.

The impact of engaged, happy and passionate employees on the company performance can be illustrated with the following important research data. There are 22 million actively disengaged employees in America, according to Gallup (Gallup Poll, 2005). Their dissatisfaction is manifested in employee absence, illness, and a variety of other big and small problems that occur when people are unhappy at work. Gallup statistics show that unhappy workers cost the American business economy up to $350 billion annually in lost labour productivity, and that earnings per share increase 2.6 times more if employees are engaged. Active engagement of employees in their jobs and work is mandatory if U.S. businesses are to enjoy high productivity in our global economy. However, Gallup research indicates that 70% of U.S. employees are not engaged at work. Companies with such a large number of dissatisfied employees "have more absenteeism and lower labour productivity—as well as 51% higher turnover rates than those with engaged employees", says James Harter, chief scientist for Gallup's international management practice. Employee disengagement is a global epidemic, see Chapter 13.

I fill this need with my products/services and brand, and I am happy that my key competitors don't have the proper concepts and tools to fill this need in a durable, holistic, and humanized way. This is making it easy for me to grab their customers. I know who my competitors are and how they are positioned.

MY KEY COMPETITORS

McKinsey, Booz Allen Hamilton, Boston Consulting Group, Kaplan & Norton, Hay Group, Franklin Covey, BSC Collaborative

Personal Brand Statement

After you have defined your Personal Ambition, brand objectives, domain, specialty, service and dominant attribute, and evaluated yourself based on your SWOT, you should formulate your Personal Brand identity in a distinctive, relevant, consistent, concise, meaningful, exciting, inspiring, and persuasive manner. Your Personal Brand identity or Personal Brand Promise is a statement that you usually use *internally* to focus your efforts on what your Personal Brand must deliver *externally* in order to satisfy the needs of others. It states what you are committed to being for others and the impact a relationship with you will have on them. It helps you focus your efforts on what you must deliver to make your customers happy. With your Personal Brand statement you want to create a particular impression in the mind of others to whom you are important and to make an emotional connection with them. It states the essence of these elements in just a few sentences: your dream, who you are, what you stand for, what you do, for whom you do it, your specialty, your service, how you create value for others, and what you are committed to being for them. It includes your Unique Value Proposition (UVP), which entails a core element what makes you more unique, more valuable, and more visible in the market. It regards what positions you as the best and only choice (your positioning); is a single powerful idea that differentiates you from everyone else in your target market and gives your potential clients a reason to buy from you. A powerful UVP will make marketing and selling yourself much easier.

Personal Brand Statement = Personal Ambition + Brand Objectives
+ Specialty + Service
+ Dominant Attribute + Domain

Personal Brand Statement = Personal Vision + Mission + Key Roles
+ Brand Objectives + Specialty + Service
+ Dominant Attribute + Domain

The formulation of your Personal Brand promise is most effective when it complies with the following criteria:

- Should be based on your Personal Ambition, personal SWOT, brand objectives, domain, specialty, service, and dominant attribute.
- Must be formulated positively, in a distinctive, relevant, consistent, concise, meaningful, exciting, inspiring, active, action-oriented, compelling, memorable, ambitious, and persuasive manner.

- Should be crystal clear about who you are and what you are not.
- The emphasis is on authenticity, integrity, consistency, relevancy, and distinctiveness.
- Should state how you will make a difference in relationships throughout your life.
- Should be short—not longer than about fifty words.
- Should include a strong slogan to position yourself and how to distinguish yourself in society.
- The four perspectives—financial, external, internal, and knowledge and learning—should be included.
- Should reflect how you provide value to others.
- Should fire your passion and make you happy.
- Should be unique to you, relevant to the market place, reflect who you really are (real you), and to be used to people at work, family, and friends (to all your relationships in your life).
- Should differentiate you and direct the way you think and behave.

Take a look at my authentic Personal Brand Statement below. It summarizes me. I have formulated this for myself to be used as guidance for my Personal Brand story and to keep me moving in the right direction. I have packaged my dream, purpose in life, key roles, passion, skills, talents, strengths, values, unique characteristics, personality, target audience, and my service into a powerful authentic Personal Brand identity that lifts me above my competitors, differentiates me and guides my career and life decisions. In this way I am trying to eliminate my competitors and to create demand for my services. My brand statement or promise is also based on my life style and my moral and behavioral code, set down by my Personal Ambition. This makes my Personal Brand more personal and continuously creates a personal touch and bond with my target audience. It provides me energy that helps me consistently build distinctive relationships with important people in my life. It also helps me to understand myself much better.

MY PERSONAL BRAND STATEMENT

Linking Human Capital to Business Success

Passionate and compassionate to inspire learning individuals to unlock their potential and dedicated to energize innovative organizations within the service and manufacturing industry. Using my holistic insight and innovative Total Performance Scorecard principles, I promise to help my customers to realize their dreams.

It matters a lot what my prospects think of me. I am therefore trying to create positive perceptions and emotions in the mind of my prospects (that I am different, special, unique, and authentic) based on my brand identity and giving them reasons to work with me. In this way I am trying to influence their perception before they make up their minds about me. It will encourage their belief that I am among the best in sustainable personal and business performance management. Every time they think or hear of me, they will associate me to this leadership role. They know me for this and they can always depend and count on me. My Personal Brand is almost similar to my Company Brand (see Chapter 10) because I am my company. I am using my brand statement to communicate my unique service that provides a sense of value for my target audience, that is in line with my dreams, life purpose, values, creativity, passion, competencies, specialization, characteristics, and things what I love doing. This will evoke strong emotions (warmth, confidence, respect) in my target market, which is exactly how I want to be perceived by my prospects.

My Personal Brand statement starts with the slogan "*Linking Human Capital to Business Success,*" which entails my position and which implies a sense of value for my target market. With my position I am categorizing my Personal Brand and influencing my target market so that they identify and label me with this single idea. In this way I am positioning myself in relation to my competitors. My dominant attribute and the link to my Personal Ambition are clearly included in the statement.

My Personal Brand statement reflects who I really am, what I do well, what I love to do, for whom I am doing it, what I care about, what my passion, values, specialty, life style, work style, and dominant attribute are, and how I create value for my clients. It's a commitment that I make to important people in my life, including my customers, about what I am willing to do on their behalf. It's clearly defined so that my target audience can quickly grasp what I stand for. I am using my Personal Brand statement to build a truly lasting relationship with my target audience and to make an emotional connection with my customers. I am also making conscious choices based on what I truly stand for and get credit for who I am and what I believe. I am not keeping my Personal Brand statement private (I am not using it silently or implicitly) because it's authentic and it reflects who I really am (my real me). I am using this to people at work, family, and friends (to all the relationships in my life). My Total Performance Scorecard principle is effectively being used in work and life. The good cause in my Personal Brand is the fact that I love making people happy, helping them to realize their dream, and by doing so helping create a better world (see also my life story and Personal Ambition in Chapter 3). This creates goodwill and understanding that I am working for more than just money.

I have included my Personal Brand statement on my website (www.total-performance-scorecard.com), my blog (rampersad.wordpress.com), in my books, articles, resume and brochures. I am using it as a compass for marketing and sales of my brand, keeping me focused, guiding me in the right direction, and defining and communicating my Personal Brand story effectively. My Personal Brand attracts attention from my domain because it's relevant to them. It's easier to convince my clients, I know what they need and want, I know and understand my Personal Brand strengths, and I just capitalize on them. I also select my customers with care and upgrade my skills continuously to satisfy them. I have found flow in my life because of my Personal Ambition and my Personal Brand.

Personal Brand Story

Your Personal Brand story is the essence of what you want to convey about your Personal Ambition, passion, unique talents, personality and your leading attribute to produce a positive emotional reaction (not the exact words in your Personal Brand statement). It should include what you do, how you do it, and how it benefits your domain. Storytelling is an important tool to communicate your Personal Brand, to explain yourself, to build credibility, and to connect with your audiences emotionally. Your brand story will enable you to present yourself (based on your Personal Brand statement) in a more confident, convincing, passionate, persuasive and compelling way to others, if they ask you "*who are you?*" "*tell me about yourself,*" or "*what do you do?*" Don't take these questions too literally and don't start describing exactly what you do. Tell them something interesting to catch their attention. By defining and formulating your Personal Brand in advance it will be much easier for you to respond fast, passionate, and strongly on these questions with a powerful story, which will reveal your personality, make you memorable (easy to visualize), build confidence, establish trust, and develop your communication skills. Use passion, examples, anecdotes, illustrations, and your own life story. You need to tell a true story that demonstrates you are the kind of person people can trust. Create a brand story that communicates your value and your market differentiation. Your story must be the answer to a question that others need the answer to. Tell your story relentlessly, and passionately to anyone who will listen. This story should be based on your Personal Ambition and your Personal Brand statement, and should promote the brand called You. Pull the critical success factors and the key words that you have used to create your Personal Brand and include these in your brand story and into everything that you say, do and publish about yourself.

According to Katharine Hansen (2007), author of *Tell Me About Yourself: Storytelling that Propels Careers*:

> Employers don't want to know merely the dry facts of what you've done. They want examples, anecdotes, illustrations ... stories. You can showcase just about any skill with a story. Using anecdotes to describe job skills is a highly effective interview technique. Truly scrutinizing the stories behind your life and career enables you to recognize patterns that reveal and reinforce who you are, what you can do, how you are qualified, what you know, what you value, what you've learned, and what you've accomplished ... Before you attempt to influence anyone you need to establish enough trust to successfully deliver your message ... the best you can do is telling them a story that simulates an experience of your trustworthiness.

A Personal Brand Story is like an Elevator Pitch; a short, clear, concise, carefully planned, and well-practiced description about your Personal Brand that people should be able to understand in the time they would take to ride up an elevator. Your Elevator Pitch clearly states to the attributes that make you unique and better qualified than others. It should be shared in a maximum of two minutes and so intriguing that they will get excited and let them easily understand and remember you and want to spend more time talking with you.

When people ask me what I do, I used to say with no passion in my voices, *I'm a consultant, trainer and coach in the performance management business.* But that didn't distinguish me and didn't set me apart from the thousands of individuals who are in the performance management business and having the same skills. Why should they remember me and choose for me? To catch their attention, stand out from the crowd, and to encourage them to want to know more about me, I am now saying with love and passion:

MY PERSONAL BRAND STORY/ELEVATOR PITCH

I am passionate to inspire others and I love to help my customers to unlock their potential by providing them excellence in integrated personal and business performance management and energizing them, based on my holistic insight and innovative Total Performance Scorecard principles ... (using anecdotes to describe this)

I am now telling people what I do in such a way that reflects my position and that add value to them. In this way I am trying to make an emotional connection to my potential clients and distinguish myself based on my brand. I am creating an aura that builds a distinctive picture of my brand in their minds, which makes me relevant to them. As a result they are eager to meet me and continue their conversations with me. My brand is related to knowledge, which gives my words high credibility. I am communicating what I stand for in a unique way that is different from others in my field and that gets inside people's mind. This gives prospects a good reason to feel good about me and what I can do for them, and makes them perceive me as beneficial to them and worth meeting. I am building a trusted relationship with my potential clients and managing their expectations and perception effectively. I am attracting substantially more attention now.

Personal Logo & Slogan

A Personal Logo is a single graphical symbol that represents and packages your Personal Brand. It tells something useful about what you do, for whom you do it, and what the benefit is. A Personal Logo consists of: a name, a slogan and an icon. Personal Logo & Slogan make your Personal Brand visible. You can use a variation of colors to improve the visibility, which depends on the mood you want to convey (Montoya, 2005a). Remember: your logo, slogan, and package can be wonderful, but it's the value provided (which reflects your values) that people care about and are attracted to.

Take a look at my Personal Logo & Slogan below. My brand name and slogan are based on my Total Performance Scorecard concept (Rampersad, 2003). My slogan "*Linking Human Capital to Business Success*" implies a sense of value to my domain and my icon is strongly related to my personal life style and my Personal Ambition (see Chapter 3). It entails the essence of my positioning. I have selected a blue color for my icon, which stands for peace, relaxation, stability, and leadership. I am using my Personal Logo & Slogan to visualize the value that I can add to my target audience and to represent my commitment to build enduring relationships with my (potential) customers that reflect my Personal Ambition and Personal Brand.

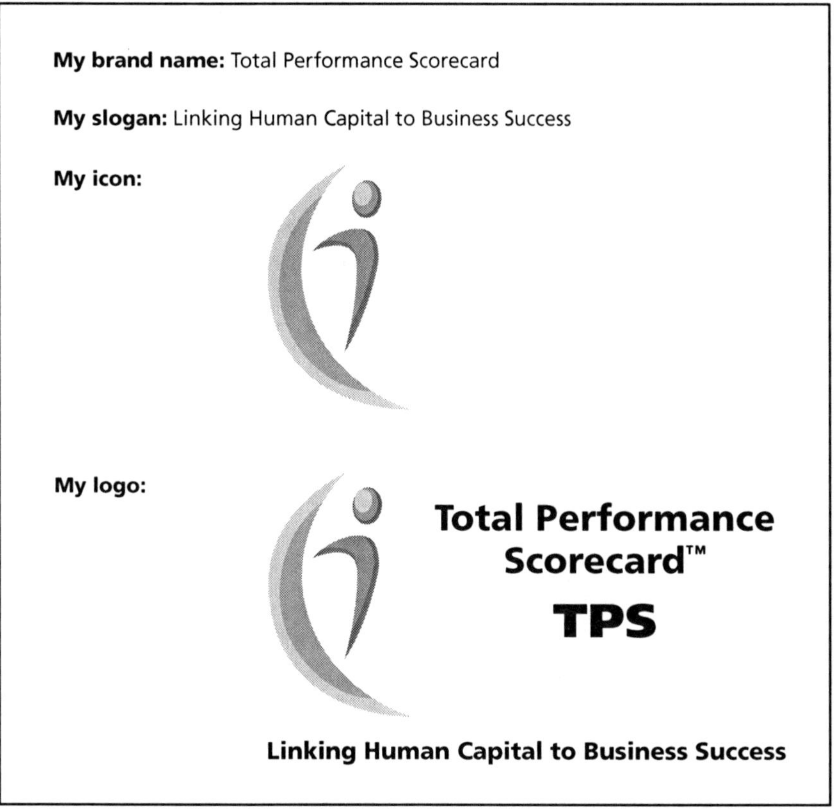

What do you think about my brand? Is it clear? Do you trust it? Do you value it? Do you like it? Do you remember it? Do you feel emotionally connected? These are the main important criteria to evaluate a brand.

ASSIGNMENT

1. Define your strengths and weaknesses and the related external opportunities and threats, based on your personal SWOT analysis and evaluate yourself. Perform the silence and breathing exercise.
2. Formulate your Personal Brand Objectives based on the SWOT analysis, related to the four BSC-perspectives.
3. Define your Specialization, Service, Dominant Attribute.
4. Define your Domain.
5. Formulate your Personal Brand Statement.
6. Create your Personal Brand Story.
7. Design your Personal Logo & Slogan.

Use the standard form in Appendix A to formulate your Personal Brand.

Ask for guidance if you need support in building your authentic Personal Brand effectively. In Appendix B you will find the Personal Brand Coaching framework and our related certification program, which is meant to be helpful for guiding you in this process. The related Personal Brand Software, described in Appendix C, will assist you to execute this process efficiently.

A nice Personal Brand without an execution plan in order to make it a reality is cosmetic and a waste of time, and will not lead to sustainable development of your potential and marketing success. This plan (PBSC) will be discussed in detail in the next chapter.

5

Formulate Your Personal Balanced Scorecard

Life is like riding a bicycle. To keep your balance you must keep moving.
— Albert Einstein

Once you've defined and formulated your Personal Ambition and Personal Brand, the next step is to translate these into your Personal Balanced Scorecard (personal branding strategy, an execution plan) in order to make your brand a reality. You need to do this in order to meet the needs and desires of your target audience and to enhance Personal Brand equity over time. Personal Branding will be of no use to you without goal setting, continuously improvement of yourself, and contributing on a day-to-day basis towards your brand, based on your Personal Balanced Scorecard (PBSC), and implementing this according to the PDAC cycle. Your Personal Ambition and Personal Brand are related to your heart (emotions) and the right half of your brain. Your PBSC, however, is related to the left half of your brain. With the left half of your brain having mainly an

Authentic Personal Branding, pages 87–109

analytical, logical and quantitative function, the right half of your brain has an intuitive, spiritual, emotional, and holistic function. One of the results of applying this holistic and authentic Personal Branding model along with the introduced tools is the balance of the left and right side of your brain and the balance of your heart and head. In this chapter I will focus on the formulation of your PBSC, which you can use to measure the progress of your brand, taking my own PBSC as example. This entails the third stage in this Personal Branding journey, see Figure 5.1.

Your PBSC translates your long term dreams, hopes, aspirations, values, and Personal Brand into short term manageable, measurable, and concrete actions in a holistic and balanced way. It entails the related personal critical success factors, objectives, performance measures, targets and improvement actions, which are divided into the four perspectives: internal, external, knowledge & learning, and financial perspectives. The PBSC is an effective tool that you can use to manage your brand, by developing improvement actions to achieve your life and brand objectives, keeping track of your progress of these actions, recording key brand information, exploring your life and brand, defining new career paths, building network of contacts, quantify and report your key accomplishments, etc. Figure 5.2 shows the framework for

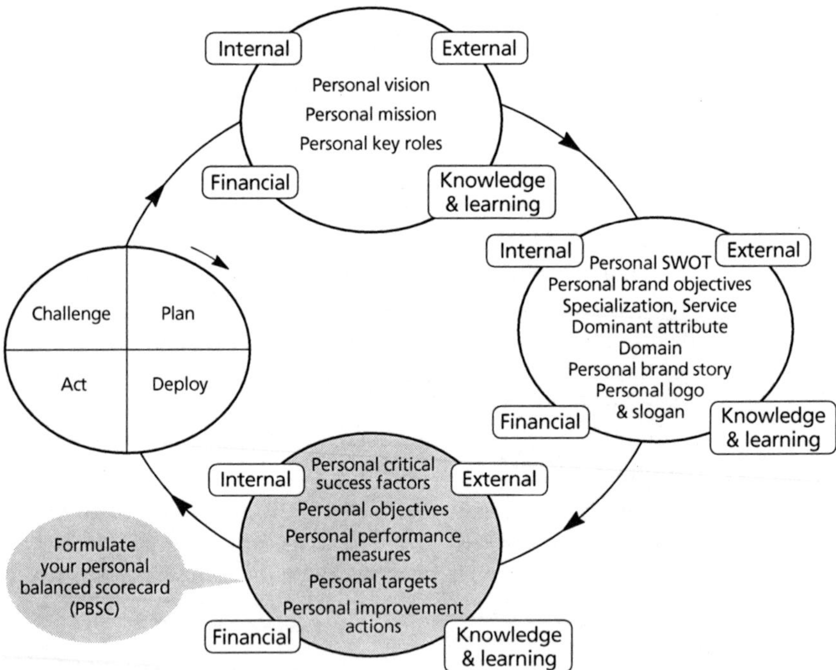

Figure 5.1 Third stage in the Authentic Personal Branding Model.

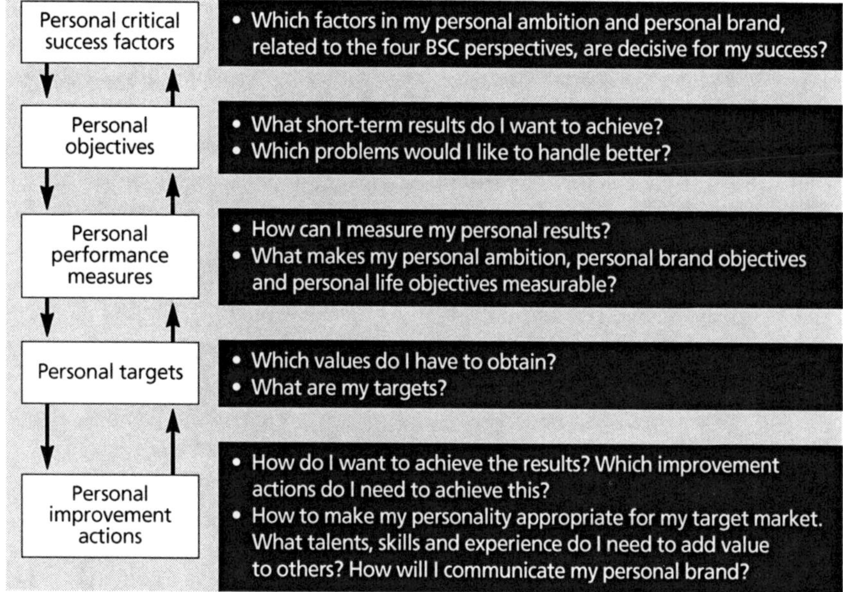

Figure 5.2 Personal Balanced Scorecard Framework (© Hubert Rampersad)

formulating your PBSC. It provides you a road map that shows how to translate your Personal Ambition and Personal Brand into actions and to capitalize on your strengths and eliminate your weaknesses. Use this framework to continuously take advantage of opportunities and challenges in your life, by selecting the critical success factors from your Personal ambition and Personal Brand statement, define your related life objectives, measures, targets and improvement actions, and prioritizing these actions to provide maximum impact. The PBSC can be defined as the following formula:

PBSC = personal critical success factors + objectives + performance measures + targets + improvement actions (divided along the four perspectives: internal, external, knowledge & learning, and financial).

In the following sections, each of the phases in the Personal Balanced Scorecard framework will be discussed in depth.

Personal Critical Success Factors

Personal Critical Success Factors (CSFs) are derived from the Personal Ambition and Personal Brand. They are related to the four perspectives, internal, external, knowledge and learning, and financial. A Personal Ambition and Personal Brand without these four perspectives results in an incomplete PBSC. The personal CSFs form the bridge between the Personal Ambition and Personal Brand (long term) and on the other side the personal objectives, performance measures, targets, and improvement actions (short term). This link is made by identifying your personal core competencies, uniqueness, genius, dominant attribute, values in your Personal Ambition and Personal Brand and translating these into concrete personal objectives. Note the following related aspects:

- A PBSC has a minimum of four CSFs (at least one per perspective)
- Every CSF has one or more related personal objectives
- Each objective has a maximum of two related performance measures
- Each performance measure has only one related target
- Each target is linked to one or more related improvement actions.

The CSFs form milestones that should be realized. They are real core competencies included in your Personal Ambition statement (the ones you actually operate from) and your idealized core competencies (the ones you think you should operate from), which you should further develop in order to make a difference and be the difference.

Some examples of personal CSFs are—financial stability, good physical and mental health, and professional ability. The crucial questions here are—What makes me unique, special and different? Which factors in my Personal Ambition and Personal Brand are decisive for my success? What are my unique talents? Which factors are important for my wellbeing? Which factors are essential for the realization of my life objectives? What are my most important competencies? These questions are related to your Personal Ambition an d Personal Brand. Figure 5.3 illustrates how each CSF in the Personal Ambition and Personal Brand is linked to the personal objectives, performance measures, targets, and improvement actions.

Personal Objectives

Your Personal Ambition and Personal Brand need to be tied to your personal objectives. These objectives should be realistic and are based on your Personal Ambition/Brand statement and the results of the self assessment executed with the help of your personal SWOT analysis. List down your life objectives to bridge the gap. The central questions here are: "Which measurable short-term personal results do I want to achieve? Which prob-

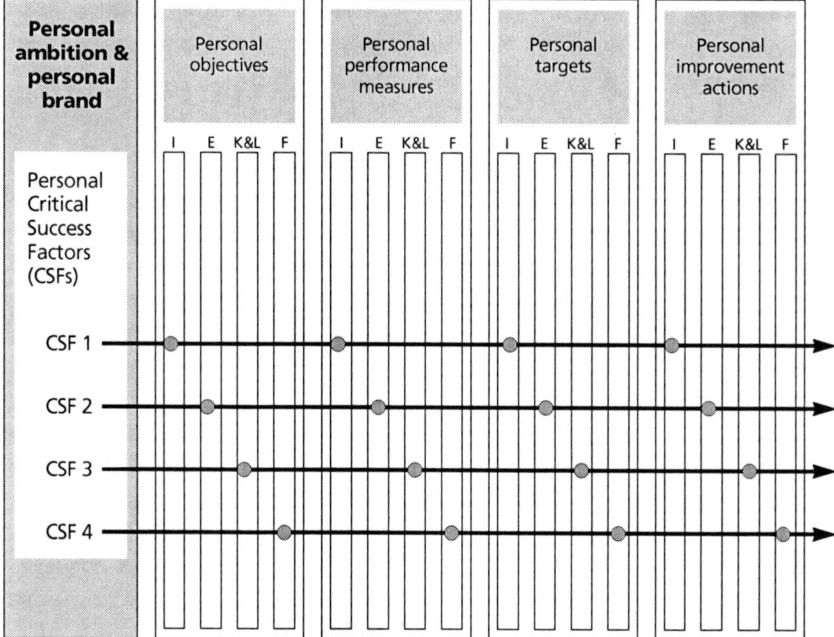

Figure 5.3 Each CSF in the PBSC is related to Personal Objectives, Performance Measures, Targets, and Improvement Actions.

lems would I like to handle better? What is my five-year career goal and life objectives?" Personal objectives describe a result that you want to achieve in order to realize your Personal Ambition and successfully launch your Personal Brand. Your ambition is aimed at the long-term future and your personal objectives at the short-term. Your personal objectives give your ambition and brand direction. The personal CSFs form the bridge between these. Your personal objectives are derived from your personal CSFs and from your SWOT analysis. Each personal CSF has one or more personal objectives that are related to one of the four scorecard perspectives, see Figure 5.3. The objectives are quantified through personal performance measures and targets. Personal objectives provide you with the criteria needed to discuss, monitor, and evaluate your performance. It specifies short-range and long-range objectives of personal importance. Personal objectives are stated in clear, concise, specific, result-oriented, challenging but realistic, relevant, and cost effective terms. Performance measures and targets make this measurable and bound by deadlines. The personal objectives form part of a cause-and-effect chain (in the strategic map), resulting in the main personal objective. Some examples of personal objectives could be—appreciation from customers, improved leadership skills, inner peace, and greater knowledge.

Personal Performance Measures

Personal performance measures are standards to measure the progress of your personal and brand objectives. With these measures, you can assess your functioning in relation to your personal critical success factors and objectives. Without performance measures and targets it is difficult to coach/ manage yourself with feedback from others. Performance measures urge you to action if they are related to your personal and brand objectives, giving you a certain direction. They measure the changes and compare this with the norm, and thus, in time, give you information about steering yourself. It is recommended that you define a maximum of two performance measures per objective. This section of the PBSC deals with the following questions—how can I measure my personal results? What makes my Personal Ambition, Personal Brand objectives and personal life objectives measurable? Table 5.1 shows an overview of possible personal performance indicators according to each PBSC perspective.

Personal Targets

A personal target is a quantitative objective of a personal performance measure. It is a value that is pursued and then assessed through a personal performance measure. Based on the personal targets you can get clear feedback about the progress of your improvement actions, which is needed to refine your Personal Brand and to better manage yourself. Your key task here is setting specific timetables and deadlines for your performance measures. Targets indicate values that you want to achieve, and depend on your level of ambition. Performance measures and targets need to comply with SMART criteria, which means that they should be

- *Specific.* They must be specifically formulated so that they can also influence behavior.
- *Measurable.* They must be formulated in such a way that they can measure the objective.
- *Achievable.* They must be realistic, realizable, feasible and acceptable.
- *Result oriented.* They must be related to concrete results.
- *Time specific.* They must be time-constrained.

Some examples of personal targets could be—increase of 15% over 2008, minimum 85% in two years, and maximum 10 lb as per March 10, 2008.

TABLE 5.1 Examples of Personal Performance Measures per BSC Perspective

Perspective	Personal Performance Measures
Internal	level of being inspired
	level of tension
	level of stress
	level of immunity to stress
	level of enjoyment
	level of laughing
	level of trust from my manager
	number of times I act with consideration versus acting without consideration
	number of times that I feel good in my skin
	number of times that I feel frustrated in my work
	level when I am irritated at work
	level of joy going to work
	number of hours jogging
	percent of mental absence
	body weight
	number of hours sleep
	frequency of sporting
	number of new challenges
	number of uncontrolled emotions at work
	number of times being mad
	hours physical rest
	percent of sick leave
	number of times fitness
	frequency breathing and silence exercise
	number of cigars per day
	fat contents
	number of km/miles per month on a bicycle
	number of stomach muscle exercise
	number of times per month playing golf
	fitness score
	cholesterol level
	number of times feeling full of energy
	percent of my life in positive shape
	number of times intuitive impulses
	alcohol consumption
	percent safety incidents
	number of times at a psychologist
	physical condition
	my delivery speed
	number of processing mistakes
	throughput time of my work
	response time to a service request
	percent delayed orders

TABLE 5.1 Examples of Personal Performance Measures per BSC Perspective (continued)

Perspective	Personal Performance Measures
External	awareness score of my Personal Brand
	percent of my revenue spent on Personal Branding
	degree of customer satisfaction
	number of activities with the children
	number of times doing something together with my partner in life
	number of donations per year
	reliability of my services
	number of successful acquisition meetings
	number of appreciating and loving remarks from spouse
	level of satisfaction of others with regard to my actions
	perception score from others with regard to my cooperation with them
	level of satisfaction of my customers
	number of warnings from my manager
	number of productive hours at my work
	number of positive changes initiated by me
	number of times positive feedback received from my clients, manager and colleagues.
	availability
	accessibility
	number of open and good conversations with loved ones
	number of committee functions in social organizations
	number of satisfied customers
	level in which I feel that I have been of added value
	number of complaints from internal and external customers
	number of hours quality time with my family
	number of family outings
	number of arguments with my spouse
	number of good conversations with my loved ones
	percent of personnel who find they are working under effective leadership
	percent of colleagues that consider me to be a good colleague
	number of times given assistance to others
	number of times positive feedback related to my ethical behavior
	customer valuation score
	time between receiving e-mails and replying to them
	number of great friends
	number of new friends
	number of offensive remarks
	delivery reliability of my services
	satisfaction score of my colleagues and employees
	time spent with real friends
	time spent at home with my children
	number of times going out with children
	number of times that my children involve me in their decisions regarding their lives

Perspective	Personal Performance Measures
External	level of appreciation by colleagues
	percent of my personnel who feel they have challenging work
	percent of my customers who want to quit because of dissatisfaction
	percent of completed, on-time deliveries, according to specifications
	time needed to fix a complaint
	percent of customers lost
	number of visits to important customers
	number of meetings with customer groups to be informed about their demands, requirements, ideas, and complaints
	number of concrete objectives with regard to customer satisfaction
	number of customer contacts
	number of customer surveys
	percent returning customers
	percent customers satisfied with communication
	degree of customer loyalty
	costs associated with losing a customer or gaining a new customer
	number of customer complaints regarding my behavior
	number of concrete objectives with regard to customer satisfaction
	perception score from others with regard to appreciation of the added value that I contribute
Knowledge & Learning	number of personal core competencies
	percent of learning objectives realized
	percent of improvement actions achieved
	number of time publicly sharing of knowledge
	number of violin lessons
	number of successful initiatives
	number of management courses followed
	percent of available management competencies
	percent of available strategic skills
	number of new management books read
	number of course days
	number of workshops and seminars attended
	number of required training courses
	number of articles published
	degree of client satisfaction with regard to my professionalism
	number of study days
	training costs
	number of effective initiatives as a manager
	number of effective initiatives implemented
	number of conscious learning moments
	sales based on newly acquired knowledge
	number of speaking engagements
	study expenditures
	percent of taxable income for investment in personal development
	ratio of number determined problems to solved problems
	number of solved problems

TABLE 5.1 Examples of Personal Performance Measures per BSC Perspective (continued)

Perspective	Personal Performance Measures
Knowledge & Learning	number of suggestions implemented number of innovative ideas which added value for others time spent on reading, debating, discussing number of books read about spirituality number of successful strategic improvement proposals number of innovative ideas number of necessary skills average time that I stay in the same position percent of communication failures lead time for product development percent sales from new products time needed to launch a new idea on the market (time-to-market) experience level of my colleagues regarding knowledge exchange
Financial	Personal Brand equity return stock investments annual turnover own company ratio earnings and expenses level pension provisions level of financial buffer percent of deviation from the budget percent of income from new orders percent revenue from new products balance savings account number of bills paid late level of debt savings balance income growth ratio of income to spending earnings salary bonus level cash flow pension disability insurance investment level profitability = sales/costs + interests received effectiveness = actual result/expected result labor productivity = result/labor costs labor costs = hours × hourly wage daily rate as consultant level of financial assets

Perspective	Personal Performance Measures
Financial	percent of income for charities
	number of successful acquisitions
	level of household expenses
	number of chargeable hours
	number of unpaid "overhead" days own consulting firm
	percent revenue from new products
	time span between two paid consultancy orders
	operational costs as a percentage of sales
	value added
	value added per work time

Source: Rampersad, 2006

Personal Improvement Actions

Personal improvement actions are strategies used to realize your Personal Ambition and Personal Brand. They are utilized to develop your skills, improve your behavior, master yourself, improve your performance, and to identify the subset of tools that will reach your target audience effectively. The central questions here are: How do I want to achieve my personal results? Which improvement actions do I need to achieve this? How to make my personality appropriate for my target market? What talents, skills and experience do I need to add value to others? How will I communicate my Personal Brand? How can I promote myself effectively? How can I develop my career successfully? How can I add value to others? How can I realize my personal objectives? How can I improve my behavior? How can I ensure that I learn continuously, individually as well as collectively? How can I get to know myself better? etc. An important action is gaining experience in areas of your brand in which you are weak.

There are two ways to define your personal improvement actions: (1) By selecting critical success factors in your Personal Ambition and Brand statement and translating these into personal objectives, performance measures, targets, and related improvement actions (according to Figure 5.3) and (2) by performing your personal SWOT analysis (see Table 4.1) and transforming your strengths, weaknesses and related opportunities and threats into personal improvement actions by using the confrontation matrix, see Table 5.2. This table shows how the internal factors related to my SWOT are combined with the external factors in a confrontation matrix. To illustrate what has been said about the Personal Balanced Scorecard, my PBSC will be discussed in the next section.

TABLE 5.2 Confrontation Matrix

Internal Environment / External Environment	**My Strengths (S)** S1: Creative and holistic insight S2: Work Experience S3: Good communicative skills S4: Enthusiastic, energetic, creative, open-minded, passionate (I love the work I do) and compassionate S5: Self-knowledge; I am aware of my personal ambition, interests, skills, personality, learning style, and values S6: Good education	**My Weaknesses (W)** W1: Impatient W2: Weak language skills W3: Diabetic W4: Weak work/life Balance
Opportunities (O) O1: Great network in Asia O2: Positive trends in outplacement field that will create more jobs O3: Organizations are investing more in human capital and employee engagement O4: Individuals are becoming aware about the importance of authentic personal branding, sustainable performance management O5: My domain is particularly in need of my set of skills O6: Opportunities for professional development in my field O7: Internet	**SO personal improvement actions (offensive)** SO1: Promote my brand more actively, publish more articles, update my website and identify subset of branding tools and branding channels that will reach my target audience effectively, based on S1-4 and O1-7 SO2: Be more helpful, inspire and encourage others to commit to their own dream, act as a role model, encourage creativity and innovation in others, and be more involved in the customer's situation, based on S1, S5, O2, O5, O6. SO3: Develop initiatives to benefit from the positive trends in outplacement field, based on S1 and O2.	**WO personal improvement actions (defensive)** WO1: Attend networking groups, network with fellow professionals, and develop network in North America, based on W2, O2, O3, O4, O5 WO2: Learn to do yoga effectively, balance the times of stress with times of pure relaxation and leisure, based on W3 WO3: Continue current diet, less candy, red wine in stead of beer, and healthy food (fruit/vegetables), based on W3. WO4: Initiate a training roster, at least 2 times a month a 20 mi bicycle trip, golf once a week, 3 times a week exercises at home, and rejoin tennis club, based on W3 WO5: Demonstrate effective emotional

	SO4: Publish 3 new books in the field of personal branding, PBSC and TPS-Lean Six Sigma, based on S1, S4, S6, O3, O4, O6 SO5: Effectively translate creative ideas into business results, based on S1, O1-6 SO6: Build effective TPS-partnerships across Asia, based on S1, S2, S6, O1 SO7: Explore opportunities for professional development in my field, based on S1-6 and O6 SO8: Initiate new initiatives due to the launch of my new Personal & Company Branding and TPS-Lean Six Sigma book, based on S1-6 and O4 SO9: Effectively anticipate on future opportunities, based on S1-6 and O1-7	responses in a variety of situations, based on W4 and O5 WO6: Act more pro-actively by being attentive of trends and developments in my domain, based on W2 and O2-6
Threats (T) T1: Weak network in North America T2: Copying behavior of competitors T3: Competitors with stronger marketing/ sales force (more money) T4: Competitors who went to Harvard Business School, MIT, Yale, and Stanford (schools with better reputation). T5: Negative trends in the US industry that diminish jobs T6: Many managers are not aware of the importance of a good work-life balance	**ST personal improvement action (adjust)** ST1: Pursue proven investment strategies, based on S1 and T3 ST2: Invest in promoting my Personal Brand and launch PBSC/Personal Branding software, based on S1-6 and T1-4. ST3: Decisive actions regarding brand promotion activities, based on S1-6 and T1-6	**WT personal improvement actions (survive)** WT1: Create work/life balance, based on W4 and T6 WT2: Show more patience, based on W1, and T3 WT3: Following a Spanish language coarse and read/speak Spanish more frequently, based on W2, T1, T3.

My Personal Balanced Scorecard

The first step in formulating my PBSC is deriving my Personal Critical Success Factors from my formulated Personal Ambition (Chapter 3) and Personal Brand statement (Chapter 4), see Table 5.3. They are related to the four perspectives, internal, external, knowledge & learning, and financial. These are factors which make me unique and in which I will further develop and distinguish myself. They have been identified in my ambition and brand statement and are in my PBSC further developed (see Table 5.4). Work/life balance and a healthy home environment are indispensable for my success. That is why this aspect is explicitly included in the external perspective of my PBSC. My personal improvement actions related to my SWOT (see Table 5.2) are added to my improvement actions, which are generated via my critical success factors, and included in my PBSC (see Table 5.4).

I am using the Personal BrandSoft, described in Appendix C, to develop, update, implement, and maintain my PBSC effectively. I am using my PBSC to improve myself continuously based on the feedback that I get from trusted friends. I am also constantly monitoring the progress of my

TABLE 5.3 My Personal Critical Success Factors, Derived from My Personal Ambition and Personal Brand Statement

Internal	External
• To live life completely, honestly, and compassionately • Enjoy physical and mental health • Experience enjoyment in my work	• Serve the needs of mankind • Passionate and compassionate to inspire others, earn their respect, and always serve out of love • Energize innovative organizations where human spirit thrives and which model the best practices in business performance and personal integrity • Love to serve learning individuals and innovative organizations to unlock their potential • Rita is the most important person in my life • Guide Rodney and Warren on the road to independence
Knowledge & Learning	**Financial**
• Enjoy the freedom to develop and share knowledge • Being full of initiative, accepting challenges continuously, and to keep on learning • Learn something new every day and always be a scholar	• Financial security

TABLE 5.4 My Personal Balanced Scorecard

Personal Critical Success Factors	Personal Objectives	Personal Performance Measures	Personal Targets	Personal Improvement Actions	Progress: In Progress	Progress: Reached my Target
			Internal			
To live life completely honestly, and compassionately	Be happy	Level of feeling happy	> 80% of my time	Accept new challenges continuously, update my PBSC frequently, ask for feedback, and be more patient.	X	
Enjoy physical and mental health	Emotionally strong	Number of hours of sleep	7 hours per day	Not endlessly continue activities but define a deadline and stick to it. Pay attention to the quality of sleep, not the quantity.	X	
	Be physically strong and fit	Weight	Per June 1, 2009 weight loss of at least 15 lbs.	Continue current diet, less candy, red wine instead of beer, and healthy food (fruit/vegetables).		X
		Body fat	Per May 1, 2009 decrease of 47.4% to 29.1%	Initiate a training roster, at least 2 times a month a 20 mi bicycle trip, golf once a week, 3 times a week exercises at home, and rejoin tennis club	X	X
Experience enjoyment in my work	No stress	Level of stress	Decrease of at least 75% within 6 months	Learn to do yoga effectively. Balance the times of stress with times of pure relaxation and leisure.	X	

(continued)

TABLE 5.4 My Personal Balanced Scorecard (continued)

Personal Critical Success Factors	Personal Objectives	Personal Performance Measures	Personal Targets	Personal Improvement Actions	Progress	
					In Progress	Reached my Target
			External			
Serve the needs of mankind	Satisfaction	Degree of satisfaction of others with regard to my actions	Satisfaction score of at least 80% within half year	Act more helpful without trying to gain profits from it. Provide positive recognitions and say "I'm sorry" and "thank you" more often.	X	
Passionate and compassionate to inspire others, earn their respect, and always serve out of love	Be of additional value to others	Appreciation score on delivered added value	Minimum 80% within one year	Be more helpful. Inspire and encourage others to commit to their own dreams. Act as a role model. Encourage creativity and innovation in others. Be more involved in their situation.	X	
Love to serve learning individuals and innovative organizations to unlock their potential	High Personal Brand awareness	Awareness score of my Personal Brand	Minimum 25% of my domain is aware of my brand within 1 year	Promote my Personal Brand more actively, publish more articles, attend networking groups, network with fellow professionals, update my website. Make effective use of Internet. Develop network in North America. Identify subset of branding tools and branding channels that will reach my target audience effectively.	X	
				Launch my Blog.	X	

		Percent of my revenue spent on Personal Branding	20% per year	Focus more on Personal Branding instead of marketing and sales. Develop initiatives to benefit from the positive trends in Personal Branding.	X	
Energize innovative organizations where human spirit thrives and which model the best practices in business performance and personal integrity	Be appreciated by my customers	Satisfaction score of my customers	Minimum 90% within 1 year	Ask feedback from customers and document this. Demonstrate effective emotional responses in a variety of situations. Encourage creativity and innovation in organizations. Develop initiatives to benefit from the positive trends in outplacement field.	X	
Rita is the most important person in my life	Be a good husband	Number of loving and appreciating feedback received from her	Minimum of once per day	Make loving remarks myself. Be open for her real needs. Go on vacation together three times a year. Create work/life balance based on this.		X
Guide Rodney and Warren on the road to independence	Be a good father	Number of times they involve me in their decisions	Whenever needed	Show more patience, listen more to them more carefully. Take an interested position, not a correcting one. Periodically inform, coach, advise and facilitate. Help them build their confidence and to deeply understand their own strengths and weaknesses.	X	

(continued)

TABLE 5.4 My Personal Balanced Scorecard (continued)

Personal Critical Success Factors	Personal Objectives	Personal Performance Measures	Personal Targets	Personal Improvement Actions	Progress: In Progress	Progress: Reached my Target
			Knowledge & Learning			
Enjoy the freedom to develop and share knowledge	Enjoyment	Level of enjoyment	Increase by at least 30% in 2009	Publish 3 new books in the field of personal branding, PBSC and TPS-Lean Six Sigma. Invest more in learning about future trends. Effectively translate creative ideas into business results. Share more.	X	
Being full of initiative, accepting challenges continuously, and to keep on learning	Being innovative	Number of new successful initiatives	At least four per month	Build effective TPS-partnerships across Asia. Explore opportunities for professional development in my field. Initiate new initiatives due to the launch of my new Personal & Company Branding and TPS-Lean Six Sigma book.		X
Learn something new every day and always be a scholar	Improved listening skills	Number of times positive feedback received from	At least 1 per week	Genuinely listen to others with more respect. Invest in ongoing personal		X

		others regarding my listening skills		development. Listening to people more patiently. Become a supportive listener.		
	Improved language skills	Time spend on learning Spanish language	At least 30 minutes per day during first Quarter 2009	Following a Spanish language course. Read and speak Spanish more frequently.	X	
			Financial			
Financial securities	Improved asset management	ROI stock portfolio	At least 8% per year	Pursue proven investment strategies		X
	Financially healthy	Revenues TPS International Inc.	20% increase in 2 years	Develop network in North America. Invest in promoting my Personal Brand, launch PBSC and Personal Branding software. Decisive actions regarding brand promotion activities. Act more pro-actively by being attentive of trends and developments in my target market. Effectively anticipate on future opportunities.	X	
	Manage expenditures	Income and expense ratio	Increase of minimum 10% per year	Be more costs conscious	X	

personal objectives, brand objectives, and personal improvement actions and tracking what works and what doesn't. Table 5.4 shows how I am monitoring the progress of my Personal Brand and my related personal objectives and improvement actions. Some important questions in this evaluation process are (see also Montoya, 2005b): Do I make more money? Do I get more referrals? Are opinions about my work stronger? Do more people know who I am, what I do, and what I stand for (brand awareness)? Am I being considered for more work? By continuously checking the data I am receiving from my own observations, I am keeping my brand relevant, focused, and emotionally connected with my target market.

My Personal Strategic Map

The position of my objectives, within the four perspectives, and their mutual relationships are made visible in Figure 5.4. In this cause effect chain my personal objectives are interrelated and affect one another. An objective is used to achieve another objective, which will result in a final objective. My final objective is to *be happy*. All my goals result in this final overall objective, which is related to my Personal Ambition and Personal Brand. I have included only the personal objectives that lead to this final objective. On the basis of this diagram, I am able to gain more insight into myself. It is

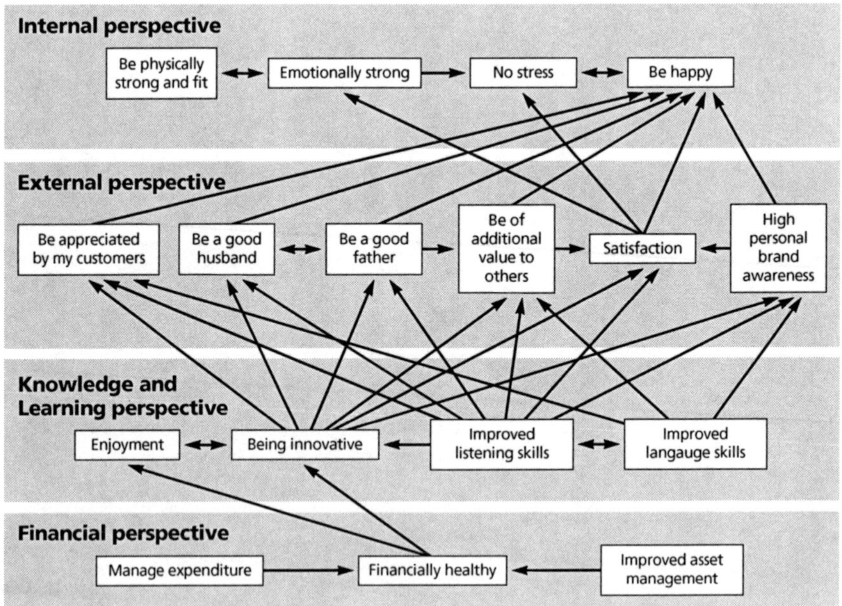

Figure 5.4 Cause-and-effect chain regarding my Personal Objectives.

also a handy tool in communicating my brand and PBSC to trusted persons. A trusted person is someone who deserves your trust, who respects you, who will guide you, who gives you honest feedback, who has consideration for you, is a mentor with your best interests in mind and offers you good guidance based on your Personal Ambition, Personal Brand and PBSC. Appendix D summarizes my Personal Ambition, the Personal Brand, the Personal Balanced Scorecard, and Strategic Map.

Giving Priority to Personal Improvement Actions

The final step in this PBSC formulation process is prioritizing your improvement actions to provide maximum impact. After all, dedication to an improvement action is much easier when the choice is clear. An other reason why it's important to prioritize your actions is that if you live by what's really important to you, you can make better time-management decisions. There are various ways to assign a priority number to the improvement actions. Here, I introduce an effective method, which has proven to be successful. In this approach, those personal improvement actions that contribute the most to the most important personal critical success factors (CSFs) receive the highest priority. The score for each improvement action is determined as follows:

- Giving a weight (W1) to the critical success factor in question.
- Giving a weight (W2) to the contribution of the improvement action in question to the critical success factor.
- Multiplying these two weights to obtain the priority score (formula: $P = W1 \times W2$).

The weights W1 and W2 are first estimated based on a number between one and five (see Table 5.5). The more important the personal CSF, the higher would be the value of the W1 factor. Similarly, the higher the contribution

TABLE 5.5 W1 and W2 Factors

The W1 factors are determined using the following scale:	The W2 factors were scaled as follows:
1 = unimportant	1 = no contribution
2 = somewhat unimportant	2 = hardly any contribution
3 = less important	3 = average contribution
4 = important	4 = high contribution
5 = very important	5 = very high contribution

of the personal improvement action to the CSF, the higher would be the W2 factor. The factor P is calculated by multiplying both average weights. Improvement actions with the highest P-factor (for instance ≥ 20) are part of the pre-selection. Then, the following criteria must be taken into consideration for the final selection of improvement actions:

- Are you passionate about this action? Do you love this action?
- Time needed for the implementation of the improvement action and the realization of the related personal objective.
- Costs related to the improvement action.
- The global costs-benefits ratio.
- The chances of the improvement action being successful (both manageable and realizable).
- It is best to start with a simple objective and the corresponding improvement actions, keeping in mind the above-mentioned aspects. Afterwards, bigger challenges can be taken on by selecting a corresponding improvement action and get going with it (see next chapter).

To illustrate this selection procedure, the priority number for each of my personal improvement actions in relation to the financial perspective is displayed in Table 5.6. It is shown that I have preselected the following financial improvement actions: *Invest in promoting my Personal Brand, decisive actions regarding brand promotion activities, effectively anticipate on future opportunities,* and *be more costs conscious.* All of these have a *p*-factor ≥ 20.

ASSIGNMENT

- Formulate your Personal Balanced Scorecard by identifying and selecting the critical success factors within your Personal Ambition and Personal Brand statement and translate these into your personal objectives with corresponding measures, targets, and improvement actions. This should be done for each of the four PBSC perspectives: internal, external, knowledge/learning, and financial.
- Draw your strategic management system (see my example in Appendix D).

Ask for guidance if you need support in formulating your Personal Balanced Scorecard effectively. In Appendix B you will find the Personal Brand Coaching framework and our related certification program, which is meant to be helpful for guiding you in this process. The related Personal BrandSoft, described in Appendix C, will assist you to execute this process efficiently.

In the next chapter I will focus on the implementation, maintenance, and cultivation of your Personal Ambition, Personal Brand and PBSC; in accordance with the Plan-Deploy-Act-Challenge cycle.

TABLE 5.6 Priority Number of Each of my Financial Personal Improvement Actions

Personal Improvement Actions	Contribution to Personal Critical Success Factor	Weight Personal Critical Success Factor W1	Contribution of Personal Improvement action to Critical Success Factor W2	Priority Number of Personal Improvement Actions P = W1 × W2
Pursue proven investment strategies	Financial securities	5	3	15
Invest in promoting my Personal Brand			5	25
Launch PBSC and Personal Branding software			2	10
Decisive actions regarding brand promotion activities			5	25
Act more pro-actively by being attentive of trends and developments in my domain			3	15
Effectively anticipate on future opportunities			4	20
Be more costs conscious			4	20

6

Implement and Cultivate Your Personal Ambition, Personal Brand, and Personal Balanced Scorecard

I get to play golf for a living. What more can you ask for—getting paid for doing what you love.

—Tiger Woods

Personal Branding will be of no use to you if you don't implement and cultivate your ambition, brand and PBSC (brand strategy) effectively. What I want to convey is that Personal Ambition, Personal Brand, and the PBSC have no value unless you implement them effectively to make them a reality. This entails the final stage in the Personal Branding journey (see Figure 6.1). To guide you with this, I will introduce the Plan-Deploy-Act-Challenge cycle (PDAC cycle) in this Chapter, which should be followed continuously to let your awareness grow gradually, to improve yourself continuously, and to deliver peak performance. To live in accordance with your

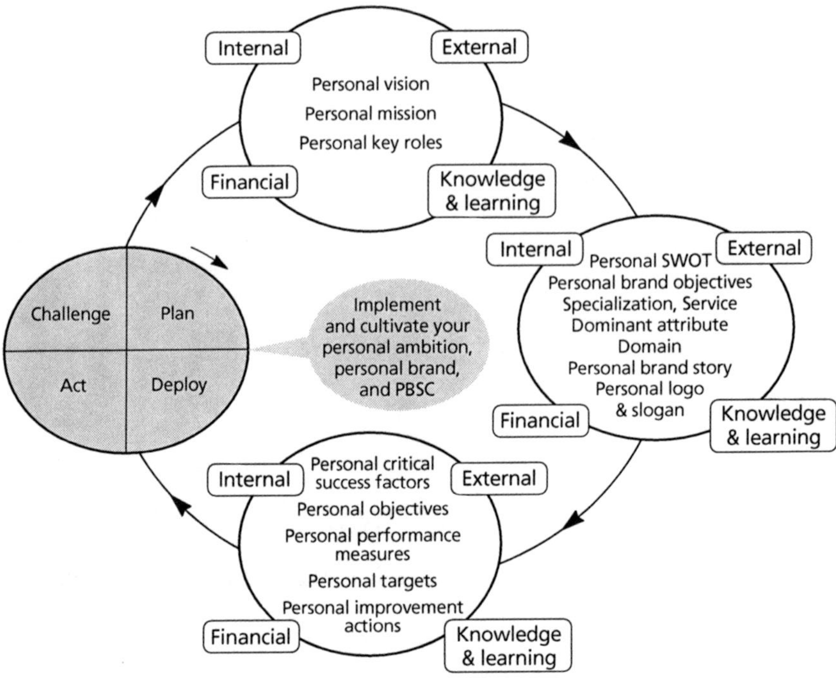

Figure 6.1 Fourth stage in the Authentic Personal Branding Model.

Personal Ambition, Personal Brand and related PBSC through its implementation using the PDAC cycle results in a journey towards self-awareness, joy, happiness, and marketing success. Once you implement and launch your Personal Brand, remember to continue maintaining and refining it. The more you strengthen, maintain, protect, and cultivate your brand, the more successful you'll be. It needs constant updating to reflect the new challenges you take, the lessons you have learned, and the growth of yourself and your brand. Personal Branding never stops. It's a continuous learning process.

In the following sections, each of the phases in the Plan, Deploy, Act, and Challenge cycle (see Figure 6.2) will be discussed in depth.

Plan

First of all you should recognize your responsibility to define, formulate, and update your authentic Personal Ambition, Personal Brand, and related Personal Balanced Scorecard. Know yourself, your core competencies, your dominant attribute, your service, your competitors, and your target audi-

Challenge

- Continually maintain and cultivate your Personal Ambition, Personal Brand, and PBSC in the light of new challenges, experiences, and insights
- Once you've got a track record, accept a larger challenge
- Be conscientious in choosing a more challenging and inspiring objective when the current improvement action starts becoming boring
- You brand needs constant updating to reflect the new challenges you take, the lessons you have learned, and the growth of yourself and your brand
- When you've accomplished all your goals, adjust your PBSC and start over
- Enjoy the experience, document what you have learned and celebrate the successes
- Repeat this PDAC cycle

Plan

- Define, formulate update your Personal Ambition
- Discover your genius and get very clear on what you want
- Fix it in your mind using the breathing and silence exercise
- List what you want to achieve and determine what you intend to give in return
- Visualize your Personal Ambition
- Evaluate yourself based on the SWOT analysis and the breathing and silence exercise
- Define, formulate, update your Personal Brand
- Create, update your Personal Brand Story and logo
- Formulate, update your PBSC
- Prioritize activities in your PBSC to provide maximum impact

Act

- Pursue with your Personal Ambition, Personal Brand and PBSC with courage and faith in yourself
- Live up to your brand promise and respond to it with love, and articulate it with passion
- Build a solid reputation within your industry and do work you love, which is consistent with your Personal Ambition and Brand
- Recognize your responsibility to improve yourself continuously and be committed to change
- Become an expert in your field and build credibility based on this
- Promote yourself, market your brand, and build effective relationships
- Communicate your brand story into everything you say and do
- Express your Personal Brand Story relentlessly, passionately, constantly and consistently and in a compelling way to everyone you meet
- Implement your personal improvement actions, assess the results, document the lessons learned, and improve and monitor your actions, behavior, and thinking continuously.

Deploy

- Focus your thoughts upon your Personal Ambition with great feeling, allow it, believe it, be open to receiving it, and give it all your positive energy
- Launch your Personal Brand on limited scale and try it out with trusted persons who can give you honest feedback
- Articulate your Personal Brand with love and passion
- Respond to your Personal Brand with love, passion courage, purpose and faith in yourself and live up to your brand promise
- Assess your Personal Brand and fine-tune this when it's not effective
- Implement your PBSC on limited scale, start with a simple objective and related improvement action with dedication, self-confidence, willpower and concentration
- Check if your improvement action is working and take action when it's not

Figure 6.2 The Plan-Deploy-Act-Challenge cycle (© H. Rampersad).

ence. Get very clear on what you want with your life, discover your genius and dream, visualize it, fix it in your mind using the breathing and silence exercise, list what you want to achieve, determine what you intend to give in return, accept personal responsibility for everything in your life, evaluate yourself based on the personal SWOT analysis, and create or update your brand story that communicates your value and market differentiation. List in your PBSC what you must do to achieve your brand and personal objectives. Specify how you are going to measure success at each step along the way. Prioritize activities in your PBSC to provide maximum impact and define the ideal communications tools and actions in your PBSC to reach your target audience effectively and to link your brand to all that you do.

Deploy

In this stage of the PDAC cycle you should focus your thoughts upon your Personal Ambition with passion. Allow it, believe it, be open to receiving it, and give it all your positive energy. Launch your Personal Brand on a limited scale and try it out with trusted persons who can give you honest feedback. Get the word out through a variety of media channels, publish articles that showcase your expertise, seek out conferences and meetings where you can give speeches and presentations. Respond to your Personal Brand with love, passion, courage, purpose and faith in yourself and live up to your brand promise. Assess your Personal Brand and fine-tune it when it's not effective. Implement your PBSC on limited scale, keeping in mind the priorities that have been identified. Start with a simple objective and related improvement action with love, dedication, self-confidence, willpower and concentration. Review the results according to the personal performance measures and targets you have defined in your PBSC. Measure your progress, and check to what extent you have realized your brand and personal objectives. Check if the improvement action is working, and take action if it is not. Make fine adjustments in your ambition, brand and PBSC if needed. As you can see in Table 5.4, I am constantly monitoring and evaluating the progress of my brand. Reflect on the following questions in this stage (see Chapter 5): Do I make more money? Do I get more referrals? Are opinions about my work stronger? Do more people know who I am, what I do, and what I stand for? Am I being considered for more work? By constantly monitoring and evaluating your personal objectives and actions you will keep your brand relevant, focused, and emotionally connected with your target market.

If you have not been able to realize your personal and brand objective, please do not worry about it. Just start again. Start with habits that restrict you, influence your brand unfavorably, and deliver poor results. Each morning when you rise, use the breathing and silence exercise, focus on a selected improvement action which you should then strive to implement during the day. Submit yourself with courage to the related objective, even when you run into resistance. Be determined in the realization of your personal objectives and don't give up. Choose individuals close to you, who you can trust, who listen effectively and give you honest feedback on your Personal Ambition, Personal Brand and PBSC; these persons could be, for example, your spouse, children, manager, colleagues or friends. Share your good intentions with them and ask them often for feedback. Use this feedback and your own observations to look for gaps and progress points, based on the personal targets in your PBSC. Act in the next stage to close the gaps. In this way you will be staying on course. It will also become a habit to do right things right the first time if you evaluate your Personal Ambition, Personal Brand and PBSC regularly with trusted persons, and learn from their experience. Think of three people, who can act as your trusted person; who give you inspiration and motivation for the realization of your objectives and improvement actions. Plan to meet with each one of them regularly. Listen enthusiastically to them, brainstorm with them, and take their counsel. Praise them for investing time and energy to offer you feedback. Find venues and a variety of media channels for communicating your Personal Brand to get your name out.

Act

Pursue your Personal Ambition, Personal Brand and PBSC with courage and faith in yourself, live up to your brand promise and respond to it with love and passion, and align your Personal Ambition and Personal Brand with your behavior and actions in order to develop personal integrity (see next Chapter). Become an expert in your field and build credibility based on this. Promote yourself and your personal code of ethics, market your brand, build effective relationships, network with fellow professionals, and express your Personal Brand Story relentlessly, passionately, constantly, consistently, and in a compelling way to everyone you meet. Find venues for your voice, express yourself, and communicate your brand story into everything you say and do. Keep your Personal Brand statement in mind when carrying out activities and dealing with others. Articulate your Personal Brand with love and passion. Improve your perceived value in the marketplace based on your PBSC and according to the PDAC cycle (putting your Personal Brand to work). You should also constantly measure your brand, evaluate your relationships, and check the status if you are reaching your brand and life objectives in order to understand what your brand stands for, how it's impacting your connection with others, if it is still relevant, if it is authentic, and if you are reaching your target audience. Take actions if there is a gap between where you are and where you want to be. It could be you who should change (learn or unlearn) and listen more carefully. Maybe you promised more than you could or maybe they expected something different from what you promised. In both cases you have to redefine your brand and/or communication.

Develop your talents and skills to achieve your personal and brand objectives. Use your PBSC to improve yourself continuously based on the feedback that you get from trusted friends. Remember what Donald Latumahina said:

> There is no such thing as instant improvement in life. And as you know in agriculture, growth can only happen little by little over time. The things that you do daily may seem small and insignificant, but over time people will be surprised to learn how much you have grown in life. Focus on the small things daily. The keyword here is daily. If you don't have the persistence to do these small things consistently, you won't be able to see the results over the long term.

Recognize your responsibility to improve yourself continuously and be committed to change. It is your ethical duty and moral responsibility to change—not only for your own good, but also for your loved ones, your work, your organization, your country, and for the world that you are part of. You should be the change. Remember what Gandhi said: "We must become the change we want to see in the world." Use this personal branding system to coach and master yourself (see Appendix B). You will improve steadily based on this. Implement your personal improvement actions, assess the results, document the lessons learned, and improve and monitor your actions, behavior, and thinking continuously. After a few weeks, you will notice small differences in yourself. In two months, the behavioral change will become firmly embedded. After five months, the important personal quality you desired will be yours and this will affect your brand positively. Also at this stage you should use the breathing and silence exercise. After all, to turn your brand into action, you need energy. Energy is increased by habitually practicing the breathing and silence exercise.

Ask for feedback about your brand from trusted friends, colleagues, customers, and others. Use your time effectively based on your PBSC, which is a plan for achieving your personal goals, actions, and priorities. Your PBSC will help you to be ruthless with time-wasting, and organize it more effectively. When something adverse happens or someone tries to pull you off course, you quickly return to your chosen path with the full knowledge that you are moving in the direction that you have stated in your ambition, brand, and PBSC.

Build a solid reputation within your industry and do work you love that is consistent with your passion, Personal Ambition and Personal Brand. To excel in your career you may need to complete additional education and training, which will enhance your brand. If you are unsure whether you need more education, seek out a personal coach, and ask for advice. He/she will assist you in achieving your goals. Ask the coach for honest and helpful feedback on your performance and growth. Promote yourself and market your brand. Express what you stand for to everyone you meet. Do this frequently and consistently. If you are inconsistent, people will not trust you. When you deliver on the brand promise you make, they will trust and value you.

Personal Branding is part of everything you do. It's about turning every part of yourself into a marketable product. Everything you do and don't do communicates the value of your brand. You should also make conscious choices about the people you associate with, the clothes you wear, and the way you speak and act. Remember also this: "The wise man, even when he holds his tongue, says more than the fool when he speaks.... A hero is someone who can keep his mouth shut when he is right" (Yiddish proverb). Surround yourself with people who share your Personal Ambition and value your Personal Brand. Everything about you should be related to your brand message. Include your brand clearly in your resume or CV. It is important to know that, according to a survey by the Society of Human Resource Managers (SHRM), over 53% of all job applicants lie to some extent on their resumes. More than 70% of all college students said they would lie on their resumes to get a job (Guarneri, 2007). For this reason many HR officers don't take resumes seriously anymore and job-seekers can no longer distinguish themselves just with a strong resume. Defining your brand based on your Personal Ambition and Personal Brand also allows job-seekers to identify companies that have similar values and beliefs and helps employees to align their Personal Brand with the company brand (see Chapter 13 and Rampersad, 2007).

You can have a great Personal Brand, but if no one knows or recognizes it, you are not going to have much success with your career. Create a representative and professional personal website that is specifically designed to deliver your brand message and showcase your key accomplishments, skills, education, successes, and summary of your career. Your website should also include your articles, speeches, awards, testimonials, etc. Use it to communicate your brand to others, and list it at every major search engine. A new trend is the fact that employers are "Googling" the names of prospective job-seekers and screening them partly based on the number of hits. Therefore your brand needs to have a strong online presence. A strong Blog will also work well in obtaining a Google score. Be aware though that the content of your blog also must adhere to your Personal Brand. My blog's domain is rampersad.wordpress.com. If you don't exist on Google, Yahoo and MSN, you don't exist. A strong "googleability" rating and online presence will enhance your Personal Brand. Be aware of the power of this new medium and the impact it has on your competitive advantage.

Design a cool-looking logo for your business card. Build a network of contacts who know your brand value and are able to communicate it, keep your network strong, keep in good contact with your network and make sure they are aware of your most recent successes. Search out new professional associations and online networking communities in order to introduce yourself to others and showcase your skills. Therefore it's important to build a strong profile on LinkedIn and share this with others. View my professional profile on LinkedIn, *www.linkedin.com/in/hubertrampersad.* It's powerful if your friends, colleagues, customers, clients, and managers talk about you and your skills, education, and accomplishments and if they help spread the word about what a remarkable contributor you are. Success also depends on good word of mouth about you. Have a clearly defined target audience for your brand message and select the proper branding channels to communicate your brand effectively. Table 6.1 shows the most important personal branding channels and tools that can be used in this stage of the PDAC cycle, see also Montoya (2005b).

I have summarized my Personal Ambition and Personal Brand statement on a card and keep this in my pocket every day (Box 6.1). I am using this as a compass for my actions and decisions, to keep me focused, to

TABLE 6.1 Personal Branding Channels and Tools

Branding Channels	Branding Tools
• Networking • Direct/E-Mailing • Advertising, commercials, banners • Tradeshows • Seminars • Client referrals (word of mouth) • Professional referrals (testimonials) • Press releases, media kit, sponsorships • Warm calling (call after having made contact with the prospect) • Publishing articles and/or books • Writing a column • Public speaking • Sharing information via LinkedIn	• Personal brochure (entails your Personal Ambition, personal life story, and Personal Brand) • Personal postcard • Personal website • Search engines; If you don't exist on Google, you don't exist • Business card • Audio tapes and CDs • PowerPoint presentation • E-Newsletter • Online discussion board (community) • They way you look, dress, talk, smile, use your hand/eyes,... (your visual "package") • Personal Ambition & Brand on a card • LinkedIn • Breathing and silence exercise • Blogging

BOX 6.1: PERSONAL AMBITION AND BRAND HUBERT RAMPERSAD

Personal Vision

To live life completely, honestly, and compassionately and to serve the needs of mankind to the best of my ability. I want to realize this in the following way:

- Enjoy physical and mental health
- Passionate and compassionate to inspire others, earn their respect, and always serve out of love
- Energize innovative organizations where human spirit thrives and which model the best practices in business performance and personal integrity
- Experience enjoyment in my work by being full of initiative, accepting challenges continuously, and to keep on learning
- Achieve financial security

Personal Mission

Enjoy the freedom to develop and share knowledge, especially if this can mean something in the life of others.

Personal Key Roles

In order to achieve my vision, the following key roles have top priority:

Spouse: Rita is the most important person in my life
Father: Guide Rodney and Warren on the road to independence
Coach: Love to serve learning individuals and innovative organizations to unlock their potential
Student: Learn something new every day and always be a scholar

Personal Brand Statement

Linking Human Capital to Business Success

Passionate and compassionate to inspire learning individuals to unlock their potential and dedicated to energize innovative organizations within the service and manufacturing industry. Using my holistic insight and innovative Total Performance Scorecard principles, I promise to help my customers to realize their dreams.

guide me in the right direction, and to help me communicate my brand story effectively.

I am broadcasting my authentic Personal Brand and logo in work and life, as defined in Chapter 4, over and over again, continuously, consistently and repeatedly, in order to embed this in the minds of my target audience, by using most of the mentioned branding tools and channels. I am expressing my brand in a way that is different from the competition. My brand statement, logo, and slogan are consistent and visible in everything I do. This creates familiarity and presumption of my quality. I make it relevant to all the relationships in my life (people at work, family, friends). I demonstrate passion and I let my target market know that I am the professional to provide them value that they can't get anywhere else and that I like what I do. I always under-promise and over-deliver, deliver what I promise and always meet deadlines. In this way I am managing the client expectations effectively. I commit myself to act according to my Personal Ambition and my Personal Brand. My brand is 100% true to what I am, I love, and my ability to perform. In this way I provide value to my customers continuously, create visibility, and make an emotional connection with them. They associate me with something valuable and new. I love my clients, treat them with care, respect, empathy, and show interest in what they are telling me. I also make connections and friends, build my network, and start relationships continuously. I add value to my clients by helping them to realize their dream and providing them free articles, free use of my on-line TPS-Life Cycle Scan (see Chapter 10), and discount on special services and products. I assess my Personal Ambition and Personal Brand continuously to check how well or how poorly I connect with what others need and expect from me. I am improving myself continuously based on this and learning also from my failures. Remember what Ralph Waldo Emerson said, "Our greatest glory is not in never failing, but in rising up every time we fail."

Challenge

Once you define, formulate, implement your Personal Ambition, Personal Brand, and PBSC, remember to continue cultivating and maintaining these in the light of new challenges, experiences and insights. You need to monitor, refine, fine-tune, and cultivate these three branding elements as you go along, figuring out which parts work and which don't, in order to create brand loyalty. You should constantly check and monitor your target market and make adjustments as necessary. You need to check whether your brand is still relevant for your target market, whether it still reflects who you really are, whether it is authentic, whether your objectives have to changed, whether your message is OK, whether the competition is copying your brand, etc. You need to refine your Personal Brand promise as you go along, figuring out which parts work and which don't, and make adjustments as necessary. You should continually refine your brand promise in the light of new insights, challenges, and experiences. Because there will always be competing brands ready to fill any gap you leave behind. The more you strengthen, maintain, protect, and cultivate your brand, the more successful you'll be. It needs constant updating to reflect the new challenges you take, the lessons you have learned, and to grow you and your brand. You should therefore update your website, personal brochure, etc. from time to time in order to keep people interested.

Once you have a track record, accept a larger challenge which is in line with your improved talents and skills and get on with it. This means select a more difficult objective and the corresponding improvement action from your PBSC and act on it with love and passion. This can make you happy. After all, when people are free to face challenges, they tend to be happier. Be conscientious in choosing a more challenging and inspiring objective in line with your improved skills when the current improvement action starts becoming boring. Remember what Tony Dorsett said: "To succeed . . . You need to find something to hold on to, something to motivate you, something to inspire you." Enjoy the experience and document what you have learned and unlearned during the execution of the improvement actions and celebrate the successes. Review your PBSC regularly and sometimes return to earlier stages to refine your ambition or brand. Also in this stage you should use the breathing and silence exercise and ask for feedback continuously. When you have accomplished all your goals, adjust your PBSC and start over and repeat the PDAC cycle. You must repeat the PDAC cycle over and over again. If you are well branded according this authentic approach and if you implement your brand according the PDAC cycle, you will attract the people and opportunities that are a perfect fit for you and realize your brand and life objectives. You will also develop self-esteem (confidence and satisfaction in yourself) that will lead to happiness.

Figure 6.3 shows how the engaging personal branding gears lead to powerful and sustainable personal branding. Since the Plan-Deploy-Act-Challenge cycle keeps on running through this, you create a stable basis for maximum brand development and personal well being. You will also constantly improve your performance and continuously satisfy others. Through this, you can work passionately toward inner and outer excellence, can decide your own fate and can become more self-confident. You will also create a feeling of inner security and will become a better person on the basis of

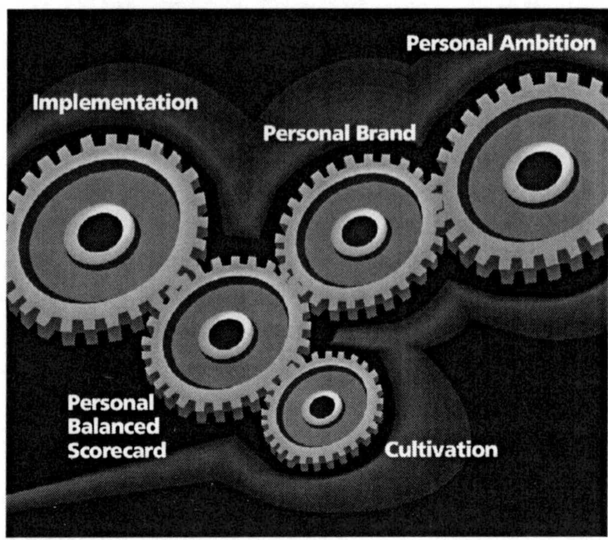

Figure 6.3 Personal Branding gears.

the match between Personal Ambition/Brand and your behavior, in combination with practice of the breathing and silence exercise.

Implementation and cultivation of your Personal Ambition, Personal Brand and PBSC in accordance with the PDAC cycle result in a process of total involvement with life. It will make you feel content with the challenging activity you are fulfilling in such a way that you will forget everything around you. This process is called *Flow* by Mihaly Csikszentmihalyi (1990). Flow is the result of a conscious effort to conquer a challenge; it is the result of a search for optimum experiences, the constant discovery of new challenges and the continuous development of new skills. Flow is controlling/managing your life without efforts. According to Csikszentmihalyi, someone is in flow when both challenges and skills are at a high level. People feel happier, more cheerful, stronger, more active, more creative and satisfied in this situation. It has been hypothesized that happy people may be healthier both mentally and physically than less happy people. It is said that happiness lies in the rhythm of life and life is a flow. Application of your Personal Ambition, Personal Brand and PBSC and implementation in accordance with the PDAC cycle produces flow. As stated before, by aligning your Personal Ambition (which is related to your destiny) with your Personal Brand and accepting this, you will become in flow and live effortlessly. You will expand your individual awareness to universal awareness, master yourself, and market your brand successfully. It will open up new horizons for you in your quest for an optimal state of health and happiness.

Formulating your Personal Ambition/Brand/PBSC and implementing this effectively according to the PDAC-cycle also result in managing your intuition effectively. Weston Agor (1998) says on this:

> Tomorrow's managers will face extremely complex situations in which they will need to make decisions under circumstances where the complete data necessary for traditional decision-making process will be unavailable, inadequate, or too costly to gather quickly. They will be dealing with a changing world and a work-force that will make increasing demands for real participation in the decision-making process. Managers will need to rely less on formal authority and more on intuitive judgment in order to handle the shift to bottom-up, horizontal organizational communication with sensibility and persuasiveness. Managers will need a new set of skills to cope with this shifting environment. Until now, the predominant management approach has been the logical, analytical, left-brain style... Intuition will become more and more valuable during the coming period of surprises, complexities, and rapid changes. Intuition becomes more efficient as we become more open to our feelings and more secure trough experience in its ability to provide the correct cues. The first rule is to believe in it. The second rule is practice makes perfect. With effort and persistence, we can develop our intuition. The third rule is to create a supportive environment in which intuitive skills are valued.

Box 6.2 shows a summary of the activities that you should consider in this process of implementation and cultivation of your Personal Ambition, Personal Brand, and PBSC. I recommend reading *The Top 200 Secrets of Success and the Pillars of Self-Mastery* by Robin Sharma and *What Got You Here Won't Get You There* by Marshall Goldsmith. They contain a wealth of wisdom and powerful insights for further developing your character and tackling your weaknesses.

BOX 6.2:
Summary of Activities in the Process of Implementation and Cultivation of Your Personal Ambition, Personal Brand, and PBSC

- Understand yourself, formulate this in your Personal Ambition statement, and manage yourself based on this.
- Identify your uniqueness, stick with it, don't lose sight of this, and maintain focus based on this.
- Recognize your responsibility to make personal improvement a routine and a continuous process.
- Regularly evaluate your need/desire to improve and the necessity of personal growth.

- Learn to learn and to unlearn; Learning and unlearning is a life long exercise.
- Implement and cultivate your Personal Brand routinely and improve and monitor your actions and thoughts continuously based on the Plan-Deploy-Act-Challenge cycle.
- Ask for trusted person's comments and perceptions. Revise, refine, update, maintain, and cultivate your Personal Ambition, Personal Brand, and PBSC based on their feedback.
- Think like a business and be the CEO of your own life.
- Communicate your brand message with love and passion. Remember: you are this message!
- Live in harmony with your Personal Ambition and Personal Brand; live your brand.
- Live up to the promise made by your Personal Ambition and Personal Brand.
- Keep promises that you make to yourself.
- Achieve behavioral changes and constantly challenge your behavior.
- Make time in your schedule to improve and to help others improve.
- Attend to your continued education and see your job as a learning experience.
- Take advantage of learning opportunities and take initiatives.
- Pursue innovation and new ideas based on your brand and the Plan-Deploy-Act-Challenge cycle.
- Be observant, a good listener, and remove the barriers you normally erect.
- Maintain a positive attitude toward life and constantly evaluate your behavior.
- Perform the breathing and silence exercise regularly.
- Learn to be still and enjoy the power of silence for at least ten minutes a day.
- Enjoy learning about everything from everyone.
- Demonstrate commitment and leadership, set an example, and act as a role model.
- Use your Personal Brand to establish yourself as an expert in your field and to build a solid reputation within your industry.
- Include your Personal Brand on your personal website. Make sure that you exist on Google.
- Regularly assess your relationships with your family, supervisor, peers, subordinates, customers, and others.

- Be authentic, consistent, and proactive; make conscious choices based on what you truly stand for.
- Think positive and be flexible.
- Make sure that your brand is relevant to the marketplace.
- Develop your communication skills and foster co-operation and communication.
- Be constantly aware of the cultural changes in your domain.
- Network, make contacts, and know your audience and their needs.
- Treat others like trusted friends; with respect, restraint and empathy.
- Turn your weaknesses into strengths.
- Specialize, focus; Focus on the one area where you are most capable of creating value and distinction.
- Empower yourself, upgrade your skills, and improve your imagination and creativity.
- Package, sell, and promote yourself based on your Personal Brand statement.
- Be passionate and spontaneous in everything you do and love what you do.
- Avoid extreme behavior and remain calm.
- Trust or believe in yourself and in your potential and boost your self-esteem.
- Trust others, be trustworthy, and show transparency and accountability; Find a balance between your personal ambition and your behavior. Live with personal integrity.
- Be the most honest person that you know; know your personal values and beliefs.
- Be truthful, patient, persevering, modest and generous; be someone with a warm heart and great character.
- Have respect for others and speak honestly and well of others.
- Judge others fairly and correctly.
- Communicate effectively; the quality of your life is the quality of your communication with others and yourself.
- Cultivate and foster new friendships, especially with those who have shared many experiences and laughs with you; relationships are essential for maintaining a healthy and successful life.
- Show compassion and sincere consideration for all your friends and develop long-lasting friendships by being a good friend.

- Contribute to others; Start with giving, than receiving.
- Treat everyone who crosses your path as if he/she is the most important person in your life.
- Develop the habit of punctuality; it reflects discipline and a proper regard for others.
- Speak less and listen more. You will learn much, as everyone we meet, every day has something to teach us. Listening is the beginning of all wisdom. Learning is listening effectively.
- Learn to always think positively; when a negative thought comes to your mind, immediately replace it with one that is positive.
- Dedicate yourself to leaving a powerful legacy to the world.
- See every opportunity as a chance to learn.
- Be an explorer; find pleasure in the things that others take for granted.
- Have courage and inspire others with your actions.
- Take anyone you think is highly effective and ethical as your role model. Visualize this person and do like him/her.
- Never feel that you have no time for new ideas, you are investing in yourself.
- Become an adventurer and revitalize your spirit and sense of playfulness. Take time out for the renewal of your mind, body and spirit.
- Follow and trust your conscience and intuition.
- Never do anything you wouldn't be proud to tell your mother.
- Know your best qualities and cultivate them.
- Never complain, be known as a positive, strong, energetic and enthusiastic person.
- Fill your mind with thoughts of serenity, positivity, strength, courage and compassion.
- Create an image of yourself as a highly competent, strong, disciplined, calm and decent individual. Include this in your Personal Ambition and your Personal Brand statement.
- Schedule relaxation time into your week; spend time in reflection, unwinding and recharging your batteries.
- Make time for the things that matter most; choose what is important and filter out what is of no value. Focus on those objectives that are truly important; read only those materials that will be useful to you.
- Create work–life balance.

- Be disciplined in following the schedule of your PBSC.
- Add at least one new thing to your resume monthly.
- Seek out knowledge. Knowledge is power. The more you know, the less you fear. The more one knows, the more one achieves.
- Read more, learn more, laugh more and love more.
- Work in harmony with others and work hard; no success comes without hard work.
- Show your appreciation and respect for your loved ones.
- The essence of a person is his character; make yours unique, unblemished and strong.
- Place greater importance on staying happy than amassing material possessions; be happy with what you have.
- Strive to be humble and live a simple, uncluttered and productive existence.
- Be committed to what you are doing and to being a better parent, friend and citizen.
- Be known as an idea person, willing to take on challenges and tackle them with passion and enthusiasm.
- Spend at least half an hour every day alone—in peaceful introspection, reading or just relaxing.
- Cultivate the habit of optimism.
- Develop a focused state of mind. Pay attention to your spiritual development so as to gain greater self-confidence.
- Give attention to the development of spirit, health, and useful activities; you cannot do good unless you feel good. When you are serene, relaxed and enthusiastic you are also more productive, creative and dynamic.
- Dedicate yourself to higher knowledge and to the development of a higher level of consciousness.
- Always pursue your personal objectives.
- Be in control of yourself and in flow.
- Do not waste energy on your ego.
- Learn to measure and understand processes and to use data that support your decisions.
- Know your target audience. You should know and understand others, not only yourself.
- Doing the right things right the first time is determined by enjoyment, love, passion, courage, self-responsibility, self-confidence, self-knowledge, self-learning, and personal integrity.

ASSIGNMENT

- Implement your Personal Ambition, Personal Brand and PBSC according to the PDAC cycle.
- Ask feedback from others.
- Meet with them regularly, listen to them, and take their counsel.
- Revise, refine, update, maintain, and cultivate your Personal Ambition, Personal Brand, and PBSC based on their feedback.

Ask for guidance if you need support in implementing and cultivating your authentic Personal Ambition, Personal Brand, and Personal Balanced Scorecard effectively. In Appendix B you will find the Personal Brand Coaching framework and our related certification program, which is meant to be helpful for coaching you in this process. The related Personal BrandSoft, described in Appendix C, will assist you to execute this process efficiently.

Having an authentic and powerful Personal Brand is not enough to be successful. You need to create trust by delivering on your brand promise. If you don't do this, personal branding will be cosmetic, selfish, and a dirty business. In the next chapter I will focus on this important step towards developing honesty, trustworthiness, credibility, transparency, and personal charisma.

7

Aligning Your Personal Ambition and Personal Brand with Your Behavior and Actions

Alignment with Yourself

Your Personal Brand is based on your values, not the other way around... Consistency is the hallmark of all strong Personal Brands. Inconsistency weakens brands and suspends belief.

—David McNally & Karl Speak

Having a great Personal Brand identity, powerful Personal Brand story, effective Elevator Pitch and strong Unique Value Proposition can make you a big winner; or a big looser if your Personal Brand doesn't reflect your true character and if you don't deliver on your related promise. Not delivering on your promise is a secure way to ruin your reputation and career. So, commit yourself to live and act according to your authentic brand promise and be careful to ensure that you can deliver. If you don't do this, personal branding will be cosmetic, selfish, egocentric, and a dirty greedy business. People relate to you on your word, and how you fulfill on that. When you say you will do something, you should do that with no excuses. Each time you make or break a promise you are affecting your Personal Brand image. You should also keep promises that you make to yourself. If you break a promise to yourself you will not have inner peace and will not develop personal charisma and transparency, which will affect your Personal Brand. You have to live your values consistently on a day-to-day basis and show transparency and accountability. A Personal Brand built on lies will crash (truth always comes out), and a brand built on the person's true character is sustainable and strong. To borrow Dwight Eisenhower's words: a *person that values its privileges above its principles soon loses both.*

Your authentic Personal Branding should reflect your true self and must adhere to a moral and behavioral code set down by your Personal Ambition. This means that who you really are, what you care about, and your passions should come out in your brand, and you should act and behave accordingly (you should be yourself) to build trust. Trust will be built faster when others believe you are real and when they witness you being true to your beliefs and aligned with who you really are. You will build trust when your values connect to your attitudes and actions and when you are true to yourself. Remember, the most important brand relationship you have is with yourself, it's not just being authentic to others. Building trust starts with being true and authentic to yourself. This involves finding the proper balance between your Personal Ambition/Brand and your behavior and actions in order to create a stable basis for trust. It's about alignment with yourself. This inner alignment is an important step towards lasting personal growth and reinforcing integrity, honesty, trustworthiness, credibility, transparency, and personal charisma. People with this perspective on life value others' lives and create a stable basis for others to feel they are credible, truthful, and trustworthy. They:

- Practice what they preach.
- Keep their word; their actions match their words and their Personal Ambition/Brand.
- Keep their brand promises; there is consistency between their Personal Brand and their behavior.
- Do what they said they would do, despite the obstacles.

When you achieve this inner authority, you also have a positive effect on the loyalty, motivation, and dedication of those around you. As a result of this, promoting yourself based on your Personal Brand will be much easier, sustainable, and successful. In this way your *Personal Image* (what others identity with you) will be in harmony with your *Personal Brand* (how others perceive you); your image will be a reflection of your brand. This alignment of your ambition/brand and your behavior is needed because if you don't deliver according to your brand promise it will negatively affect your reputation and damage your Personal Brand. Therefore it's advisable to under-promise and over-deliver always.

As noted earlier, a nice Personal Ambition and Personal Brand statement and a related PBSC without personal integrity is cosmetic and will not lead to your sustainable development and your brand's. It will also not create a stable basis for effective personal leadership. I am referring to Miller and Pruzan (2003):

> There is such a need for a complete rebirth of trust in our business leaders. Somewhere along the line leaders lost their humility and in doing so they have lost their compassion and empathy, and their inner connection to God.

The most intimate relationship you have is with yourself. You will strengthen this relationship and build personal integrity by aligning your Personal Ambition and Personal Brand with your behaviour and actions—with who and what you really are. "*Authentic you*" means your personality, spirit, character. This aligning process is about the interaction between your dream, aspirations, intentions, purpose, and values—in other words, your Personal Ambition and your Personal Brand—and how others interpret you (your personal behavior). Your values (which are part of your Personal Ambition and Personal Brand) are the principles by which you live your life, and affect the way you think, feel, act, and behave. When your actions, behavior, and thoughts reflect your values, the result is personal integrity. This affects your relationship with others and yourself positively.

There is a potential difference between how you see yourself (who you want to be), and how others judge you (how you are perceived by others). While we judge ourselves by our invisible behavioral patterns, others judge us by our visible behavioral patterns—what we do and say and how we act. These judgments are the perceptions of you in the heads of others. The more distinctive your actions, the better your brand becomes for them. To become the person envisioned in your Personal Ambition and Personal Brand, you also have to know how others see you and what they think of you. When you know this, your self-knowledge increases and you will be able to improve the effectiveness of your actions. As a result your brand will be stronger. Therefore, this process of authentic Personal Branding involves also the establishment of a balance or fit between your Personal

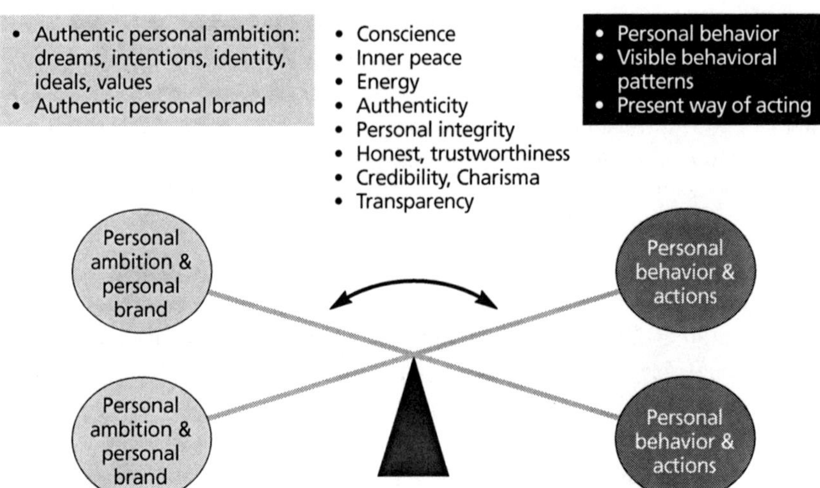

Figure 7.1 Aligning Personal Ambition and Personal Brand with Personal Behavior and Actions.

Ambition and Personal Brand (which envisions a higher level of consciousness) and your personal behavior (which refers to your present behavior and actions), see Figure 7.1.

As I have discussed, your Personal Ambition and Personal Brand are also shaped by your mindset. Behind these opinions, your motives and inner needs as expressed through your behavior are hidden. In order to achieve sustainable personal improvement and growth, and to distinguish yourself from the crowd, it is necessary to find a balance between your Personal Ambition/Brand and your personal behavior/actions:

Personal Ambition & Personal Brand = Personal behavior & actions

Personal Vision + Mission + Key Roles + Specialty + Service +
Dominant Attribute + Domain = Personal behavior + Actions

You should reflect during this alignment process on the following questions:

- Do I act in accordance with my conscience and my values?
- Is there consistency between what I am thinking and what I am doing?
- How do my ideals, ambitions, intentions, needs, deepest desires, and Personal Brand fit my present actions?

- Are my thoughts and my practices the same?
- Do I act consistently in accordance with my Personal Ambition and Personal Brand?
- Do my Personal Ambition and Personal Brand reflect my desire to act ethically?
- Are there contradictions in my Personal Ambition and Personal Brand?
- In what way does my behavior influence my views, and vice versa?
- Do I keep promises that I make to myself?
- How do others perceive me and my values?
- Do they witness me being true to my core beliefs and me staying in alignment with who I really am?

Your Personal Ambition/Brand and your practices must be the same. When you find harmony between your Personal Ambition/Brand and your personal behavior, you will not come into conflict with your conscience. Then you can work authentically and purposefully at launching your brand without wasting energy and with inner peace. In this way you will enhance your charisma, be transparent and become trusted. Robin Sharma said, "Be the master of your will but the servant of your conscience." G.P. Gupta believes that

> Consciousness is the "inner aspect" of life. It's made up of two elements: (1) awareness of self and things, (2) forces and conscious power. Awareness is the first necessity; you have to be aware of things in the right consciousness, in the right way, seeing them in their truth. But awareness by itself is not enough. There must be a Will and Force that make the consciousness effective... If one changes one's consciousness the whole world itself changes for you... Based on consciousness, management has to be developed "Within-to-Without."

According to Selvazajan Yesudian,

> our conscience is the inner voice that talks to us with firm conviction to help us distinguish between right and wrong, between fact and fiction. It is a voice that whispers to us what we can do best and guides us in our daily activities. It is a voice that we can trust and on which we can build our existence. It is the only reliable compass to follow if there is a conflict between the mind that reasons and the heart that decides.

Harmony between your Personal Ambition/Brand and your personal behavior/actions ensures that your deeds are in accord with your conscience. You will gain better insight into your behavior, your strengths and weaknesses and your related brand/personal objectives. It has also an impact on your solidarity with others. Remember what Albert Schweitzer said: "The first step in the evolution of ethics is a sense of solidarity with other human beings." Harmony between Personal Ambition/Brand and personal behavior also has to do with attentiveness, namely, to continuously perceive what you do and be aware of the influence of your behavior and actions on human beings, animals, plants and the environment (social responsibility). As this attentiveness develops, your ethical behavior will increase. The breathing and silence exercise previously introduced and reflection on the match between your Personal Ambition/Brand and your personal behavior/actions will help to stimulate your attentiveness. You will also become a better human being and a strong brand.

THE BEST WAY TO LOOK AT SUCCESS IS TO ASK:

- Have I followed my conscience consistently?
- Have I followed my Personal Ambition consistently?
- Have I followed my Personal Brand consistently?
- Have I given it my best effort consistently?
- Have I done what was right consistently?

The ability to look at oneself honestly and openly is the most powerful and important skill in becoming a strong and trusted Personal Brand. Others will trust you if they experience consistent trustworthy behaviors and if you act right. It's therefore important to ensure that who you are, what you say you are and what others experience from you are always the same. As a result of this your relationship builds *brand equity*, which entails the cumulative levels of credibility, trust, and value (McNally & Speak, 2003).

Formula for Right Personal Action

Aligning your Personal Ambition and Personal Brand with your behavior and actions ensures that your actions in society are always *right* and in accordance with your conscience. Thomas Huxley has said, "Learn what is true in order to do what is right." According to Debashis Chatterjee (2002), right action is one that flows from our being. He defines being as the very spirit of action. I am of the opinion that being is related to your personal mission and that you also should have insight into yourself on the basis of your authentic Personal Ambition and Personal Brand and that these should be in balance with your personal behavior and actions (alignment with yourself) to be able to act right. "Acting" is also of importance as you will develop your skills based on this and enter into new challenges constantly (see Plan-Deploy-Act-Challenge cycle in Chapter 6). I have therefore defined right personal action as follows:

Right personal action = Authentic Personal Ambition +
Authentic Personal Brand + Acting + Aligning with yourself

Remember what Thomas Jefferson said: "Do you want to know who you are? Don't ask. Act! Action will delineate and define you." Also remember what Johann Wolfgang Von Goeth said: "To think is easy. To act is difficult. To act as one thinks is the most difficult." Defining yourself based on your authentic Personal Ambition and Personal Brand is strongly related to self-knowledge.

Formula for Self-Knowledge

Without knowing who you are, it's very difficult to love yourself and others. Self-knowledge is *implicit knowledge,* which is inside your head. This is strongly related to your authentic Personal Ambition and Personal Brand. The PBSC transforms this self-knowledge into *explicit knowledge,* whereby you are better able to develop and manage your self-knowledge. Making the *implicit* knowledge *explicit* has a favorable influence on your creativity. I have defined self-knowledge as a function of four core elements: *Authentic Personal Ambition, Authentic Personal Brand, Thinking, and Acting* (see Figure 7.2). Therefore, self-knowledge is a function of *Authentic Personal Ambition, Authentic Personal Brand, Thinking and Acting.*

<Self-knowledge> = *f* (<Authentic Personal Ambition>,
<Authentic Personal Brand>, <Thinking>, <Acting>)

The function *f* specifies the relation between self-knowledge and authentic Personal Ambition, authentic Personal Brand, thinking and acting. The Personal Ambition and Personal Brand components are related to your awareness and consist of information about yourself. They are connected to your dream, motives, values, genius, uniqueness, specialty, and dominant attribute, which are the basis of your behavior and actions. Thinking is necessary to provide you this insight, to which end I have introduced the breathing and silence exercise in Chapter 3. In fact, breathing and the ability to think have the same origin in the human brain. Thought control follows breath control and vice versa. On the basis of the breathing and silence exercise, you can turn your attention inward and gain control over

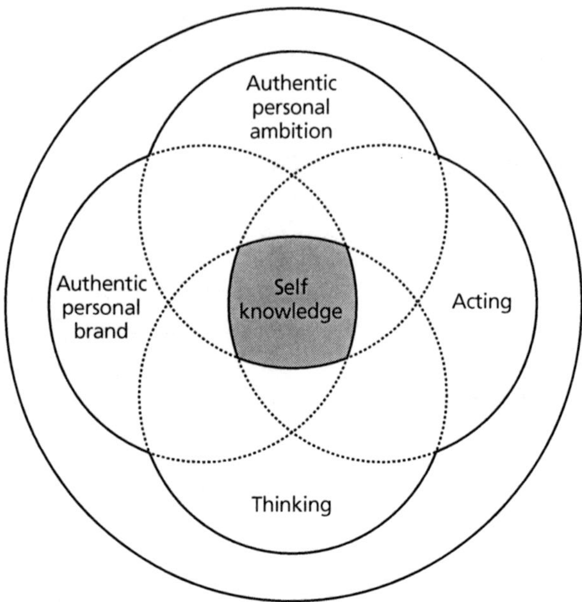

Figure 7.2 Self-knowledge serves as the binding tie.

your awareness. Silence comprises the sharpening and better understanding of your spirit and results in a calm state of mind, which leads to clear thinking. This thinking process helps you bring the left side of your brain in balance with the right side and will help you think out of the box. Remember what Albert Einstein said: "We can't solve problems by using the same kind of thinking we used when we created them." Acting is necessary to implement your Personal Ambition/Brand via the PBSC, to make it a reality, to develop your skills on the basis of experience, to learn from this and to constantly enter into new challenges. For this purpose I have introduced the Plan-Deploy-Act-Challenge cycle in Chapter 6. Learning by doing is necessary, because your Personal Ambition and Personal Brand do not only rely on insight about yourself, but also on reality and the feedback that you receive from others. Acting is therefore related to your capabilities, skills, and personal experiences; in other words, what you are able to do, know and understand. To be effective, one has to keep on learning. Learning is a continuous personal transformation. It is a cyclic and cumulative process of actualizing your self-knowledge (adding new information to your knowledge repertory) in order to qualitatively improve your actions. It is a permanent change of self-knowledge as a result of repeated actions and experiences. In the scope of increasing shifts of *lifetime employment* to lifetime *employability*, you must ensure that your self-knowledge is up-to-date. After all, one is more successful if one can learn quicker and is able to implement self-knowledge quicker. A person who does not learn continuously, and is unable to continually develop, mobilize, cultivate, evaluate, utilize and maintain his/her self-knowledge, will not be able to operate effectively in this ever more complex society. This forms a stable basis for your education. Remember what Albert Einstein said: "Education is what remains after one has forgotten everything he learned in school."

So, to achieve optimum learning, it is important that people have the opportunity to act. Learning can be categorized as self-learning and shared learning (organizational learning). Self-learning, which I have discussed above, is the source of all learning. For this, insight into your Personal Ambition and Personal Brand is indispensable. People who do not have this insight are poor learners. Without self-learning, shared learning cannot exist. With self-learning, employees learn separately and experience an individual behavioral change. For shared learning, insight into the Company Ambition and Company Brand is indispensable, which will be discussed in Part 2 of this book.

To develop and cultivate shared knowledge and create a stable basis for shared learning define and formulate the Company Ambition, Company Brand, and Company BSC as well and align these with your Personal Ambition, Personal Brand and Personal BSC (alignment with your company) in order to reach a high degree of compatibility (best fit) between personal and company goals and mutual value adding, which stimulates employee engagement, love, happiness, commitment, devotion, passion, and enjoyment in the company. This will be discussed in Part 2 of this book.

PART 2

Authentic Company Branding

A product is something made in a factory; a brand is something that is bought by the customer. A product can be copied by a competitor; a brand is unique. A product can be quickly outdated; a successful brand is timeless.

—Stephen King, WPP Group

8

An Authentic Company Branding Model

The idea that business is just a numbers affair has always struck me as preposterous. For one thing, I've never been particularly good at numbers, but I think I've done a reasonable job with feelings. And I'm convinced that it is feelings—and feelings alone—that account for the success of the Virgin brand in all of its myriad forms.

—Richard Branson

This chapter emphasizes the introduction of an organic authentic Company/Corporate Branding model, which provides an excellent framework and roadmap for formulating and implementing a sustainable, powerful, authentic Company Brand. This model has a similar base as the Personal Branding model that I described in part 1 of this book. Because of the fact that Personal Branding has become more important than Company Branding, I will focus in Part 2 of this book just briefly on Company Branding. The authentic Company Branding process starts also with determining the Company Ambition, which is based on the company dream, vision, mission, and core values. The Company Ambition is the soul, starting point, core intention and the guiding principles of the Company Brand. As with the Per-

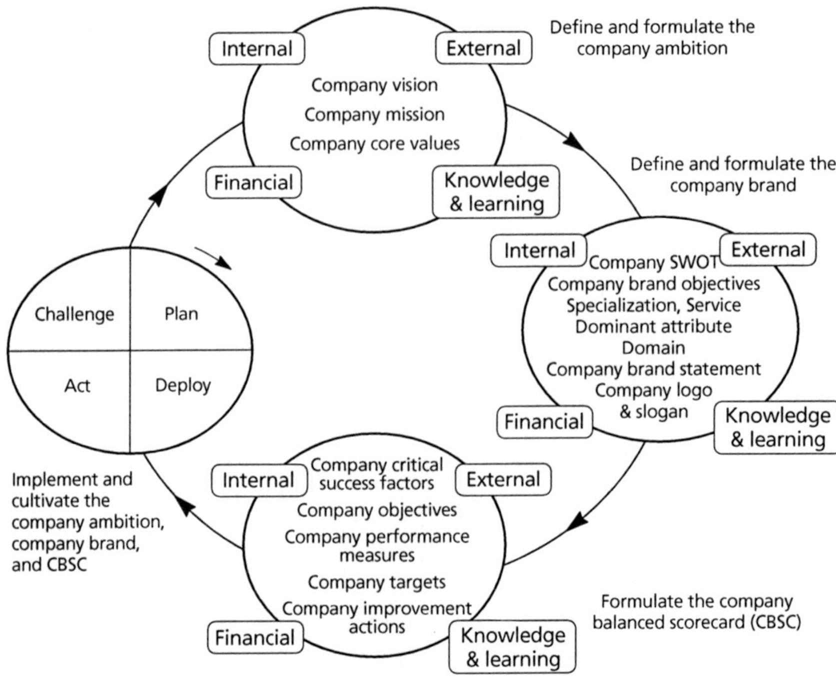

Figure 8.1 Authentic Company Branding Model (© Hubert Rampersad).

sonal Branding model, sustainable, authentic, consistent, and memorable Company Branding is related to the important criteria, which I discussed in Chapter 2. The related Company Branding model consists of the following four phases (see Figure 8.1):

1. **Define and Formulate the Company Ambition**: This phase involves defining and formulating the shared Company Ambition. The Company Ambition is the soul of and the fuel for the Company Brand. It encompasses the company vision, mission, and core values, related to the four perspectives, which should be in balance. As with the Personal ambition, the following 4 basic perspectives have been chosen, however, the contents have different meanings: internal, external, knowledge & learning, and financial perspectives (see also Figure 8.2).
2. **Define and formulate the Company Brand**: This phase involves defining and formulating an authentic, distinctive, relevant, concise, inspiring, compelling, enduring, and memorable Company Brand promise, which is in harmony with the Company Ambition, and used as the focal point of company's culture and

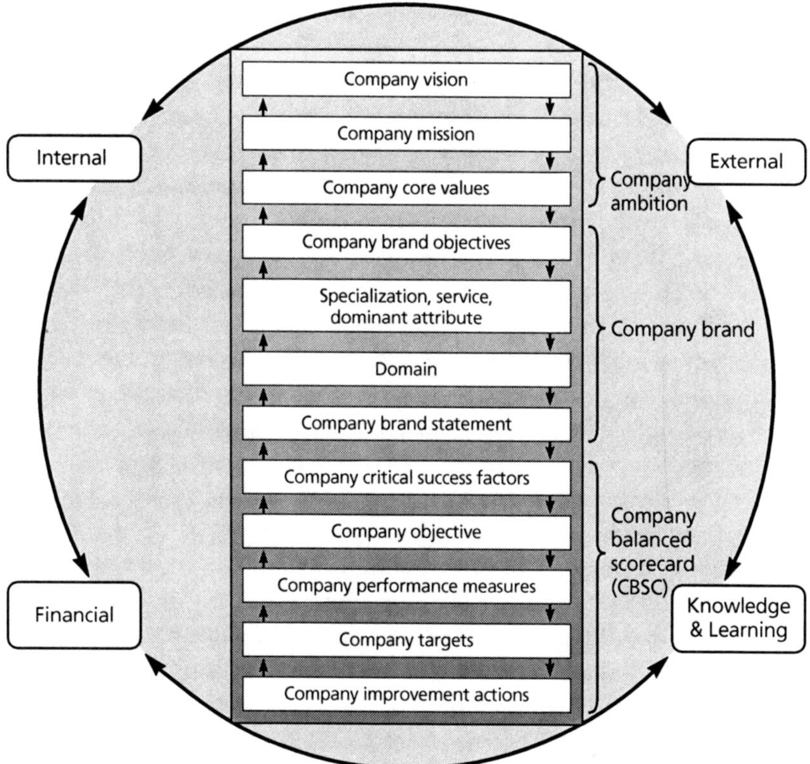

Figure 8.2 Authentic Company Branding Framework (© Hubert Rampersad).

actions. As with the Personal Brand, first of all you should perform a company SWOT analysis and evaluate the performance and culture of the company. This relates to the Company Brand objectives. The Company Brand objectives entail the results the Company Brand should accomplish, which should be related to the four perspectives: internal, external, knowledge & learning, and financial (see Figure 8.2). The company should also determine its specialization, what its main specific services are, what its most powerful attribute is, and what its audience (domain) and their greatest needs are. The Company Brand Statement entails the total of Company Ambition, brand objectives, specialty, service, dominant attribute, and domain. It also includes a Unique Value Proposition (UVP). The next step is to define the Company Brand Story (Elevator Pitch), which is the essence of what you want to say about the Company Brand in order to produce a positive emotional reaction. Finally you should design the Company Logo, which is a single graphical symbol that represents the Company Brand.

3. **Formulate the Company Balanced Scorecard (CBSC)**: as with the PBSC, the Company Ambition and Company Brand have no value unless you don't take actions to make these a reality. Therefore the emphasis in this stage is developing an integrated and well balanced action plan based on your Company Ambition and Company Brand to reach the company objectives. It's about translating your Company Ambition and Company Brand into your CBSC (action). The CBSC entails the related company critical success factors, objectives, performance measures, targets and improvement actions (see Figure 8.2). It's divided into four perspectives: internal, external, knowledge & learning, and financial perspectives. The CBSC is needed to improve the business processes continuously based on the Company Ambition and Brand in order to satisfy its customers and to make them happy.
4. **Implement and Cultivate the Company Ambition, Company Brand and CBSC**: as with Personal Branding, Company Ambition, Company Brand, and the CBSC have no value unless you implement them to make it a reality. Therefore the next step is to implement, maintain, and cultivate the Company Ambition, Company Brand, and CBSC effectively in order to deliver peak performance and to create competitive advantage. To guide you in this process I have introduced the Plan-Deploy-Act-Cultivate cycle (PDAC cycle), which should be followed continuously. This is necessary to let the Company Brand awareness grow gradually. Once you implement and launch the Company Brand, it should be maintained continuously. The more you strengthen, maintain, and cultivate the Company Brand, the more successful the company will be. To operate in accordance with the Company Ambition, Company Brand and related CBSC, through its implementation using the PDAC cycle, results in a journey towards business success.

The effective combination of all these four tools and phases makes a strong, solid, and trusted Company Brand. This new model shows you how all Company Branding elements fit together in a coherent and holistic whole, taking the following into account:

- Company Ambition is the soul, starting point, core intention and the guiding principles of the Company Brand.
- Company Brand without Company Ambition is not authentic.

- Company Brand and Company Ambition without Company Balanced Scorecard is not effective.
- Company Brand, Company Ambition, and Company Balanced Scorecard without implementing these according to the Plan-Deploy-Act-Cultivate is waste of time.
- Company Brand, Company Ambition, Company Balanced Scorecard, and implementation according to the Plan-Deploy-Act-Cultivate cycle is the Company Brand Manifesto.

As we can see from Figure 8.1, the Company Branding model gives you insight into both the way authentic Company Branding can be developed effectively and the coherence between its different aspects. After the last phase is complete, the cycle is again followed in order to fine tune the Company Ambition, Company Brand, and CBSC with its surroundings on a continuous basis. By doing this the company will constantly improve it brand and performance, and thus continuously satisfy it clients. In the following chapters, each of the phases in the authentic Company Branding model will be discussed in depth.

9

Define and Formulate the Company Ambition

My most important wish is that the global business community could adopt a shared vision for the next 10 to 20 years about what you want the world to look like, and then go about trying to create it in ways that actually enhance your business, but do so in other people as well. I think the factor about globalization that tends to be underappreciated is, it will only work if we understand it genuinely means interdependence. It means interdependence, which means that none of us who are fortunate can any longer help ourselves unless we are prepared to help our neighbors. And we need a more unifying, more inclusive vision. Once you know where you're going, it's a lot easier to decide what steps to take to get there. If you don't know where you're going, you can work like crazy and you would be walking in the wrong direction.

— Bill Clinton, former President of the USA

As with the Personal Ambition, before you can clearly define and describe your Company Brand, you need to look at the big picture first. You need to start with the company dream or vision, purpose, values, and competencies. As stated before, the Company Ambition is the starting point, core

Authentic Personal Branding, pages 147–156

intention and the guiding principles of the Company Brand. It's the fuel for the Company Brand. The first phase in the Company Branding model therefore involves defining and formulating the Company Ambition. It encompasses the company vision, mission, and core values, see Figure 9.1.

The Company Ambition expresses the soul of the Company Brand. A successfully formulated Company Ambition shows employees how their activities contribute to the larger whole. People working together towards strategic objectives often produce better performances. They feel pride in making a useful contribution towards something worthwhile. The Company Ambition directs an organization and function both as its compass and its road map. They also make employees proud of their organization, letting them focus on relevant activities and in turn create value for customers, thus eliminating unproductive activities. In an organization without a Company Ambition, employees are exposed to ad hoc decisions and short-term plans. The Company Ambition functions as a lighthouse keeping the company steadily on the course of its dream. Organizations without a clear inspiring shared ambition—or with a wrong one—create a lot of suffering for their stakeholders.

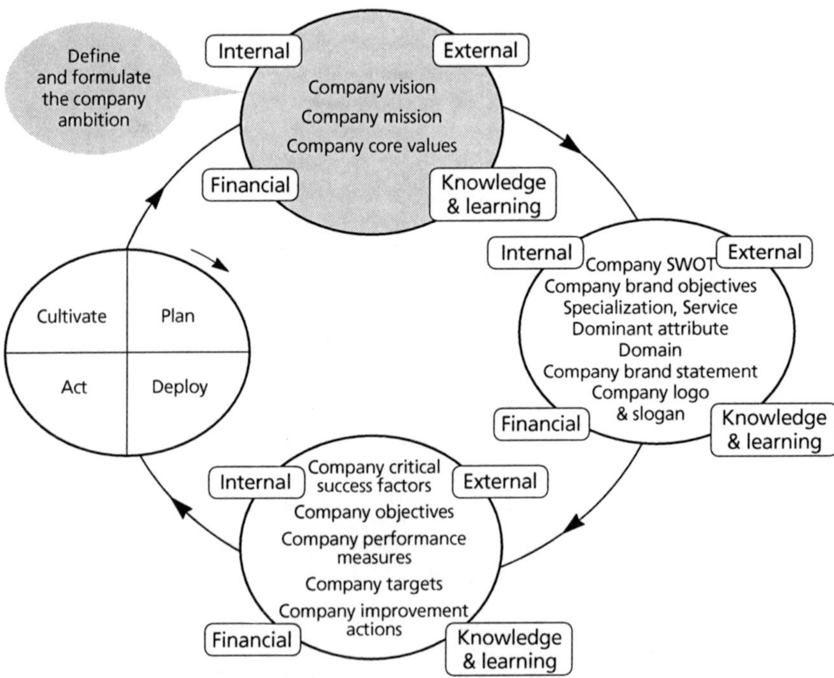

Figure 9.1 First stage in the Authentic Company Branding Model.

The four result domains in the Company Ambition include categories of business results, which are of essential importance for survival. As with the Personal Ambition, the following four basic perspectives have been chosen; however, the contents have different meanings.

1. *Internal*: Process control. How can we control the primary business processes in order to create value for our customers? In which processes do we have to excel to continuously satisfy our customers?
2. *External*: Customer satisfaction. How do customers see the company? What does it mean for our customers?
3. *Knowledge and learning*: Innovation. Skills and attitudes of the employees and the organizational learning ability. How can the company remain successful in the future? How should we learn and improve, and through this continuously realize our shared ambition?
4. *Financial*: Financial soundness. How do shareholders see the company? What does it mean for our shareholders?

These four basic perspectives also cover the consequences for the community. Figure 9.2 shows the Company Ambition framework, including the related ambition questions.

The Company Ambition can be defined as the following formula:

Company Ambition = company vision + mission + core values
(divided along the four perspectives: internal, external,
knowledge & learning, and financial).

Every element in this formula will be explained in detail below. The formulation of the Company Ambition is most effective when it complies with the following criteria.

- The Company Mission is aimed at *being* (is an articulation of what the company is all about), and Company Vision at *becoming*.
- The Company Vision motivates the employees, the Company Mission inspires them and the Core Values guide them.
- The vision is ambitious and challenging; it gives an attractive view of the final objective, gives guidance to initiatives and creativity, appeals directly to people, and joins forces within the organization.
- The vision gives direction; it determines today's actions in order to achieve an optimal future.

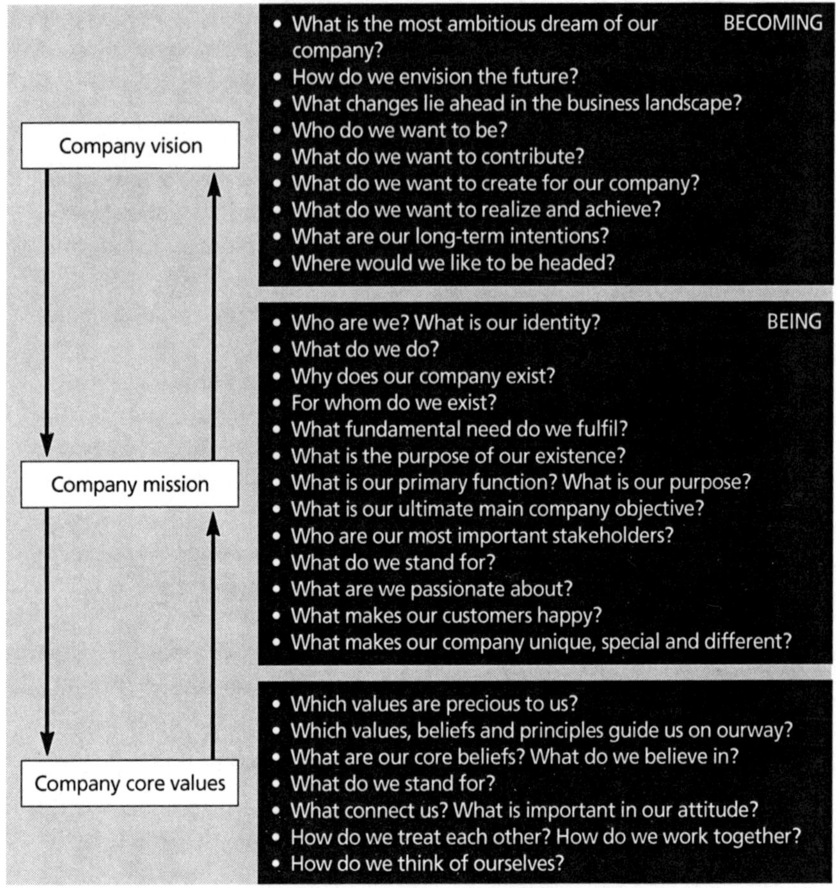

Figure 9.2 Company Ambition Framework (© Hubert Rampersad).

- The vision, in contrast to the mission, is tied to a timeline.
- The emphasis is on unselfishness.
- The mission is short, concrete, and simple; it is understandable and clear to everyone in the company so that it can be used as a concrete guide for taking action.
- The mission is not focused explicitly on profitability or on any other financial element, and it describes the *why* rather than the *what.*

- The mission and vision appeal to the largest group of stakeholders and are formulated in positive terms.
- The mission and vision are realistic and recognizable for everyone; their feasibility is not open for discussion.
- The mission and vision are organization specific; their emphasis is on those elements that distinguish it from other companies. At the same time the borders of the mission specifically are broadly defined to allow for the development of new initiatives.
- The mission and vision include ethical starting points and cultural components, such as respect for the individual, contributions to society, helping people to develop their possibilities, and so on.
- The vision is complete; it takes into consideration all four scorecard perspectives: financial, customers, internal processes, and knowledge & learning.
- The vision advances; its elements are based on continuous improvement, learning, and development. It should be revised every ten years in order to keep it fresh. An effective vision can generally give the organization successful direction for decades.
- The vision, mission and values can be visualized by means of a drawing.

In the following sections, each of the phases in the Company Ambition framework will be discussed in depth.

Company Vision

The Company Vision contains the most ambitious dream of the organization. It provides a shared vision of a desired and feasible future, as well as the route needed to reach it. It indicates what the organization wants to achieve, what is essential for its success, and which critical success factors make it unique. Standards, values, and principles are also part of the organizational vision (see Figure 9.2). An effectively formulated Company Vision guides personal ambitions and creativity, establishes a climate that is fertile for change, strengthens the organization's belief in the future, and therefore releases energy in people. Take a look below at the vision of our company, TPS International, which is strongly related to my Personal Ambition and Personal Brand.

TPS INTERNATIONAL'S COMPANY VISION

To be the best at helping our customers to realize their dreams. We will accomplish our mission by:

- Achieving excellent financial results through the successful introduction of our unique Total Performance Scorecard concept.
- Providing excellence in integrated personal and business performance management for our customers and offer them opportunities to realize sustainable competitive advantage.
- Creating organizations where human spirit thrives and which model the best practices in performance, quality, creativity, and integrity.
- Innovating wisely and improving our business processes continuously.
- Fostering a mutually supportive, inspiring, and learning environment within our organization and working with talented and creative people who care for the needs of the society.

Also take a look at Coca Cola's Company Vision, the world's most valuable brand. This company created a clear and recognizable set of distinctive, relevant, and consistent competencies and built a powerful brand that guides the way it does business.

COCA COLA'S COMPANY VISION

To achieve sustainable growth, we have established a vision with clear goals:

- *Profit*: Maximizing return to shareowners while being mindful of our overall responsibilities.
- *People*: Being a great place to work where people are inspired to be the best they can be.
- *Portfolio*: Bringing to the world a portfolio of beverage brands that anticipate and satisfy peoples' desires and needs.
- *Partners*: Nurturing a winning network of partners and building mutual loyalty.
- *Planet*: Being a responsible global citizen that makes a difference.

Company Mission

The Company Mission consists of the organization's identity and indicates its reason for existing (see Figure 9.2): Why, to what extent, and for whom does it exist? What are the primary function and the ultimate objective of the organization? Which basic need does it fulfill, and who are its most important stakeholders? An effectively formulated Company Mission creates a sense of unity in the behavior of employees, strengthens their like-mindedness, inspires them, and improves both communication and the atmosphere within the organization. The mission of TPS International is shown below, which is strongly related to my Personal Ambition and Personal Brand.

TPS INTERNATIONAL'S COMPANY MISSION

We are devoted to serving learning individuals and innovative organizations in order to achieve their full potential and to link human capital to business success.

Also take a look at Coca Cola's Company Mission.

COCA COLA'S COMPANY MISSION

Everything we do is inspired by our enduring mission:

- To Refresh the World . . . in body, mind, and spirit.
- To Inspire Moments of Optimism . . . through our brands and our actions.
- To Create Value and Make a Difference . . . everywhere we engage.

Company Core Values

The Company Ambition is also based on a set of shared values that are used to strengthen the like-mindedness, commitment, and devotion of employees and to influence their behavior positively. These Company Core Values determine how one must act in order to realize the Company Vision and Mission. They function as the guiding principles that support people's behavior at work. They have an important impact on the relationship between the employees and the organization. Core values hold people together if they act and think along the lines of these values. They articulate the way we treat each other and how we see customers, employees, shareholders, suppliers, and the community. When the principles, norms, and values of the employees match those of the organization, then their efforts and involvement would be optimal. Therefore, core values are strongly related to the personal ambition of the individual employees. After all, with a Company Vision and Mission based on shared values, the personal objectives of individual employees will correspond closely to those of the organization. The core value must be ethical in order to pass the test of moral scrutiny. Everyone within the company should act in accordance with these principles and moral standards. Jack Welch formulated five core values to change General Electric

> loathing bureaucracy and all nonsense associated with it; understanding what is meant by responsibility and devotion and decisiveness; determining aggressive objectives and realizing them with energetic integrity; having the faith to empower others; and nothing is a secret.

The core values of TPS International Inc. are shown below, which are strongly related to my Personal Ambition and Personal Brand.

TPS INTERNATIONAL'S CORE VALUES

We are guided by the following core values:

- *Integrity*: We keep commitments, deliver at all times the promised quality, and are responsible and accountable for our results.
- *Joy*: We thoroughly enjoy our work and always act and serve out of love.
- *Passion*: We are passionate in everything we do.

Coca Cola's Core Values:

COCA COLA'S CORE VALUES

We are guided by shared values that we will live by as a company and as individuals:

- *Leadership*: "The courage to shape a better future"
- *Passion*: "Committed in heart and mind"
- *Integrity*: "Be real"
- *Accountability*: "If it is to be, it's up to me"
- *Collaboration*: "Leverage collective genius"
- *Innovation*: "Seek, imagine, create, delight"
- *Quality*: "What we do, we do well"

How to Develop the Company Ambition

The company ambition development process begins with the management team formulating the Company Ambition conceptually, and then communicating it during several sessions to all stakeholders. In practice, this dissemination of the Company Ambition is done more and more through in-house conferences, where large groups of participants are briefed, and then discuss the ambition statement with each other. Based on this feedback adjustments are made and a definitive ambition statement is then formulated to which nearly everyone can subscribe. Afterwards, every business unit formulates its own vision based on the Company Ambition. After employees have familiarized themselves with the vision of the business unit, they will use it as a guideline for the formulation of their own team's vision. This process of ambition development is done at all organizational levels, with the active participation of all stakeholders at an early stage. This learning process is intuitive, iterative, and cyclic as well as democratic; it is based on the exchange of insight, creativity, and ideals. Treat everyone equally, strive for single-mindedness (absolute consensus is not required), stimulate interdependence and diversity; and concentrate on the process (not only on the formulation of the ambition statement). With the development of the shared ambition, past and present insights and activities are aligned with future expectations. By exchanging thoughts with employees (*brainstorming* in a team, whereby each team is representative of the entire company), employees and managers get better insight into the company course to follow. This will benefit the support and commitment within the whole organization. The development process is therefore more important than the statement itself. When assessing the company ambition, the following questions are central:

- Does it give you direction, energy, strength, motivation, something to hold on to, and a feeling of warmth?
- Do you feel like implementing your knowledge intensively and sharing it with others because of it?
- Do you feel personally involved with it?
- Does it provide perspective to all stakeholders?
- Does it give an orientation to all key activities? Does it relate to you? Does it make you enthusiastic?
- Do you believe in it?
- Does it give you a feeling of direction?
- Will you work with all your might to realize it?

By asking and answering these questions you make choices that will gradually give greater and greater shape to the Company Ambition. Top management starts this process, whereby the results are propagated from top to bottom. It's a top down and bottom up process. In order to do this effectively, the management must give direction and support, show commitment, as well as coach and think together with everyone instead of doing the thinking for the employees. They must help and train the individuals on how to raise the energy in an environment of mutual respect, trust, and commonly shared ambition.

In the next chapter, I will show you how to successfully connect your Company Ambition to your Company Brand in a way that can have a profound impact on the company performance.

10

Define and Formulate the Company Brand

A company brand is like a reputation for a person. You earn reputation by trying to do hard things well.
—Jeff Bezos, founder and president of Amazon.com

The second stage in the Company Branding journey is primarily concerned with defining and formulating a sustainable, strong, authentic, consistent, and memorable Company Brand identity, which is in harmony with the Company Ambition (see Figure 10.1).

Figure 10.2 shows the framework and the building blocks for defining and formulating the Company Brand. As with the Personal Brand, first of all you should perform a company SWOT analysis and assess the company. This relates to the Company Brand objectives. These should also be related to the four perspectives: internal, external, knowledge & learning, and financial. Based on the brand objectives you need to determine the company's specialization (core competencies), what the company's main

Authentic Personal Branding, pages 157–173

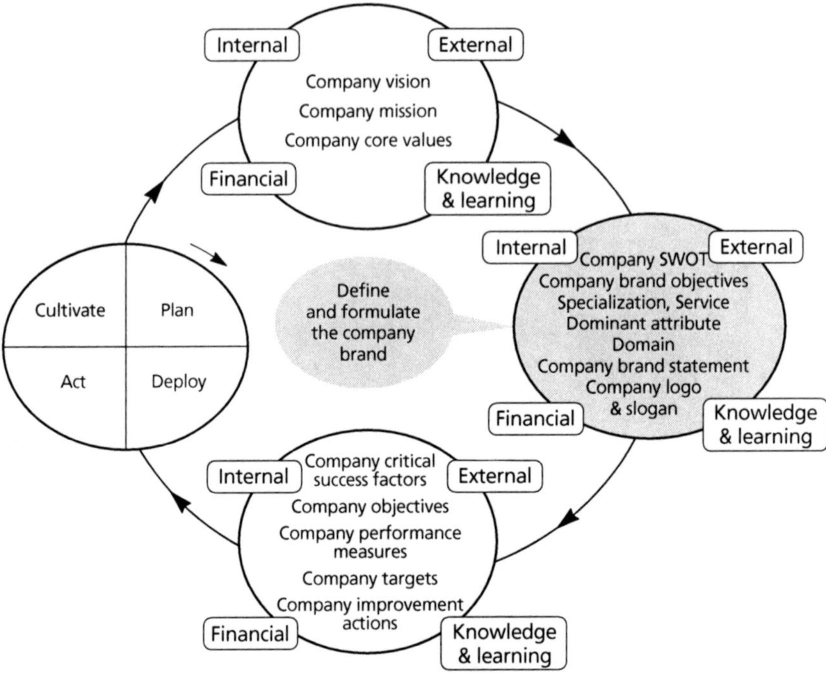

Figure 10.1 Second stage in the Authentic Company Branding Model.

services are, what its leading and most powerful attribute is, who is the audience (domain) and what are their greatest needs. The Company Brand Statement entails the total of Company Ambition, brand objectives, specialty, service, dominant attribute, and domain. The company's Unique Value Proposition (UVP) is part of this. The next step is to define the Company's Brand Story (Elevator Pitch), which is the essence of what you want to say about the Company Brand in order to produce a positive emotional reaction. Finally you should design the Company Logo, which is a single graphical symbol that represents the Company Brand.

In the following sections, each of the phases in the Company Branding framework will be discussed in depth.

Company SWOT Analysis

The company SWOT analysis forms the basis of the brand and company objectives, by examining its strengths and weaknesses in the internal environment and opportunities and threats in the external environment. To illustrate this, I will share our TPS International's SWOT with you, see Table 10.1.

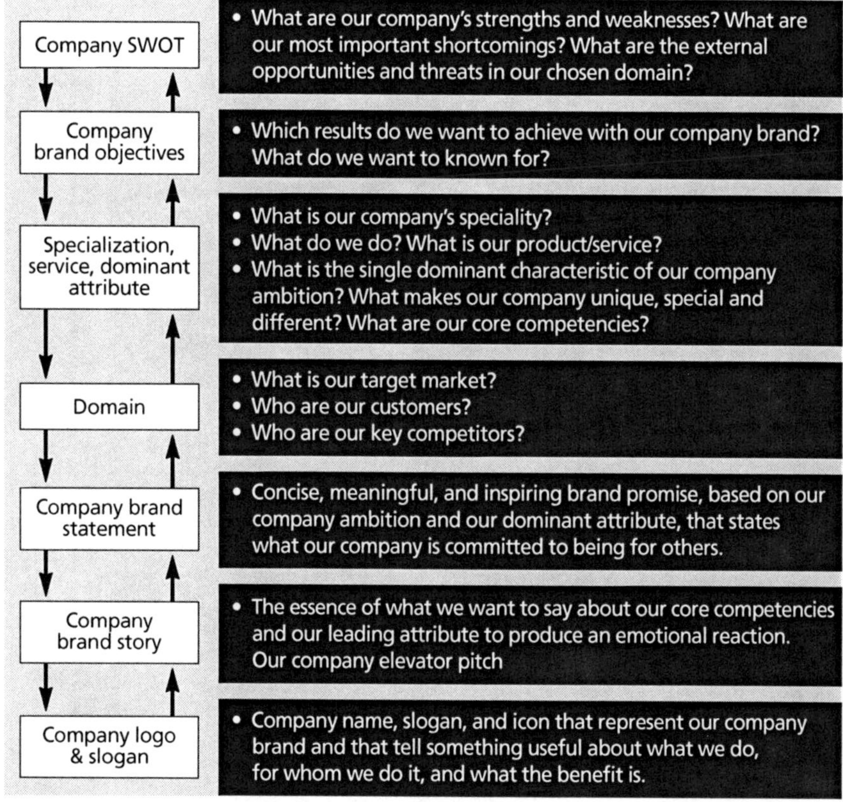

Company SWOT
• What are our company's strengths and weaknesses? What are our most important shortcomings? What are the external opportunities and threats in our chosen domain?
Company brand objectives
• Which results do we want to achieve with our company brand? What do we want to known for?
Specialization, service, dominant attribute
• What is our company's speciality?
• What do we do? What is our product/service?
• What is the single dominant characteristic of our company ambition? What makes our company unique, special and different? What are our core competencies?
Domain
• What is our target market?
• Who are our customers?
• Who are our key competitors?
Company brand statement
• Concise, meaningful, and inspiring brand promise, based on our company ambition and our dominant attribute, that states what our company is committed to being for others.
Company brand story
• The essence of what we want to say about our core competencies and our leading attribute to produce an emotional reaction. Our company elevator pitch
Company logo & slogan
• Company name, slogan, and icon that represent our company brand and that tell something useful about what we do, for whom we do it, and what the benefit is.

Figure 10.2 Framework for defining and formulating the Company Brand (© Hubert Rampersad).

Company Assessment

To assist you with the SWOT analysis, I have introduced the TPS Life Cycle Scan, which is a new integrated tool for systematic self diagnosis/assessment that can be used to understand the gaps and to determine areas of opportunity, which then should be included in the Company Balanced Scorecard (Rampersad, 2006). The TPS Life Cycle Scan is an innovative performance excellence model and measuring rod aimed at increasing individual and organizational performance in the direction of Total Performance. It consists of five development levels and eight dimensions that follow the TPS concept. The five development levels are: basic, improving, moderate, advanced, and total performance. Each higher level, i.e., towards total performance, can be considered as an increase in the organization's abilities to adapt and react to

TABLE 10.1 TPS International's SWOT Analysis

	Positive aspects	Negative aspects	
Internal	**Our strengths** Internal positive aspects that are under control and upon which we may capitalize in our CBSC • Professional and happy workforce • Innovative • Unique Total Performance Scorecard, Personal Balanced Scorecard, Personal Branding, and TPS-Lean Six Sigma concept • Knowledge of new technologies • New Personal & Company Branding and TPS-Lean Six Sigma book	**Our weaknesses** Internal negative aspects that are under our control and that we may plan to improve (strategic objectives and related improvement actions in our CBSC) • Weak sales force • Low marketing budget • Location of our business	Aspects that are under our control
External	**Opportunities in Our Domain** Positive external conditions that we do not control but of which we will plan to take advantage (strategic objectives and related improvement actions in our CBSC) • Positive trends in outplacement field • Organizations are investing more in human capital and employee engagement • Individuals are becoming aware about the importance of personal development and personal branding • Internet	**Threats in Our Domain** Negative external conditions that we do not control but the effect of which we will be able to lessen (strategic objectives and related improvement actions in our CBSC) • Weak network in North America • Copying behavior of competitors • Negative trends in the US industry that diminish jobs • Many managers and human resources officers don't understand the importance of a good work-life balance of their employees • Competitors have superior sales force and marketing budget	Aspects that are not under our control

external and internal necessity for improved performance. The eight dimensions are: Personal Management, Strategic Management, Business Values management, Talent Management, Process Management, Knowledge Management, Team Management, and Change Management.

We have applied the TPS Life Cycle Scan for our own company, TPS International, to define in which development level it finds itself. I am president, CEO, and majority shareholder of this company. The results of the company scan are shown in Figure 10.3. This figure clearly shows the gaps and the areas of opportunity. By making our performance management measurable in this way, it will be easier to manage related performance processes and to increase the score year by year in order to realize our brand objectives.

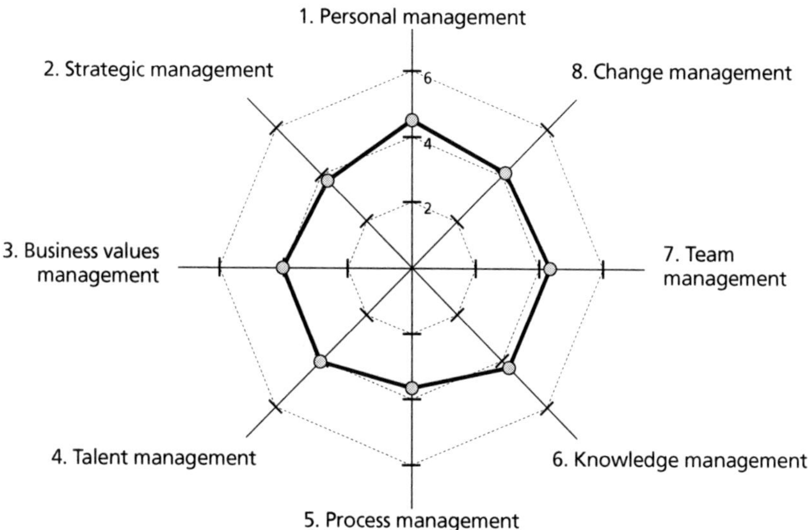

Figure 10.3 Assessment of TPS International based on the TPS Life Cycle Scan.

This makes it possible to steer our improvement actions systematically, always aiming for higher levels of personal and business excellence. The result of this self-assessment forms the input for the Company BSC, which will be discussed in the next chapter. You can execute the self assessment for your own company via our website www.Total-Performance-Scorecard.com.

While assessing the company, you should reflect on the following questions:

- How do we relate to our clients?
- What are our strongest areas? Do they add value to our domain?
- For what core competencies are we best known?
- What is the value that our clients associate with us most?
- What do our clients say about us?
- How are we perceived?

The answers on these questions are also important to formulate the company Ambition effectively.

Company Brand Objectives

The Company Brand objectives are based on the company strengths, weaknesses, related threats and opportunities, and the results of the self-assessment. For this, you should reflect on the following questions:

- What should the Company Brand accomplish?
- What does the company want to be known for? What do we want our clients to think about us?
- What emotions should the Company Brand produce in others?

The Company Brand objectives should be related to the four mentioned perspectives: internal, external, knowledge & learning, and financial. Take a look at TPS International's Brand objectives below.

TPS INTERNATIONAL'S COMPANY BRAND OBJECTIVES

High Company Brand awareness, greater degree of trust from our employees and customers, innovative image, higher turnover, higher positive cash.

Specialization

The next step is determining the company's specialization. The company should focus on its area of specialization, concentrated on its core competencies and tailor its service to the target market, in order to be unique, special, and different. Take a look at TPS International's specialization below. We have narrowed down the scope of what we do, which are in line with our strengths. We don't want to be all things to all companies, such as most competitors in our field. This is our niche that we love, that we are passionate about, and which is related to our Company Ambition.

TPS INTERNATIONAL'S SPECIALIZATION

Providing integrated personal and business performance management services with an authentic human focus

Also take a look at Coca Cola's specialization.

COCA COLA'S SPECIALIZATION

Developing soft drinks, both carbonated and non-carbonated, and non-alcoholic beverages.

Service

After defining the company's specialization, you should determine its service and tailor this to your target market (domain). Reflect on the following questions:

- What do we do?
- What are our company's specific services?
- What is our company's culture?
- How do we want prospects in our target market to view our service?

Take a look at TPS International's service, its culture, and what it does.

TPS INTERNATIONAL'S SERVICES

Integrated personal and business performance management consulting, training, coaching, and certification, based on our holistic and authentic Total Performance Scorecard (TPS) principles.

TPS INTERNATIONAL'S CULTURE

Creative, passionate, love what we do, result-oriented, open-communication, teamwork, happy workforce

WHAT TPS INTERNATIONAL DOES

We love to provide integrated personal and business performance management consulting, training, coaching, and certification services to learning individuals and innovative organizations.

Also take a look at Coca Cola's products, service, and culture.

COCA COLA'S PRODUCTS AND SERVICE

"The Coca-Cola Company is the world's largest nonalcoholic beverage company. We offer a portfolio of world class quality sparkling and still beverages, starting with Coca-Cola® and extending through over 400 soft drinks, juices, teas, coffees, waters, sports and energy drinks that refresh, hydrate, nourish, relax and energize. Within our more than 400 brands are nearly 2,400 beverage products. Four of the world's top-five soft-drink brands are ours: Coca-Cola, Diet Coke®, Sprite® and Fanta®. In 2005, we ranked No. 1 worldwide in sales of sparkling soft drinks and No. 1 in sales of juice and juice drinks. We are the world's No. 2 producer of sports drinks, and the No. 3 producer of bottled water."

COCA COLA'S WORKPLACE CULTURE

"We are focused on strategic workplace programs that help assure the success of our commitment to embracing the similarities and differences of people, cultures and ideas."

Dominant Attribute

You should also define the company's main attribute; the elements that make the company unique, special and different and you should know what attracts customers to buy the company's products. The company should be unique and fill a special niche to be successful in the marketplace. For this, you should reflect on the following questions:

- What are our company's core competencies which are very clear to our clients and prospects and which add value to them?
- What are the top five characteristics that reflect our Company Brand?
- What is the single leading and most powerful attribute of our Shared Ambition?
- What separates our company from the mass?
- What makes our company distinctive?

Take a look below at TPS International's top five characteristics and dominant attribute.

TPS INTERNATIONAL'S TOP FIVE KEY CHARACTERISTICS

Innovative, creative, passionate, teamwork, happy workforce

TPS INTERNATIONAL'S DOMINANT ATTRIBUTE

Innovative

My single most dominant attribute is *passionate* (see Chapter 4) and our company's single most dominant attribute is *innovative*. *We* have chosen this characteristic because this is who we are as a team, what reflects our organizational culture, what makes our company distinctive, what correlates to our core values, and it appeals to and values our target market. This is what makes our Company brand unique. Also take a look at Coca Cola's dominant attribute.

COCA COLA'S DOMINANT ATTRIBUTE

Creativity in developing soft drinks and non-alcoholic beverages

Domain

The next step is defining the company's domain (which is in harmony with the Company Ambition, brand objectives, specialty, service, and dominant attribute) and gaining knowledge about its audience and their greatest needs. In this inside-out approach, you should reflect on the following questions:

- In what arena do we want to achieve our Company Brand objectives?
- What is our target market? Does it have the potential to make money? Do we enjoy working in this target market?
- Who are our customers?
- What are their greatest needs? What do they want? What do they value? What do they expect? What are they worried about?
- What are the values of our domain?
- Who will find the company's unique strengths valuable in the marketplace?
- Which core competencies does the domain value most? What experience will be valuable to our domain? What qualities does it value most?
- Is our company suited to the domain's culture?
- What communication channels dominate in our domain?
- Who are our key competitors? What makes our company different from them?

Take a look at TPS International's main domain, the greatest needs of its customers, and its key competitors.

TPS INTERNATIONAL'S DOMAIN

Learning individuals and innovative organizations within the service and manufacturing industry

We are focusing on people and companies that are willing to learn and improve consciously and don't want to waste time and energy to help people and companies who are not committed to change and learning. We have selected the service and manufacturing industry because of the growth potential of this target market, its wealth, size, and need for our service. We enjoy working in this industry, learning a lot about it, to understand it much better, and we are aware of the value this industry perceives in our Company Brand.

GREATEST NEEDS OF TPS INTERNATIONAL'S CUSTOMERS

Personal effectiveness & growth, employee engagement, happy and passionate workforce, high labor productivity, awareness for integrity

Employee engagement, a happy and passionate workforce, personal effectiveness & growth, high labour productivity, and awareness for integrity are very important to our target market (see Chapter 4 and Chapter 13). We fill this need with our products/services. Our key competitors don't have the proper concepts and tools to fill this need in a durable, holistic, and humanized way. This is making it easy for us to serve their customers. We know who they are and how they are positioned.

TPS INTERNATIONAL'S KEY COMPETITORS

Booz Allen, Boston Consulting Group, George Group, KPMG, Kaplan & Norton, Hay Group, Franklin Covey, BSC Collaborative

Company Brand Statement

After you have defined the Company Ambition, brand objectives, specialty, service, dominant attribute, domain, and assessed and evaluated the company, you should formulate the Company Brand identity in a distinctive, relevant, consistent, meaningful, exciting, and persuasive manner. As with the Personal Brand, the Company statement entails a concise, meaningful, and inspiring brand promise that states what the company is committed to being for others. The formulation of the Company Brand promise must comply with the criteria discussed in Chapter 4. It states: the company's dreams, what it stands for, what it does, for whom it does it, its specialty, service, how it creates value for customers, and what it is committed to being for them. It can include a slogan and a Unique Value Proposition (UVP). The UVP entails a core element what makes the company more unique, more valuable, and more visible in the market. A powerful UVP will make marketing and sales much easier. FedEx dominated the package shipping market based on the following UVP: "Federal Express: When it has to be delivered overnight."

Company Brand Statement = Company Ambition + Brand Objectives + Specialty + Service + Dominant Attribute + Domain

Company Brand Statement = Company Vision + Mission + Core Values + Brand Objectives + Specialty + Service + Dominant Attribute + Domain

Take a look at TPS International's Brand Statement below. Our Company Brand statement starts with the slogan "*Linking Human Capital to Business Success,*" which entails our company position. This is to categorize our Company Brand and to influence our target market so that they identify and label our company with this single idea. We are using this Company Brand statement as guidance for our Company Brand story and to keep us moving in the right direction. We have packaged our Company Ambition, brand objectives, specialty, service, dominant attribute, and domain into a powerful authentic Company Brand identity that lifts us above our competitors, differentiates our company, and guides us in our decisions. In this way we are trying to eliminate our competitors and to create demand for our services. It provides us energy that helps us deliver top performances.

TPS INTERNATIONAL'S BRAND STATEMENT
Linking Human Capital to Business Success

We are passionate in providing excellence in integrated personal and business performance management to learning individuals and innovative organizations within the service and manufacturing industry. Using our innovative Total Performance Scorecard principles, we promise to help our customers to achieve their full potential and to offer them opportunities to become a best practice in financial performance, quality, creativity, and integrity.

Also take a look at Coca Cola's Brand Statement.

COCA COLA'S BRAND STATEMENT

We develop soft drinks and non-alcoholic beverages that create value for our company, our bottling partners, and our customers. We promise to:

- Refresh the World . . . in body, mind, and spirit.
- Inspire Moments of Optimism . . . through our brands and our actions.
- Create Value and Make a Difference . . . everywhere we engage.
- Bring to the world a portfolio of beverage brands that anticipate and satisfy peoples' desires and needs.

Another nice example is JVC's shared Ambition (see Figure 10.4) and its related Brand Statement below.

JVC'S BRAND STATEMENT

The Perfect Experience

To create truly moving experiences and provide total satisfaction for our customers. Using our superior technologies to create new products, JVC promises to:

- Inspire people
- Expand the possibilities for creative expression
- Provide customers with the potential for personal enrichment
- Provide customers with a lifetime of satisfaction

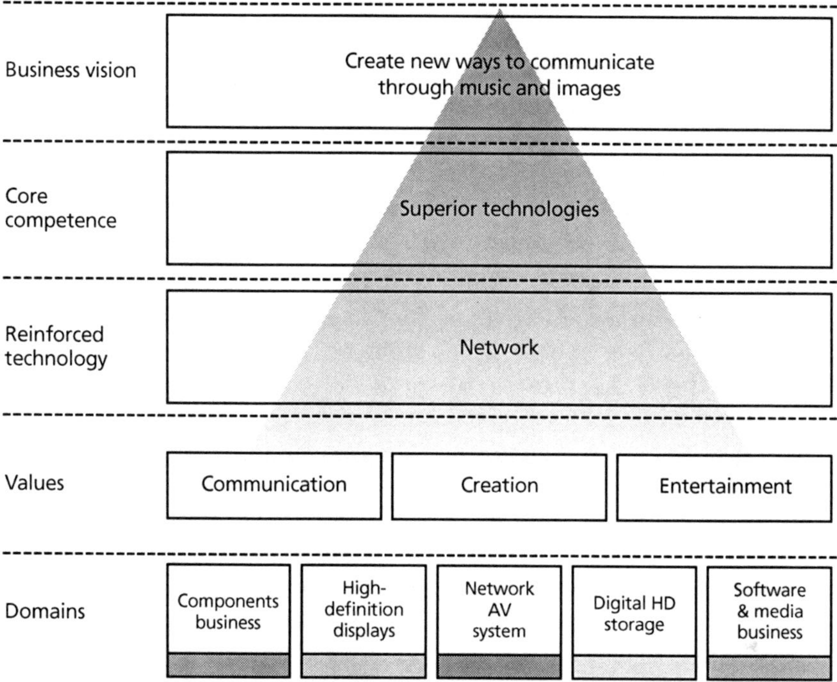

Figure 10.4 JVC's shared ambition.

FedEx's Brand statement is: "An unrelenting commitment to deliver." It's being used to guide all FedEx employees in their work to focus on the customers to whom the boxes and envelopes should be delivered.

Company Brand Story

As with the Personal Brand story, the Company Brand Story is the essence of what executives and employees, especially sales people, want to say to others about the uniqueness of the company and about its leading attribute, in order to produce a positive emotional reaction. This is not the exact words in the Company Brand statement. Telling a story is an important sales tool to communicate the Company Brand, to build credibility, and to connect the company with its audiences emotionally. The Company Brand story will enable the Sales department to present the company (based on the Company

Brand statement) in a more confident, convincing, passionate, persuasive and compelling way to customers, if they ask you "*tell me about your company*" or '*what does your company do*?' By defining and formulating your Company Brand in advance it will be much easier for you to respond fast and strongly on these questions with a powerful story, which will reveal the company's uniqueness, build confidence, and establish trust. So, create a Company Brand story that communicates the company's value and its market differentiation. Pull the critical success factors and the key words that you have used to create the Company Ambition and Company Brand statement and include these in the Company Brand story and into everything that you say about your company. Tell this story relentlessly and passionately.

A Company Brand story is like an Elevator Pitch; a short, clear, concise, carefully planned, and well-practiced description about the Company Brand that customers and other stakeholders should be able to understand in the time they would take to ride up an elevator. The Company Elevator Pitch clearly speaks to the attributes that make the company unique and better qualified than competitors. It should touch very briefly on the products or services the company sells, what market it serves, and the company's competitive advantage. It's a quick and concise way to communicate the core competencies of the company, what it does, why it's the best, and how it distinguishes itself from competitors. It should be shared in maximum 2 minutes and so intriguing that prospects and customers will get excited and let them easily understand and remember the company.

Take a look at TPS International's Brand Story/Elevator Pitch below.

TPS INTERNATIONAL'S BRAND STORY/ELEVATOR PITCH

We provide integrated professional services in a result oriented and pragmatic manner and are devoted to helping our customers to become successful. We distinguish ourselves though our expertise, creativity, professionalism, passion and integrity. The results of the implementation of our innovative Total Performance Scorecard principle are high performance culture, increased profitability and customer satisfaction, and related unique competitive advantage...

We are telling our clients and prospects what our company does in such a way that reflects our company position and that add value to them. In this way we are trying to make an emotional connection to them, distinguish our company, and build a distinctive picture of our Company Brand in their minds, which makes our company relevant to them. As a result they are eager to meet us and continue their conversations with us. We are communicating what our company stands for in a unique way that is different from competitors in our field, which gives prospects good reasons to feel good about our company and what we can do for them. This makes them perceive our company as beneficial to them.

Company Logo & Slogan

As with the Personal Logo, a Company Logo is a single graphical symbol that represents the Company Brand. It tells something useful about what the company does, for whom it does it, and what the benefit is. A Company Logo consists of: a company name, a slogan or UVP and an Icon. It makes the Company Brand visible. Take a look at TPS International's Logo & Slogan below. Our Company Brand name and slogan are based on my Total Performance Scorecard concept (Rampersad, 2003). Our company slogan "*Linking Human Capital to Business Success*" implies a sense of value

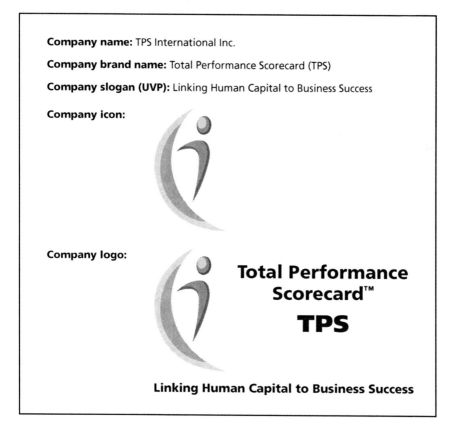

Company name: TPS International Inc.

Company brand name: Total Performance Scorecard (TPS)

Company slogan (UVP): Linking Human Capital to Business Success

Company icon:

Company logo:

Total Performance Scorecard™

TPS

Linking Human Capital to Business Success

to our domain and our icon is strongly related to my Personal Ambition and Brand (see Chapters 3 and 4). It entails the essence of our company positioning. We are using this Logo & Slogan to visualize the value that our company can add to our target audience and to represent our commitment to build enduring relationships with our (potential) customers that reflect our Company Ambition and Company Brand.

Also take a look below at some other examples:

Microsoft's new slogan: "Get less for more!"

Nike's slogan: "Just do it"

Nokia's slogan: "Connecting People"

BMW's slogan: "The Ultimate Driving Machine"

PHILIPS's slogan: "sense and simplicity"

ASSIGNMENT

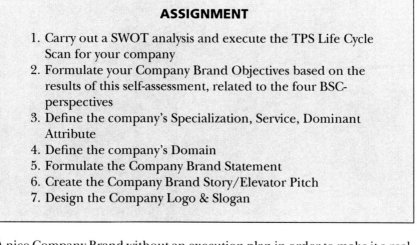

1. Carry out a SWOT analysis and execute the TPS Life Cycle Scan for your company
2. Formulate your Company Brand Objectives based on the results of this self-assessment, related to the four BSC-perspectives
3. Define the company's Specialization, Service, Dominant Attribute
4. Define the company's Domain
5. Formulate the Company Brand Statement
6. Create the Company Brand Story/Elevator Pitch
7. Design the Company Logo & Slogan

A nice Company Brand without an execution plan in order to make it a reality and without continuous improvement of the business processes and the learning ability based on the Company BSC (CBSC) is cosmetic and waste of time, and will not lead to sustainable competitive advantage. I therefore will discuss the CBSC in the next chapter in detail.

11

Formulate the Company Balanced Scorecard

Your premium brand had better be delivering something special, or it's not going to get the business.

—Warren Buffett

Once you have defined and formulated your Company Ambition and Company Brand, the next step is to translate these into your Company Balanced Scorecard (Company Branding strategy, an execution plan) in order to make the Company Brand a reality. You need to do this in order to enhance Company Brand equity over time, which will lead to sustainable competitive advantage. Company Branding will be of no use to you without goal setting, continuous process improvement, and contributing on a day to day basis towards the Company Brand, based on the Company Balanced Scorecard (CBSC), and implementing this according to the PDAC cycle. In this chapter I will focus on the formulation of the CBSC, taking TPS International's company BSC as example. This entails the third stage in the Company Branding journey, see Figure 11.1.

Authentic Personal Branding, pages 175–189

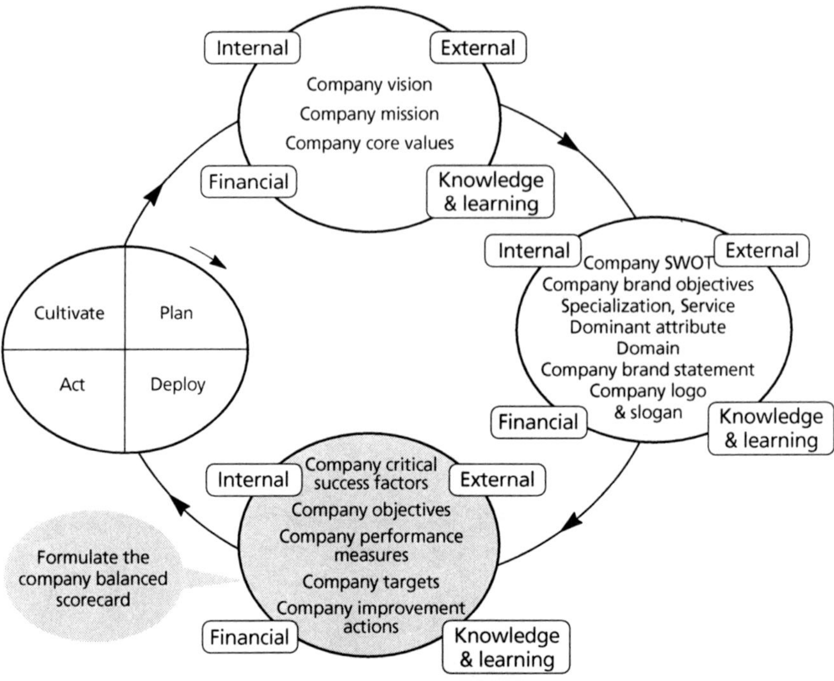

Figure 11.1 Third stage in the Authentic Company Branding Model.

The CBSC is a participatory approach that provides a framework for the systematic development of business strategy based on the Company Ambition and for making this ambition operational at all organizational levels. It makes the long term Company Ambition and Company Brand measurable and translates these systematically into short term manageable, measurable, and concrete actions in a holistic and balanced way. The CBSC system differs from the basic BSC concept of Robert Kaplan and David Norton (2000, 2003), developed in the early 1990s, see Rampersad (2003, 2006). The CBSC entails the company critical success factors, objectives, performance measures, targets and improvement actions, which are divided into the four perspectives: internal, external, knowledge & learning, and financial perspectives. The CBSC is an effective tool to manage the Company Brand, by developing improvement actions to achieve the brand objectives, keeping track of the progress of these actions, reporting your key accomplishments, etc. Figure 11.2 shows the framework for formulating the CBSC. It provides a road map to translate the Company Ambition and Company Brand into actions and to capitalize on the strengths and eliminate the weaknesses. The CBSC can be defined as the following formula:

CBSC = company critical success factors + objectives +
performance measures + targets + improvement actions
(divided along the four perspectives:
internal, external, knowledge & learning, and financial).

In the following sections, each of the phases in the Company Balanced Scorecard framework will be discussed in depth.

Company Critical Success Factors

The company critical success factor (CSF) is one in which the organization must excel in order to survive, or one that is of overriding importance to organizational success. Such strategic issues determine the competitive advantage of a company. They are factors in which the company wants to differ and makes itself unique in the market, and as such are related to its core competencies. CSFs are real core competencies included in the Company Ambition statement (the ones the company actually operates from) and the idealized core competencies (the ones the company thinks it should operate from), which the company should further develop in order to *make a difference and be the difference.* The crucial questions in this process are: What

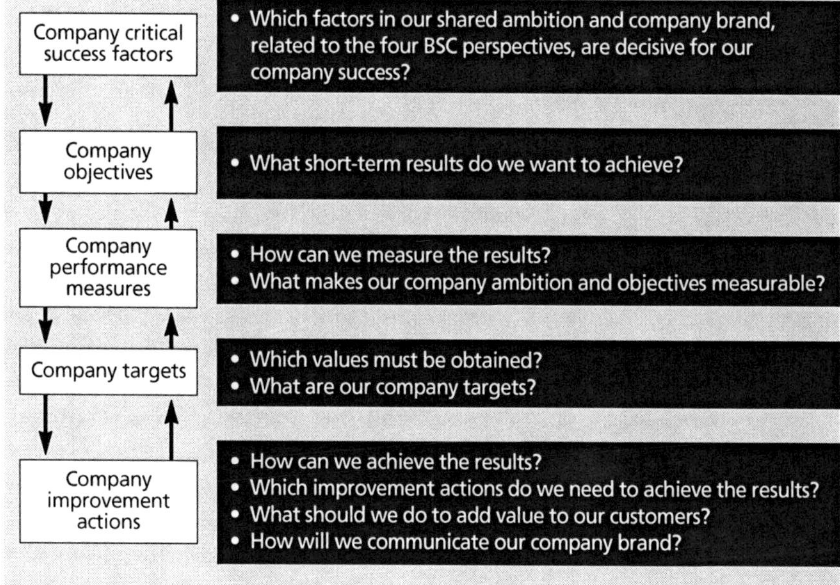

Figure 11.2 Company Balanced Scorecard Framework (© Hubert Rampersad).

makes our company unique, special and different? Which factors in our Company Ambition and Company Brand are decisive for our competitiveness? Which factors are essential for the realization of our company objectives? What are our core competencies? Company critical success factors are related to the four BSC perspectives and thus form an integral part of the shared Company Ambition and Company Brand. The company CSFs form the bridge between the Company Ambition and Company Brand (long term) and on the other side the company objectives, performance measures, targets, and improvement actions (short term). This link is made by identifying the company's core competencies, uniqueness, values in the Company Ambition and Company Brand and translating these into concrete company objectives. As with the PBSC, a CBSC has a minimum of four CSFs (at least one per perspective), and every CSF has one or more related company objectives; each objective has a maximum of two related performance measures, while each performance measure has only one related target; each target is linked to one or more related improvement actions. Examples of company critical success factors are: financial strenght; well-motivated personnel; a happy workforce; skilled employees; teamwork; customer orientation; good customer service; strong brand; and high product quality. Figure 11.3 illustrates how each CSF in the Company Ambition and Company Brand is linked to the company objectives, performance measures, targets, and improvement actions.

Company Objectives

As with Personal Branding, the Company Ambition and Company Brand need to be tied to the company objectives. Company objectives describe the expected results that should be achieved within a short time in order to realize the long-term Company Ambition and successfully launch the Company Brand. The company objectives give the Company Ambition and Brand direction. The SWOT analysis and the self-assessment based on the TPS Life Cycle Scan form the input for the company objectives. Each CSF has one or more company objectives that are related to one of the four scorecard perspectives, see Figure 11.3. The company objectives are quantified through company performance measures and targets. These objectives are derived directly from the critical success factors and form realistic milestones. Quantifying objectives is avoided in the CBSC; it will take place at a later stage via performance measures and targets. The objectives form part of a cause-and-effect chain (strategic map), resulting in the main company objective. The main question here is, what comes first, shareholders, customers, employees, society, . . . ?

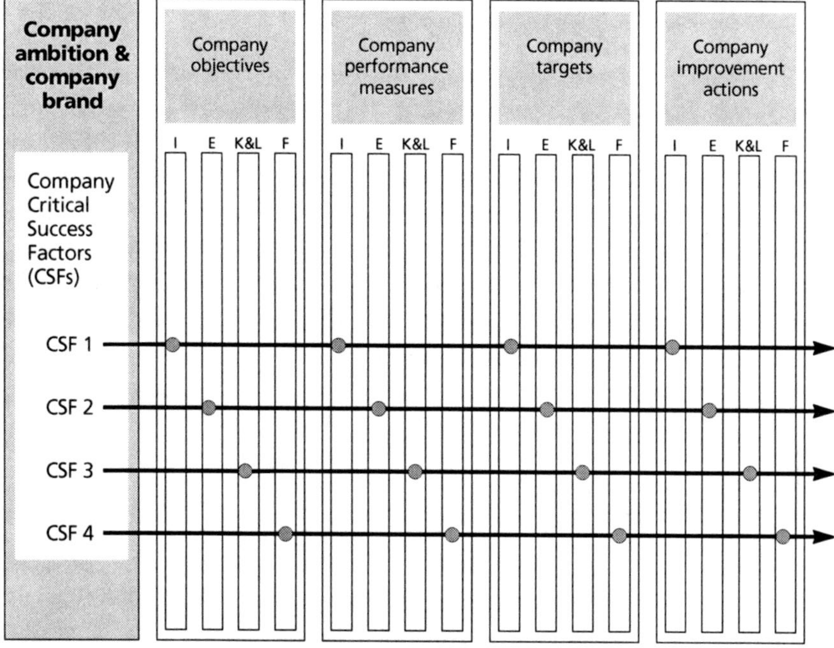

Figure 11.3 Each CSF in the CBSC is Related to Company Objectives, Performance Measures, Targets, and Improvements Actions.

In my view employees come first, the customers come second, the society is in the third place, and the shareholders are in forth place. You will not improve the quality of life of your customers and shareholders and make them happy if you do not first improve the quality of life of your employees and make them happy. The company should be *stakeholder-oriented* instead of *shareholder-oriented.* A study performed by Harvard Business School found that companies that were stakeholder-oriented (meaning that they paid explicit attention to their responsibilities towards their stakeholders, such as employees, customers, society, and their shareholders) showed four times the growth rate and eight times the employment growth of those companies that only focused on increasing the wealth of their shareholders (Miller and Pruzan, 2003). Wealth creation is not a major objective; it's the means by which we can serve the society. Also remember what Konoshuke Matsushita (founder of Matsushita Electric) said: "Profit should not be reflected of corporate greed but a vote of confidence from society that what is offered by the firm is valued."

Company Performance Measures

A company performance measure is an indicator, related to a company critical success factor and a related company objective, and is used to judge the functioning of a specific process. These indicators are the standards by which the progress of the objectives is measured. They are essential for putting the Company Ambition and the Company Brand into action. They provide management with timely signals of guidance, based on the measurement of (process) changes and the comparison of the measured results to the norms. Therefore, performance measures make the Company Ambition and the Company Brand measurable.

Table 11.1 displays an overview of possible company performance indicators according to each CBSC perspective.

Company Targets

A company target is the quantitative objective of a performance measure. It is a value that a company aspires towards, the realization of which can be measured by means of a performance measure. In other words, targets indicate values to be obtained. In this stage you should set specific timetables and deadlines for each performance measure. As with Personal performance measures, company performance measures and targets need to comply with SMART criteria (see Chapter 5).

Company Improvement Actions

Company improvement actions are strategies undertaken to realize the Company Ambition and Company Brand. The *how* is central here. Alternative strategies are formed on the basis of the aforementioned CBSC-steps, and from this, actions are chosen which result in the greatest contribution to the critical success factors. The central questions here are: How we want to achieve our objectives? Which improvement actions do we need to achieve this? How do we add value to our customers? How will we communicate our Company Brand? etc.

As with the PBSC, there are two ways to define company improvement actions: (1) By selecting critical success factors in the Company Ambition and Brand statement and translating these into company objectives, performance measures, targets, and related improvement actions and (2) by performing the company SWOT analysis (see Table 10.1) and transforming the company's strengths, weaknesses and related opportunities and threats

TABLE 11.1 Possible Company Performance Measures per BSC Perspective

Perspective	Company Performance Measures
Financial	• Company Brand equity • Shareholders value • Return • Return on investment • Investment level • Cash flow • Revenue growth • Sales • Operational costs as a percentage of sales • Margin • Profitability = sales / costs + interests received • Percent of deviation from the budget • Productivity = output / input = result / costs • Actual productivity = actual result / actual costs • Expected productivity = expected result / expected costs • Result = output = (all produced units × sales price) + dividends • Labor productivity = result / labor costs • Labor costs = man hours × hourly wage • Capital productivity = result / capital costs • Capital costs = annuity value of used capital goods • Material productivity = result / material costs • Material costs = purchased material – storage costs • Miscellaneous productivity = result / miscellaneous costs • Miscellaneous costs = energy, maintenance, insurance, etc. • Integral productivity = result / (labor costs + capital costs + material costs + miscellaneous costs) • Effectiveness = actual result / expected result • Gross value added = sales – used raw material, goods, and services needed to produce these products • Net value added = gross added value – depreciation (consumption of durable capital goods) • Value added per annual sales • Purchase share as percent of sales • Circulation velocity of stock • Percent inventory • Purchasing price versus market price • Purchase share in relation to sales • Number of suppliers • Percent revenue from new products

TABLE 11.1 Possible Company Performance Measures per BSC Perspective (continued)

Perspective	Company Performance Measures
External	• Company Brand awareness • Market share • Market growth • Percent of customers who terminate their relationship with the organization due to dissatisfaction • Number of highly satisfied customers • Degree satisfaction of customers • Number of potential customers • Potential revenues • Time needed to answer a complaint • Time needed to solve a complaint • Degree of customer loyalty • Number of "nonsales" • Costs associated with losing a customer or gaining a new customer • Sales loss as a result of dissatisfied customers • Number of visits to important customers • Number of meetings with customer groups to be informed about their demands, requirements, ideas, and complaints • Number of concrete objectives with regard to customer satisfaction • Number of guidelines related to optimal customer satisfaction • Percent of cases where the telephone is answered within three rings • Accessibility • Costs of marketing • Sales marketing department • Level of satisfaction of internal customers • Delivery time (between placing an order and delivery) • Time needed to make an offer • Percent of orders delivered late • Response time to a service request • Number of customer contacts • Number of customer surveys • Number of warranty claims • Number of customer complaints • Percent customer returns • Percent customers satisfied with communication
Internal	• Efficiency = expected costs / actual costs • Process throughput time = processing time + inspection time + movement time + waiting/storage time • Manufacturing cycle effectiveness = processing time / throughput time • Down time • Number of breakdowns • Availability = MTBF / MTTR • MTBF = Mean Time between Failures

Perspective	Company Performance Measures
Internal	• MTTR = Mean Time to Repair • Failure rate = (number of failures / total number of products tested) × 100% • Failure rate = (number of failures / operating time) × 100% • Actual processing times versus waiting times • Machine availability = {(production time – stoppage time) / production time} × 100% • Throughput time of failures = dispatch time – notice time • Invoicing speed • Delivery time (between order and delivery) • Time needed to present an offer • Percent of delayed orders • Response time to a service request • Lead time for product development • Percent sales from new products • Time needed to launch a new product on the market (time-to-market) • Percent of sick leave • Percent of latecomers • Satisfaction degree of employees • Percent of personnel turnover • Percent of personnel who find that they are working under effective leadership • Percent of personnel who find that they do challenging work • Percent of forms filled in correctly • Percent correctly performed function-oriented behavior • Quality grade = {(production quantity – number of defects) / production quantity} × 100% • Percent rejects or percent approved • Percent scrap • Percent damaged • Percent returned • Percent injuries due to dangerous work • Percent safety incidents • Percent environmental incidents • Percent of processes that are statistically controlled • Percent of processes with real-time quality feedback • Percent delayed orders • Delivery reliability; percentage deliveries completed on time and according to the specifications • Quality costs consisting of: – *Internal failure costs*: costs linked to correcting mistakes before delivery of the product, such as scrap, rejects, adjustments, downtime of equipment, labor sitting idle while waiting for repairs, and sales discounts for inferior products. – *External failure costs*: costs that regard the adjustments of malfunctions after delivery of the product, such as repair costs, travel and lodging expenses, replacement costs, stock spare parts, lost goodwill of customer, guarantee and warranty costs, and dispatchment costs.

TABLE 11.1 Possible Company Performance Measures per BSC Perspective (continued)

Perspective	Company Performance Measures
Internal	– *Prevention costs*: costs that are related to occurrence of the above mentioned costs, such as designing the product and the related process for quality, planning the quality control process, preventive maintenance costs, capital costs, quality training, and standard working procedures. – *Judgement costs*: costs that have to do with measuring and evaluating products and processes to guarantee that these meet certain standards, such as input check, laboratory tests, acquiring special testing equipment, receiving inspection, reporting on quality, and ISO audits.
Knowledge & Learning	• Labor productivity = result / labor costs • Value added per labor costs • Value added per number of employees • Value added per labor time • Revenue per employee • Sales per employee • Availability of strategic information • Experience level of employees regarding information exchange • Percent of communication failures • Percent of available competences • Number of necessary skills • Number of required or followed training courses • Percent of qualified employees • Percent of employees that are trained in essential skills • Percent of employees with the need for crucial skills • Training costs of employees • Training costs of executives and managers • Training costs as a percentage of sales • Number of solved problems • Number of suggestions per employee • Number of suggestions implemented • Usable strategic information as a percent of available information • Percent of employees with a competence profile • Degree of existence of innovative technology • Percent of available strategic skills • Average time that someone stays in the same position • Percent of personnel with personal ambition linked to shared ambition of the organization

Source: Rampersad, 2003

into company improvement actions by using the confrontation matrix, just like in Table 5.2.

To illustrate what has been said about the CBSC, I will share TPS International's CBSC with you, which is based on the related Company Ambition and Company Brand, described in Chapter 9 and Chapter 10 respectively.

TPS International's Company Balanced Scorecard

As with the PBSC, the first step in formulating the CBSC is deriving the Critical Success Factors from the formulated Company Ambition (Chapter 9) and Company Brand statement (Chapter 10), see Table 11.2. They are related to the four perspectives, internal, external, knowledge & learning, and financial. They have been identified in the Company Ambition and Company Brand statement and are further developed in the CBSC (see Table 11.3).

TPS International's Strategic Map

The position of TPS International's objectives, within the four perspectives, and their mutual relationships are made visible in Figure 11.4. In this cause effect chain the company's objectives are interrelated and affect one anoth-

TABLE 11.2 TPS International's Critical Success Factors, Which Are Derived from TPS International's Company Ambition and Company Brand Statement

Internal	**External**
• Innovating wisely • Improving our business processes continuously	• Serving individuals and organizations to achieve their full potential • Creating organizations where human spirit thrives and which model the best practices in performance, quality, creativity, and integrity • Providing excellence in integrated personal and business performance management for our customers and offer them opportunities to realize sustainable competitive advantage
Knowledge & Learning	**Financial**
• Fostering a mutually supportive, inspiring, and learning environment and working with talented and creative people	• Achieving excellent financial results through the successful introduction of our unique Total Performance Scorecard concept

TABLE 11.3 TPS International's Company Balanced Scorecard

Company Critical Success Factors	Company Objectives	Company Performance Measures	Company Targets	Company Improvement Actions
		Internal		
Innovating wisely	Newly developed products and services	% of Sales from new products and services	10% increase per year	Develop personal branding software Offering personal branding coaching services
		Time needed to launch a new product and service on the market (Time-to-Market)	Shortened with 15% in 2 years	Structure our organization more efficiently
Improving our business processes continuously	Efficient organization	Efficiency	30% increase in 3 years	Implement lean management Introduce intranet
		External		
Serving individuals and organizations to achieve their full potential	Improved customer satisfaction	Degree of satisfaction of our customers	At least 80% in 2 years	Ask feedback from customers and document this. Develop Guidelines for Optimal Customer Satisfaction
Creating organizations where human spirit thrives and which model the best practices in performance, quality, creativity, and integrity	High brand awareness	Awareness score of our Company Brand	Minimum 25% of our domain is aware of our Company Brand within 3 years	Promote our brand more actively, redesign our website. Decisive actions regarding brand promotion activities. Strengthen our sales force. Select new company location.
Providing excellence in integrated personal and business performance management for our customers and offer them opportunities to realize sustainable competitive advantage	Greater degree of trust from our customers regarding in the services we provide	Degree of Customer Loyalty	30% increase in 2 years	Measure the degree of customer loyalty Benchmarking with regard to customer loyalty. Introduce customer complaints procedure

		Knowledge & Learning		
Fostering a mutually supportive, inspiring, and learning environment and working with talented and creative people	Passionate workforce	Labor productivity of personnel	At least 20% increase in 2009	Coaching our employees based on the PBSC Provide training in effective leadership
	Creative employees	Number of innovative ideas per employee	At least 15% increase in 2010	Provide Training on teamwork, coaching, problem solving, and interpersonal communication skills Introduce effective talent management system
	A learning culture	Number of improvement suggestions executed by marketing employees	At least 20% increase in 2009	Make inventory regarding knowledge and skills lacking in marketing personnel.
		Financial		
Achieving excellent financial results through the successful introduction of our unique Total Performance Scorecard concept	Higher turnover	Turnover	20% increase in 2 years	Expand our activities in Asia. Develop network in North America. Launch PBSC software. Effectively anticipate on future opportunities. Implementing E-business tools. Market and promote my new Personal & Company Branding and *TPS-Lean Six Sigma* book Develop the outplacement market in the US Stay focused on human capital and employee engagement.
	Higher positive cash flow	Operational costs	10% decrease in 2009	Outsourcing accounting business activities

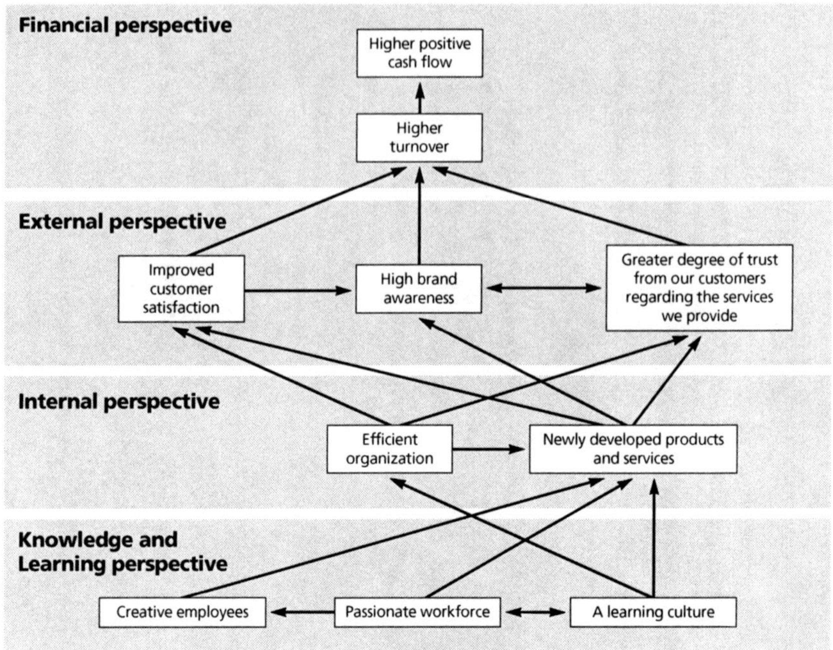

Figure 11.4 Cause-and-effect chain regarding TPS International's objectives.

er. The final objective is *higher positive cash flow.* All company goals result in this final overall objective, which is related to the Company Ambition and Company Brand statement. This diagram is a handy tool in communicating the Company Ambition and Brand to the stakeholders.

Giving Priority to Company Improvement Actions

The final step in this CBSC formulation process is prioritizing the company improvement actions to provide maximum impact. In Chapter 5, I have introduced an effective way to assign a priority number to the personal improvement actions. This can be used for company improvement actions (CBSC) as well.

ASSIGNMENT

Formulate the Balanced Scorecard of your company by identifying and selecting the critical success factors within the Company Ambition and Company Brand statement and translate these into the company objectives with corresponding measures, targets, and improvement actions. This should be done for each of the four CBSC perspectives: internal, external, knowledge/learning, and financial.

In the next chapter I will focus on the implementation of the Company Ambition, Company Brand and CBSC; in accordance with the Plan-Deploy-Act-Cultivate cycle.

12

Implement and Cultivate Your Company Ambition, Company Brand, and Company Balanced Scorecard

The companies that survive longest are the ones that work out what they uniquely can give to the world not just through growth or money but their excellence, their respect for others, or their ability to make people happy. Some call those things a soul.
— Charles Handy

Company Branding will be of no use to you if you don't implement and cultivate the Company Ambition, Company Brand and Company Balanced Scorecard effectively. These thee elements have no value unless you implement them effectively to make them a reality. This entails the final stage in the Company Branding journey (see Figure 12.1). For this, I introduce the Plan-Deploy-Act-Cultivate cycle (PDAC cycle) in this Chapter, which should be followed continuously to let the Company Brand equity and Company Brand awareness grow gradually.

Authentic Personal Branding, pages 191–197

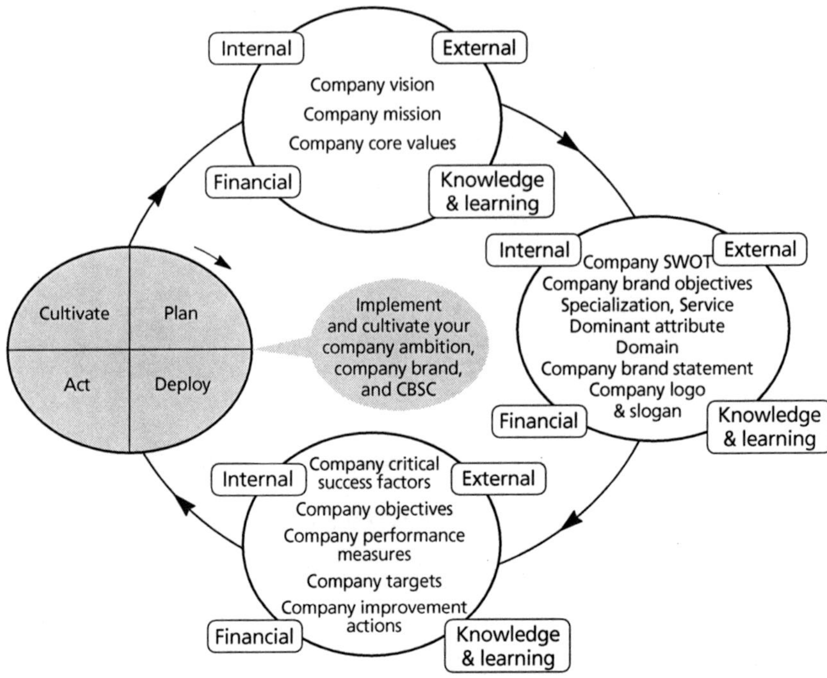

Figure 12.1 Fourth stage in the Authentic Company Branding Model.

In the following sections, each of the phases in the Plan, Deploy, Act, and Cultivate cycle (see Figure 12.2) will be discussed in depth.

Plan

First of all the company should recognize its responsibility to define, formulate, and update its authentic Company Ambition, Company Brand, and related Company Balanced Scorecard (CBSC). It should assess itself, for which the TPS Life Cycle Scan can be used, execute a SWOT analysis, and create or update its brand story that communicates the company's value and market differentiation. The CBSC also specifies the communications tools and actions in order to reach the target audience effectively, how to measure success at each step along the way and prioritized activities to provide maximum impact. In this stage it's also important to understand the customers.

Cultivate

- Continually maintain and cultivate the Company Ambition, Company Brand, and CBSC in the light of new challenges, experiences, and insights
- The Company brand needs constant updating to reflect the new challenges the company takes, the lessons learned, and the growth of the brand
- Once the selected business process has been improved, enjoy the experience, document what the company has learned, celebrate the successes, and select a new business process to improve
- When the company has accomplished all its CBSC goals, adjust the CBSC and rpeat this PDAC cycle

Plan

- Define, formulate, update the Company Ambition
- Evaluate the company based on the TPS Life Cycle Scan and the SWOT analysis
- Define, formulate, update the Company Brand
- Create, update the Company Brand Story and logo
- Formulate, update the CBSC
- Prioritize activities in the CBSC to provide maximum impact
- Understand the customers

Act

- Persue with the Company Ambition, Company Brand and CBSC with courage
- Live up to the Company Brand promise and respond to it with love, and articulate it with passion
- Express the Company Brand Story relentlessly, passionately, constantly and consistently and in a compelling way to stakeholders
- Promote the Company Brand and market the brand
- Improve the percived value in the marketplace based on the CBSC
- Improve selected business processes, improve related products and services, monitor the process performance, eliminate waste, streamline business processes, identify non-value-added activities, and stripping out waste through continuous improvement of business processes, based on TPS-Lean Six Sigma techniques

Deploy

- Launch the Company Brand on limited scale and try it out
- Articulate the Company Brand with passion
- Live up to the Company Band promise
- Assess the Company Brand and fine-tune this when it's not effective
- Implement the CBSC on limited scale and check if the improvement action is working and take action when it's not
- Map critical business processes
- Select most important business process for improvement
- Evaluate and analyze process performance

Figure 12.2 The Plan-Deploy-Act-Cultivate cycle (© Hubert Rampersad).

Deploy

Launch the Company Brand on limited scale and try it out. Assess and fine-tune it when it's not effective. Articulate the Company Brand with passion and live up to the Company Brand promise. Implement the CBSC on a limited scale, keeping in mind the priorities that have been identified. Review the results according to the performance measures and targets defined in the CBSC, measure the progress, and check to what extent the company has realized its brand and company objectives. Check if the improvement action is working, and take action if it is not. If you have not been able to realize the objective, please do not worry about it. Just start again. In this stage it's also important to map critical business processes, select most the important business process for improvement, and evaluate the process performance, based on TPS-Lean six Sigma techniques (Rampersad & El-Homsi, 2007).

Act

Pursue with the Company Ambition, Company Brand and CBSC with courage, live up to the Company Brand promise, respond to it with love, articulate it with passion, and align employee's Personal Ambition/Brand with the Company Ambition/Brand in order to develop employee engagement and a happy workforce (see Chapter 13). Promote the Company Brand, market the brand, and express the Company Brand Story relentlessly, passionately, constantly and consistently and in a compelling way to stakeholders. Improve the perceived value in the marketplace based on the CBSC and according to the PDAC cycle, and build a solid company reputation within the industry. Improve selected business processes, based on the CBSC, improve related products and services, monitor the process performance, eliminate waste, streamline business processes, lower inventory levels, avoid redundant steps, reduce lead times, identify non-value-added activities (waste) in the value stream, and strip out this waste through continuous improvement of business processes, using TPS-Lean six Sigma techniques described in the book *TPS-Lean Six Sigma; Linking Human Capital to Lean Six Sigma (A New Blueprint for Creating High Performance Companies)*, Information Age Publishing (Rampersad & El-Homsi, 2007).

We have summarized our Company Ambition and Company Brand statement on a card for all our associates (see Box 12.1). We all are using this as a compass for our company actions and decisions, to keep us focused, to guide us in the right direction, and to help us communicate our Company Brand story effectively.

Cultivate

Once you define, formulate, and implement the Company Ambition, Company Brand, and CBSC, it's important to continue cultivating and maintain-

BOX 12.1: COMPANY AMBITION AND BRAND TPS INTERNATIONAL

Company Vision

Total Performance Scorecard™

TPS

Linking Human Capital to Business Success

To be the best at helping our customers to realize their dreams. We will accomplish our mission by:

- Achieving excellent financial results through the successful introduction of our unique Total Performance Scorecard concept.
- Providing excellence in integrated personal and business performance management for our customers and offer them opportunities to realize sustainable competitive advantage.
- Creating organizations where human spirit thrives and which model the best practices in performance, quality, creativity, and integrity.
- Innovating wisely and improving our business processes continuously.
- Fostering a mutually supportive, inspiring, and learning environment within our organization and working with talented and creative people who care for the needs of the society.

Company Mission

We are devoted to serve learning individuals and innovative organizations to achieve their full potential and to link human capital to business success.

Core Values

We are guided by the following core values:

- *Integrity*: We keep commitments, deliver at all time the promised quality, and are responsible and accountable for our results.
- *Joy*: We thoroughly enjoy our work and always act and serve out of love.
- *Passion*: We are passionate in everything we do.

Company Brand Statement

Linking Human Capital to Business Success

We are passionate in providing excellence in integrated personal and business performance management to learning individuals and innovative organizations within the service and manufacturing industry. Using our innovative Total Performance Scorecard principles, we promise to help our customers to achieve their full potential and to offer them opportunities to become a best practice in financial performance, quality, creativity, and integrity.

ing these in the light of new challenges, experiences and insights. You need to refine, fine-tune, and cultivate these three branding elements as you go along, figuring out which parts work and which don't. You should make adjustments as necessary. The more you strengthen, maintain, protect, and cultivate the Company Brand, the more successful the company will be. It needs constant updating to reflect the new challenges the company takes, the lessons learned, and the growth of the Company Brand. Once the selected business process has been improved, enjoy the experience, document what the company has learned, celebrate the successes, and select a new business process to improve. When the company has accomplished all its CBSC goals, adjust the CBSC and repeat this PDAC cycle.

Figure 12.3 shows how the engaging company branding gears lead to powerful and sustainable Company Branding. Since the Plan-Deploy-Act-Cultivate cycle keeps on running through this, the company will create a stable basis for maximum brand development, constantly improve its performance, and thus continuously satisfy all stakeholders. Strategy formation, brand development, process improvement, development of human potential, and learning are all part of this perpetual process. Progressing through the PDAC cycle will result in the continuous improvement of business results through the years. Through this approach, the customer is satisfied, and the organization is able to come to know itself and its surroundings on an ongoing basis.

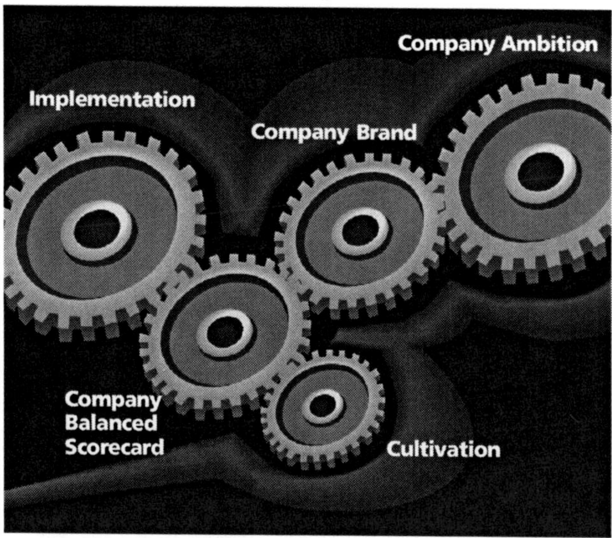

Figure 12.3 Company Branding gears.

ASSIGNMENT

- Implement your Company Brand and CBSC according to the PDAC cycle.
- Cultivate your Company Brand.

Having an authentic and powerful Company Brand is not enough to become successful. The company should make its people happy, motivated, engaged, and committed, in order to realize durable competitive advantage. In the next chapter I will therefore focus on the balance between employee's Personal Ambition/Brand and the Company's Ambition/Brand, in order to realize the "best fit" between employee and organization and therefore to create a real learning organization.

13

Aligning Personal Ambition and Personal Brand with Company Ambition and Company Brand

Alignment with your Company

In the 21st century great companies will figure out how to tap into people's hearts—their passion and their desires to make a difference through their work. Those companies that link these passions to the generation of innovative ideas will have the capacity to sustain their growth for decades.

— Bill George, former Chairman of Medtronic Inc.

The final step in this authentic Personal & Company Branding model is aligning and synchronizing the employee's Personal Ambition and Personal Brand with the Company's Ambition and Company Brand, for the purposes of employee engagement and creating a challenged and happy workforce (see Figure 13.1). It's about alignment with your company. This

Authentic Personal Branding, pages 199–215

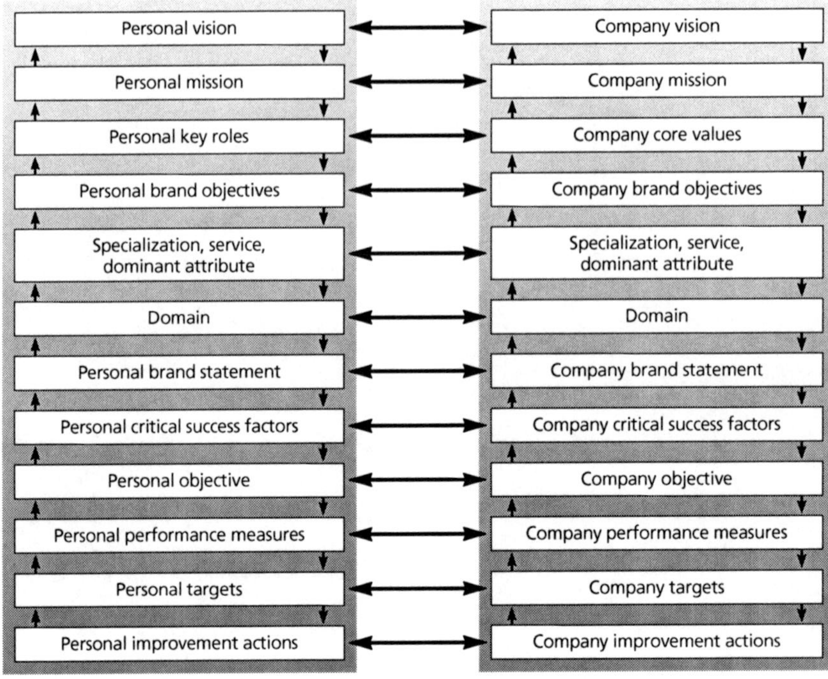

Figure 13.1 Aligning Personal and Company Ambition/Brand/BSC.

is needed because staff members don't work with devotion or expend energy on something they do not believe in or agree with. If there is an effective match between their interests and those of the company, or if their values and the company's values align, they will be engaged and will work with greater commitment and dedication towards realizing the company objectives. Identification with the Company Ambition and Company Brand is the most important motive for them to dedicate themselves actively to the company objectives and to maximize their potential. When your Personal Ambition and Personal Brand are in harmony with your company's (are compatible) and combined in the best interest of both parties, the results will be higher Personal and Company Brand equity, brand loyalty, and happy stakeholders. Doing work related to your Personal and Company Brand that is interesting, exciting and provides learning opportunities has become a key personal driver. The emphasis here lies in intrinsic motivation. Intrinsic motivation is inherently pleasurable and it arises from within; most people do something because they enjoy doing it and love it. People work harder and better when they perceive that they are treated as human beings and when they do interesting and challenging work.

Increasingly, successful companies are beginning to recognize that good brand relationships with their employees are more important than good brand relationships with their customers; employees should be happy first in order to make the customers happy. Company Brand loyalty starts with employee's happiness; with the linkage between employee's ambition/brand/BSC and employer's ambition/brand/BSC. You should put both ambitions/brands/BSC's side by side to check if there are similarities or not, as shown in Figure 13.1. Both don't have to match exactly but should align in key places, such as the ambition and brand statement.

Aligning Personal Ambition/Brand with the Company Ambition/Brand has an impact on the organizational bonding of the employees. The alignment of the employee's ambition/brand with the company's ambition/brand energizes them and gives them the proud feeling that they count (that they are being paid attention), that they are appreciated as human beings and that they make a useful and valuable contribution to the organization. Employees are stimulated in this way to commit and focus on those activities that create value for clients. This will create a strong foundation of peace and stability upon which creativity and growth can flourish, and life within the company will become a more harmonious experience. The alignment of the Personal Ambition/Brand with the Company Ambition/Brand has to do with reaching a high degree of compatibility between personal and company branding, as shown in Figure 13.2. This has an important impact

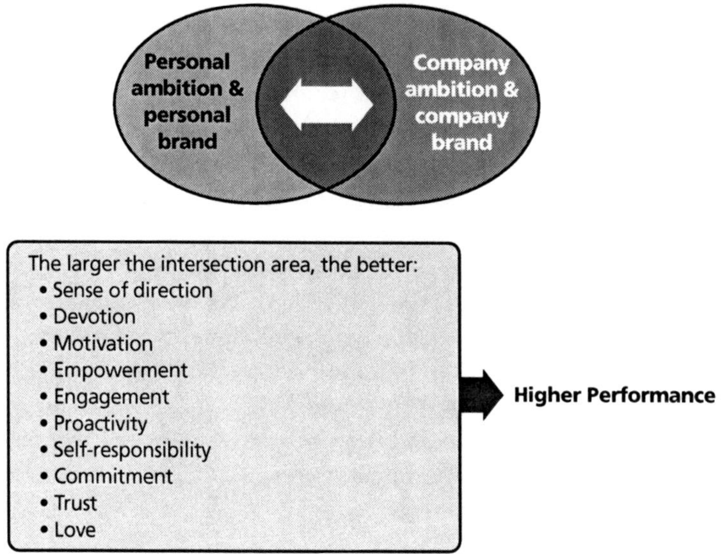

Figure 13.2 Matching the Personal Ambition/Brand with the Company Ambition/Brand.

on employee engagement. I will first discuss the importance of employee engagement, before focusing in detail on the alignment process.

Employee disengagement is a global epidemic (see also Chapter 4). According to the latest Gallup poll information:

- 61% of the British workforce, 67% of the Japanese workforce, and a whopping 82% of the workforce in Singapore is not engaged.
- Disengaged Employees Cost Singapore $4.9 Billion; the country's workforce ranks among the lowest in the world in employee engagement.
- 20% of Australian workers are actively disengaged at work and this costs the economy an estimated $31.5 billion per year; the survey of 1,500 Australian workers, found that only 18 % are engaged at work and thus providing their employers with high levels of productivity, profitability and customer service.
- The percentage of engaged employees in organizations is less than 20% in Europe.
- The highest recorded levels of engaged employees are in Brazil (31%) and Mexico (40%). The lowest recorded levels are in Asia.

Furthermore, a recent Conference Board study showed that 53% of American workers are unhappy in their jobs. In seven countries (UK, USA, Sweden, Netherlands, India, Hong Kong and Australia) SHL, the world leader in providing psychometric assessment techniques, asked hundreds of managers how much time they spend managing 'poor performers'. In its 2004 research study, it was found that the cost of bad performance by employees costs as much as US$ 32 billion in the UK. New research shows that poor performance of disengaged employees can actually "infect" their co-workers and put a drag on an entire company's morale. Sirota Survey Intelligence (Salary.Com Research, May 2006) found that many managers fail to realize the tremendous impact that poor performance of a few employees has on the entire company's operations. Out of 34,330 employees polled for this study, 33 percent of managers and 43 percent of non-management employees think their companies aren't addressing poor performers in an appropriate manner. This has a tremendous negative impact on motivation and productivity, says David Sirota:

> It has to do with employees being frustrated by co-workers. It's indicative of management that's really not managing. People want management to care

> about performance. If somebody's not working, it's a real detriment to everyone's performance.

Consequently, when companies do address poor performance, employee engagement and productivity increase. According to Sirota research (Salary.Com Research), nearly three-quarters (73 percent) of employees who think their company is doing a good job of addressing poor performers identify themselves as "favorably engaged" at work. To take advantage of all these findings, companies need to make lagging employees understand that performance is taken seriously, match their ambition/brand with the company's ambition/brand and let them go if they do not improve with coaching.

Matching the Personal Ambition/Brand with the Company Ambition/Brand has to do with reaching a higher degree of compatibility between personal and company objectives and mutual value addition (as shown in Figure 13.2). A study, by CO2 Partners (2007), found that 30% of US workers values mismatch with the company:

- One in three U.S. workers said their employer's core values are not consistent with their own.
- 44 percent said their values were consistent.
- 11 percent said they were uncertain about their own core values but never uncomfortable working for their employer.
- 10 percent said they didn't feel their core values had much connection to the work they do.

Another study, by Towers Perrin (2005), found that in stead of matching the right employee to the right position for long-term success, most US companies and H/R departments put the emphasis on simply filling the position as quickly as possible. As a result, American businesses are losing money as fast as they are losing employees.

It has become essential to get the optimal fit and balance between the Personal Ambition/Brand and the Company Ambition/Brand in order to enhance labor productivity and to stimulate engagement, commitment, love, and passion in the company, see Figure 13.3. This has to do with reaching a higher degree of compatibility between personal and organizational objectives and mutual value addition. People do not work with devotion or expend energy on something they do not believe in or agree with. Clarity and uniformity of personal and organizational values and principles are therefore essential for the active involvement of employees. Research has shown that when an individual has some input regarding the shared ambi-

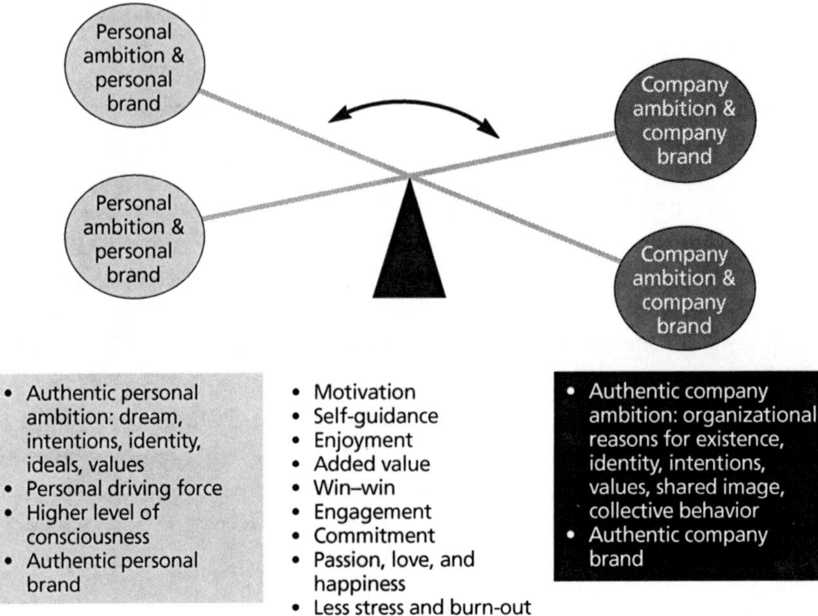

Figure 13.3 Aligning Personal Ambition and Personal Brand with the Company Personal Ambition and Company Brand.

tion that affects his or her work, the person will be more supportive, motivated, and receptive towards organizational change. Experience teaches us that identification with the company is the most important motive for employees to dedicate themselves actively to the company's objectives and to maximize their human resource potential. Workers are often willing to work together towards the goals of the organization with dedication when there is a match between their personal ambition and the company ambition. All people have different personal values and principles that we must try to understand and link to the company values. The experience of applying the personal and company branding concept in the past years has shown that most employees want to be content and happy at their workplace; that they really enjoy going to work; that they strive for a balance between work and life and that they want to give 100% to the organization. A study by Towers Perrin (2005), found that while many people are keen to contribute more at work, the behavior of their managers and culture of their organizations is actively discouraging them from doing so. It shows that there is a vast reserve of untapped "employee performance potential" that could drive better financial results if only companies could tap into this reserve. Remember what Peter Drucker said: "So much of what we call management consists in making it difficult for people to work."

How to Create Employee Engagement by Aligning the Personal Ambition/Brand and the Company Ambition/Brand

It is recommended to encourage managers and employees to formulate their personal ambition/brand and to let them reflect about the balance between their own personal ambition/brand and the company ambition/brand. I, therefore, recommend introducing an *ambition meeting* within companies between the line-manager or superior and his/her employees. The ambition meeting is a periodical, informal, voluntary and confidential meeting of a maximum duration of one hour between line-manager and his/her employees, with the employee's Personal Ambition/Brand/PBSC and the Company Ambition/Brand/CBSC as topics. *Why informal? Because they will learn more from informal than from formal meetings.* It is recommended that the meeting is held structurally at least once every two months, preferably more often. The outcome of these informal meetings should be highly confidential and should be kept out of the personnel file and not be used against the employee. The line-manager or supervisor plays a crucial role in worker well-being and engagement. He/she should act as a trusted person, coach, and role model in this process. *Why as a trusted person? Because if there is distrust and fear, there will be no sharing and learning.* To be able to talk about the employee's Personal Ambition/Brand/PBSC, one needs a confidential, informal and friendly atmosphere, an atmosphere of trust and open communication. This is essential as human values will be discussed. Experience has shown that this intimate atmosphere can be reached if the manager formulates his/her own Personal Ambition/Brand/PBSC beforehand and shares it with his/her employee. The implementation of the employee's Personal Ambition/Brand/PBSC comes up for discussion, and includes private matters, as well as work-related aspects. At least those private matters that have an impact on job performance can be discussed confidentially. During the alignment process, the manager should act as a trusted and informal coach and provide social support to the employees by being a good listener, providing help, and being someone the employee can rely on. In Appendix B you will find the Personal Brand Coaching framework and our related certification program, which is meant to be helpful for guiding you in this process, in order to become an effective coach.

The Ambition meeting will help you clarify if your Personal Ambition/Brand and those of your company are in harmony and where they are in conflict. It determines how closely your employer's Ambition/Brand aligns with your Ambition/Brand. The line-manager can make a selection of the following ambition questions, which he/she can use during in the ambition meeting with you.

- Does your Personal Ambition/Brand correspond with the Company Ambition/Brand?
- Can you identify yourself with the Company Ambition/Brand? In doing this, do you feel personally involved and addressed by the Company Ambition/Brand? Is your Personal Ambition/Brand to be found in the Company Ambition/Brand? If not, do they have to be expanded or adjusted? Are they acceptable? How can they flourish within the organization?
- Is it possible that your Personal Ambition/Brand level or that of the company should be lowered?
- Does your Personal Ambition/Brand match the Company's Ambition/Brand? Where do they align and where do they contradict each other? Do they conflict? Are there compatibilities? Are there linkages?
- Are your most important personal values done justice here? Which points in your Personal Ambition/Brand are strengthened and which are in conflict with the Company Ambition/Brand? Which ones are neglected?
- Is there a win-win situation between your own interests and the ones of your company?
- What makes you feel good at work?
- Are you proud of working for the company?
- Whose life is improved because of your work?
- Which skills do you need to be a pillar of the organization and thus realize the Company Ambition/Brand? What do you want to gain through this?
- Are your developmental expectations in tune with those of the company?
- Do your job requirements match your capabilities and needs?
- How is the implementation of your ambition/brand/PBSC going? Did you reach your target? Could it be better? Where did it go wrong? What have you learned? What did you unlearn?
- What motivates you? What demotivates you? What makes you happy or sad? What do you enjoy the most?

- What contribution are you trying to make to the realization of our Company Ambition/Brand? Which job do you aspire? What are your wishes? What do you strive for? What are your concerns?
- Have you considered a job change?

Don't expect a perfect match or alignment, but the more alignment the better. You should decide, based on the results of this alignment process, to stay and struggle or to leave. If your ambition/brand doesn't align at all with the company's brand/ambition, and if it probably never will finding an other job where there is a better fit is the best option. Some of my customers decided to look for another job after they discovered that their ambition/brand did not well align with their employer's ambition/brand. It prevented stress and burnout. Sometimes this can be the best option for both yourself and the company.

As discussed, the alignment process also has an important impact on the level of stress and burnout at work. The International Labour Organization (ILO) defines organizational stress as "Harmful physical and emotional responses that occur when the job requirements do not match the capabilities, resources or needs of the workers." Burnout is a physical, mental, and emotional response to constant levels of high stress. It produces feelings of hopelessness, powerlessness, cynicism, resentment and failure—as well as stagnation and reduced labor productivity. Research shows that when employees have tense or strained relationships with their manager or colleagues, this could increase their levels of stress. Organizations that understand the connections between worker stress and health and wellbeing can help their employees manage stress and find balance in their work and personal lives. When they do, productivity and engagement improve (*Gallup Management Journal,* 2005). As shown in Chapter 5, the PBSC is an excellent tool for finding balance in your work and personal lives in order to reduce stress and burnout. The impact of stress and burnout is high. According to the National Institute for Occupational Safety and Health (1983):

- Stress is linked to physical and mental health, and decreased willingness to take on new and creative endeavors.
- Job burnout is experienced by 25% to 40% of U.S. workers.
- Stress has a major negative impact on productivity.
- Depression, only one type of stress reaction, is responsible for more days lost than any other single factor.
- $300 billion, or $7,500.00 per employee, is spent annually in the U.S. on stress related compensation claims, reduced productivity, absenteeism, health insurance claims, and direct medical expenses (nearly 50% higher for workers who report stress symptoms).

The authentic Personal and Company Branding system introduced in this book will help you to reduce organizational stress and burnout. This happens through aligning the Personal Ambition/Brand with the Company Ambition/Brand in concordance with the introduced breathing and silence exercise. This exercise will give you energy and have a restful effect on you to produce a calm state of mind free from stress. Experience has shown that deeper involvement and harmonious working relationships created among employees through the PBSC method also reduces organizational stress and burnout. Public health scientists at University College London have found that a happy state of mind can lead to a healthier heart and lower levels of stress-inducing chemicals. They have found that people who have more moments of happiness over a day produce less harmful chemicals such as cortisol and so are likely to be healthier in the long run and less likely to suffer from heart disease. Some executives and managers, instead of creating happiness, create distrust and fear within the organization. They have an enormous destructive impact on the health of their people and their company, and true learning is not stimulated in an atmosphere of distrust and fear. Research shows that more than half of all employees in Europe have changed jobs or organizations at least once because of their manager's behavior—in other words mismanagement is the reason for their poor performance on the job. You will drive out fear from your company by introducing the ambition meeting between the line manager and his/her employees. In this way the line manager will give employees the feeling that they count for something and that they are appreciated as human beings. Consequently they will create a firm foundation of peace and trust upon which creativity and growth can flourish. Trust is the most important ingredient for successful personal and Company Branding. Ralph Waldo Emerson said: "Trust men and they will be true to you; treat them greatly and they will show themselves great." According to Simon Dolan (2007):

> When others trust us and give us freedom to act, our self-esteem improves and we tend to become more productive. This is the basis for empowerment... People with appropriate self-esteem experience themselves better, they are and feel alive, they are more willing to go beyond themselves and take care of others. They establish certain interpersonal bonds easily, they don't feel alone, they manage their lives with ease and are relaxed towards their own destiny, towards their own happiness.

The discussed alignment process is an opportunity to create warmth, pleasure, passion, heartfelt commitment, self-direction within companies, and motivation, which is often missed. Management has two general options of rewards regarding motivation: extrinsic (such as salary, money) and intrinsic (for example, recognition, appreciation, and praise). Intrinsic motivation is that which is inherently pleasurable, while extrinsic motivation is not. Intrinsic motivators are those that arise from within—doing something because you enjoy it—while extrinsic motivators mean people are seeking a reward, such as money. Money has lost its impact on employee's motivation, as it is a short-term incentive. Therefore, organizations must reward employees intrinsically, too. A climate of learning, challenges, enjoyment, happiness, trust, creativity, self-actualization, self-development, esteem, and inner involvement is often more important to employees than salary. Mihaly Csikszentmihalyi (1990) did large-scale research in the United States about dissatisfaction of employees. It was established that American employees named three important reasons why they were dissatisfied with their job. These reasons had to do with the quality of the experience on the job, and not with salary and other material interests. The first and most important reason was about the lack of variations and challenges (dull and senseless). The second reason was related to conflicts with other people at work, in particular with bosses. The conflict is often because of someone's defensive attitude, which results from fear of failure. The third reason has to do with exhaustion (especially in managers); too busy, too much stress, too much tension, too little time for themselves, insufficient balance between work and life, and family problems.

Stimulating employees and making a job more enjoyable are the changes managers have to make in order to attract and engage workers whose fundamental views about work have been shifting radically over the past ten years. The solution for this is: Formulating your Personal Ambition, Personal Brand, and PBSC, creating work-life balance with the PBSC (in the external perspective), implementing these according to the PDAC-cycle, and aligning yourself with the company. On the basis of this you will also be able to set priorities and effectively manage your spare time in a more structured fashion so that you can enjoy optimum experiences and new challenges at home. This will also help with your hobbies, which require specific skills, behaviors and inner discipline. Robert Park, the prominent American sociologist said 60 years ago, "I suspect that the biggest waste of American life flows from squandering of our spare time." Relevant to this are some important statements made by Mihaly Csikszentmihalyi:

> Together we squander the equivalent of millions of years of human consciousness. The energy which can be used for concentration on complex objectives, personal growth and feeling well, is being dissipated on incentives which do not do more than imitate reality... Work and spare time can also provide for our needs. People, who learn to enjoy their work, and use their spare time the right way, often have the idea that their lives have become more valuable.

> The future is not only for the learned person, but also for the person who has learned to use his spare time effectively.

Valuable energy is wasted in spending time on activities that are of no value and on daydreaming. There are many important and fun things to do in life. The challenge is to respect time, so that we can achieve a fuller, more satisfying life. According to Robin Sharma:

> True happiness comes from only one thing: achievement of goals, whether they are personal, professional or otherwise. You are happiest when you feel you are growing. When you feel that you are contributing and advancing in the direction of your dreams, you will notice that you have boundless energy and vitality. Time spent on activities which offer little reward aside from a fleeting feeling of relaxation (television watching is the best example), is time lost forever. Relaxation is essential but choose the most effective means of renewal and spend your time in productive pursuits that will slowly move you along the path of accomplishment. Happiness comes from doing—not sleeping.

Also remember what Charles Darwin said, "Anyone who dares to waste one hour of life has not discovered the value of life."

Many of the above-mentioned spare time activities are often not challenging and do not result in an optimum flow experience, because challenges and skills needed for these are not always on a high level. Chances to be happier, more joyful, more creative, more satisfied, and to stimulate personal growth in spare time are often missed in pursuit of these activities. Therefore it is recommended that you systematically apply the introduced Personal Branding method not only at your workplace but also in your spare time and with your family. You will then be able to realize your family objectives and to breathe more life into your relationships with your spouse and children. Hence, assist your family members in formulating their Personal Ambition, Personal Brand, and related PBSC, let them share this amongst themselves, and stimulate them to perform the breathing and silence exercise. You will thus create conditions so that you can enjoy life with your family and be happy together. Work-life balance is also an important issue that employers must offer in order to retain and develop talent. Many companies in North America and Europe have been successful in allowing employees to schedule their own shifts, so as to be able to meet family commitments. Research shows that one of the reasons why partners broke up was that they spent too much time on their careers (http://www.asanet.org/media/ timewarp.html). People want more time for themselves and their kids now. According to U.S. Census figures, the average male is stated to have worked 43.5 hours a week in 1970 and 43.1 hours a week in

2000, and the average female 37.1 hours in 1970 and 37.0 hours in 2000. See Chapter 5 how the PBSC method will help you create a stable basis for work-life balance. It will also help you to set priorities in your life and manage yourself and your time effectively.

It was proven through Mihaly Csikszentmihalyi's research that the average American devotes 10% of working hours on irrelevant matters, such as daydreaming and gossiping with colleagues. In some cases, this even goes as high as 25% of work time. A more recent study, by America On-line and Salary.com, found that the average U.S. worker wastes more than two hours a day, and that's not including lunch. This means companies spend as much as $759 billion (U.S.) on salaries annually for which they receive no apparent benefit. Americans who feel bored and underpaid do work hard—at surfing the Internet and catching up on gossip, according to a recent survey of Salary.com (2007). This survey found U.S. workers waste about 20 percent of their working day. The online survey of 2057 employees by the online compensation company found about six in every 10 workers admit to wasting time at work with the average employee wasting 1.7 hours of a typical 8.5 hour working day. "While a certain amount of wasted time is built into company salary structures, our research indicates that companies with a challenged and engaged workforce can expect more productivity in return," said Bill Coleman, chief compensation officer at Salary.com.

To take advantage of all these findings, executives should introduce the ambition meeting and should help their employees to improve the quality of their life, not only at the workplace, but also in their spare time on the basis of the methods and techniques presented here. Following such practices would encourage employees to continuously feel free and safe, and able to accept bigger challenges, and through this, provide enjoyment in work and experience well-being and happiness. This attitude will also have its effect on customers and shareholders, improving their quality of life and adding to their well-being and satisfaction. It is therefore critical that managers realize that their employees' home situation (healthy or not) has an impact on their work performance. This can no longer be ignored, in the interests of the health and happiness of employees.

Company Integrity

An important final step in this sustainable and holistic personal and Company Branding process is to integrate the personal integrity of individuals (see Chapter 7) into a system called *company integrity* or *business ethics*. It's about aligning authentic Personal Branding with authentic Company Branding, see Figure 13.4. Company integrity defines how a company integrates its

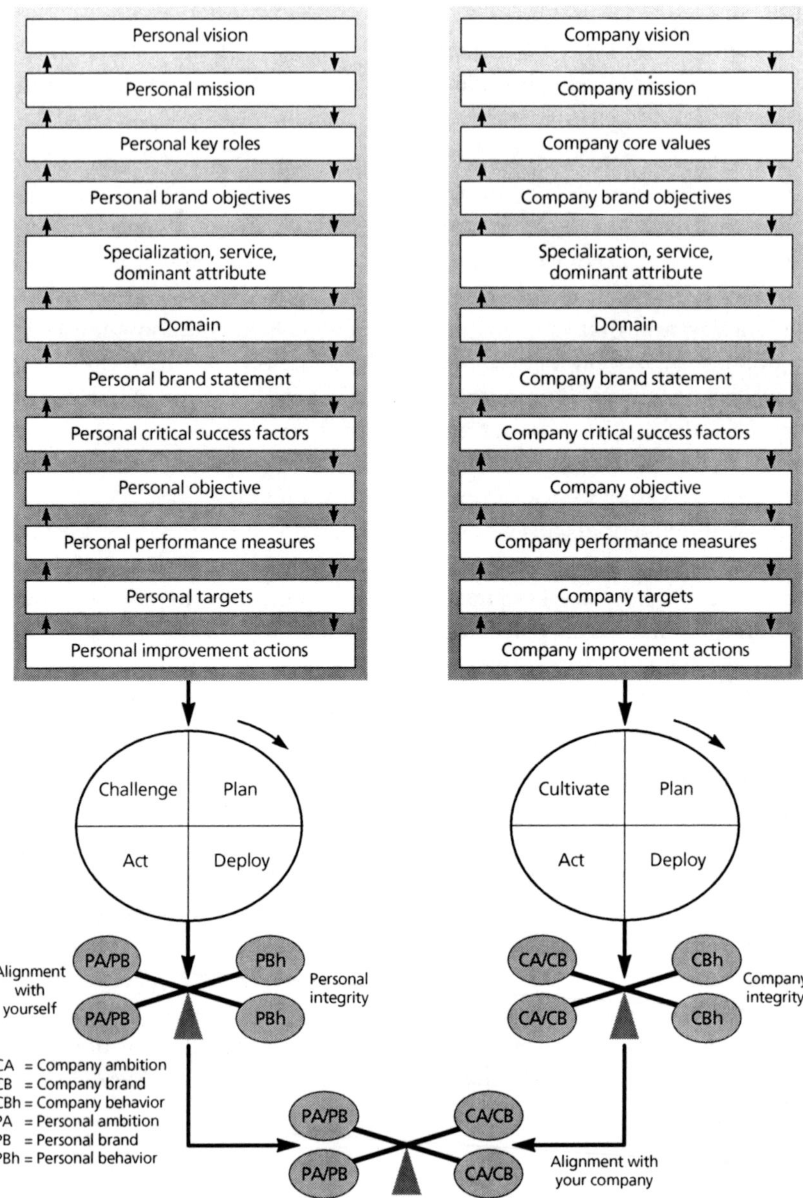

Figure 13.4 Aligning Personal Branding with Company Branding.

Company Ambition and Brand and the personal integrity of all individuals into its policies, practices, and decision-making. This can be developed by aligning the Company Ambition and Brand with the company behavior.

The behavior allowed in companies comprises the company culture, or shared values and beliefs which result in a certain way of doing things and in a distinct environment. Aligning Company Ambition and Brand with the company behavior can be done by (Rampersad, 2006):

- Building ethics into the Company Ambition and Brand and helping managers and employees to understand that values and ethical standards are integral to all company operations activities.
- Stimulating everyone within the company to align their Personal Ambition with their behavior and actions (to align themselves with themselves, see Figure 13.4). They should care about ethics and corporate social responsibility, and ensure that their actions reflect integrity and high ethical standards.
- Top management must be openly committed to ethical conduct and everyone within the company must be made aware of the core values. Involvement and commitment of personnel at all organizational levels is important in order to develop higher levels of trust and pride.
- Integrating ethics into all aspects of corporate communications and develop communication programs with emphasis on corporate ethics to inform all stakeholders.
- Developing an ethics code, which tells employees and managers how to act in various situations.
- Executing the TPS Life Cycle Scan (see Chapter 10) to ensure personnel compliance on at least an annual basis. This performance excellence model will guide you in this process of continuous business ethics improvement.
- Setting up board ethics and corporate social responsibility committees—let ethics officers or other senior managers with ethics responsibilities report directly to the board.
- Top management should act as a role model. Remember what Alan Greenspan said: "Our market system depends critically on trust—trust in the world of our colleagues and trust in the world of those with whom we do business... I am saying that the state of corporate governance to a very large extent reflects the character of the CEO."
- Strengthen employee loyalty and commitment by aligning the employees with the company (see Figure 13.4). In my TPS International company I have passed along and shared my Personal Ambition and Personal Brand with my employees, via a monthly

> ambition meeting. In this way they help spread our Company Ambition and Company Brand in everything they do.

Company integrity should not only be based on formal regulations and exhaustive guidelines, but on actual practices. As demonstrated by Enron and others, ethics programs provide no protection from potentially catastrophic ethical failures. Company integrity starts with personal integrity. It must be an informal self-learning process, a way of life based on alignment with yourself and alignment with your company. This ethical thinking should be promoted and communicated within the whole company. In this way ethical behavior will become a routine in the whole organization, and leaders and employees will gain more understanding about their responsibility with regard to ethical behavior. They will understand that it is their responsibility to act ethically, on duty as well as off-duty. This is a more sustainable, comprehensive and holistic approach to ethics and social responsibility. This integrated authentic Personal and Company Branding approach as shown in Figure 13.4 will create a paradigm shift in the company and will continually impact the employee's transformational process. It will work as a catalyst to accelerate the transformation of satisfied workers into committed employees. It will also create a real learning organization. As discussed in Chapter 7, learning can be categorized as self-learning and shared learning (organizational learning), see Figure 13.5. Self-learning, which I have discussed in Chapter 7, is the source of all learning. For this, insight into your Personal Ambition and Personal Brand is indispensable. People who do not have this insight are poor learners. Without self-learning, shared learning cannot exist. With self-learning, employees learn separately and experience an individual behavioral change. For shared learning, insight into the Company Ambition and Company Brand is indispensable. With shared learning people learn together, with and from each other. When shared learning occurs the whole company learns, and undergoes a shared behavioral change, or organizational change. This reflects the company behavior. This process applies to knowledge as well—Self-knowledge needs to be cultivated first before you can acquire knowledge of the world. It's therefore important to make self-knowledge your best friend.

In Appendix B, I will introduce the Personal Brand Coaching framework and our related certification program, which is meant to be helpful for coaching yourself and others to develop and implement a sustainable and authentic Personal Brand. The Personal BrandSoft, described in Appendix C, will assist you in this process and help you manage and steer yourself on performance.

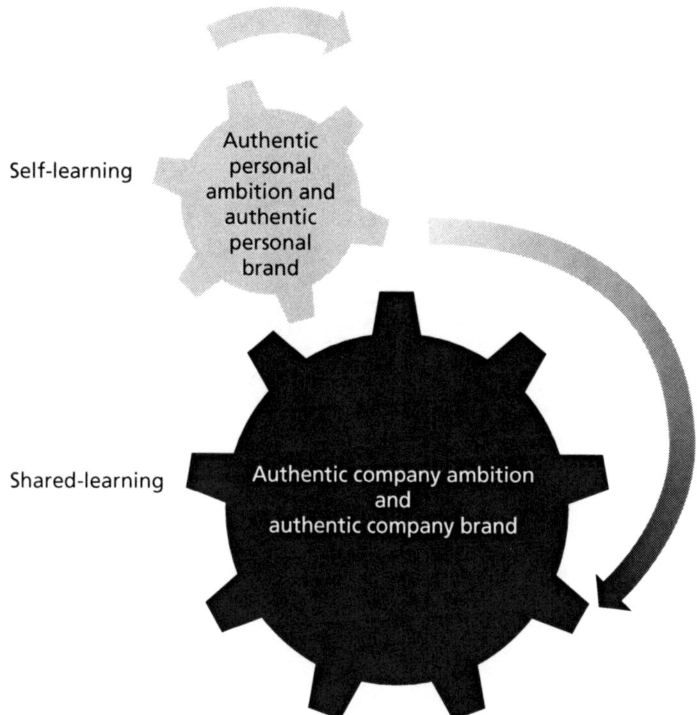

Figure 13.5 Self learning and shared learning.

Epilogue

An image is not simply a trademark, a design, a slogan or an easily remembered picture. It is a studiously crafted personality profile of an individual, institution, corporation, product or service.

— Daniel J. Boorstin, prolific American historian, professor, attorney, and writer

I wrote this book because I am an international crusader for individual's and company's happiness and empowerment. By way of this book, I want to provide individuals and companies a breakthrough formula and some practical tools, successfully tested in practice, to develop, implement, maintain, and cultivate an authentic Personal and Company Brand identity. Part 1 of this book is for everyone who wants to build, implement, maintain, and cultivate a strong authentic Personal Brand, separate themselves from the crowd, and deliver peak performance. This part is useful for everyone. Part 2 is for organizations that want to build, implement, maintain, and cultivate an effective authentic Company Brand, to create a happy workforce, to improve their competitiveness based on this. Part 1 can be used separately from Part 2. Personal Branding has become more important than Company Branding. Consequently, in this book I have focused in more detail on Personal Branding than on Company Branding.

Everyone has a Personal Brand but most people are not aware of this and do not manage this strategically and effectively. It's about time to focus on authentic Personal Branding, in order to be happy and successful in life. It is your ethical duty and responsibility to build, implement, maintain, and cultivate an authentic Personal Brand, for your own good, your loved ones,

Authentic Personal Branding, pages 217–219

your organization, your country, and the world we are part of. Without a strong Personal Brand, you look just like everyone else. Be the CEO of your life and take control of your brand and the message it sends and how it affects the way others perceive you. This is the key to success in today's online, virtual, and individual age. I have therefore introduced an organic, holistic and authentic Personal Branding model which will help you to build, implement, maintain, and cultivate an authentic, distinctive, relevant, consistent, concise, meaningful, crystal clear, and memorable Personal Brand, which forms the key to enduring personal success. The related tools will guide you to deliver peak performance and to create a stable basis for trustworthiness, credibility, and personal charisma. If you are branded in this holistic way your Personal Brand will be strong, distinctive, relevant, consistent, concise, meaningful, exciting, inspiring, compelling, enduring, crystal clear, persuasive and memorable. You will also create a life that is fulfilling, automatically attract the people and opportunities that are a perfect fit for you. The introduced authentic Company Branding model, which is similar to the authentic Personal Branding model, has the same effect for your company.

I believe this book differs from other branding books. It is up to you, the reader, to judge whether this is true. I gladly welcome any reactions and suggestions from you regarding this book. Please send your feedback by e-mail to h.rampersad@tps-international.com. The development of this authentic Personal and Company Branding concept and the writing of this book have been a continuing learning process for me. If you would like to keep track of the latest developments in this field, please visit my blog rampersad.wordpress.com and my website at *www.Total-Performance-Scorecard.com.* Authentic Personal Branding™ is a worldwide registered trade mark. We are devoted to helping individuals and organizations to develop a strong authentic brand, by providing integrated professional services (coaching, consulting and training) based on our proven principles. The results are personal and organizational effectiveness and a related unique competitive advantage. For more information about our Authentic Personal & Company Brand Management concept, or the international office closest to you, please write to:

TPS International Inc.
P.O. Box 601564
North Miami Beach
Florida 33160, USA
Phone: +1-786-537-7580
Fax: +1-714-464-4498
h.rampersad@tps-international.com
hubert@personalbrandinguniversity.org
www.total-performance-scorecard.com
www.rampersad.wordpress.com
www.linkedin.com/in/hubertrampersad
Skype: h.rampersad

Personal Branding University
P.O. Box 601564
North Miami Beach
Florida 33160, USA
Phone: +1-786-537-7580
Fax: +1-714-464-4498
h.rampersad@tps-international.com
www.pbuniversity.wordpress.com
www.personalbrandinguniversity.org

Afterword

Now that you have finished reading this outstanding book, you are probably wondering "what does this all mean?" It is nearly impossible to retain all the details of four stages of the authentic personal branding model, you will want to remember some of the messages of this book and how they can be applied to you and your personal and professional life. Of course, you may want to refer back to some of the simple and elegant models for personal and company ambition, objectives, critical success factors, and actions. Hubert Rampersad has a knack for preparing comprehensive frameworks for analyzing important issues. You may also want to reflect on many of the self and organization diagnostic questions that offer you insight into your brand and your company's brand. These mental models and their related investigative questions will help you know where you are today so you can get to where you want to be tomorrow.

We tend to like books and ideas that confirm and inform our thinking. Both of these are true for me of this book. With my colleagues Wayne Brockbank, Norm Smallwood, and Jon Younger, we have thought, debated,

Authentic Personal Branding, pages 221–226

and written about issues related to firm, leadership, and personal brand.[1] We have tried to understand how to help leaders develop leadership within their companies, how to build talent throughout a company, and how to use HR practices to create and sustain value. Many of the themes in this book confirm our thinking. But, this work also informs our thinking and helps us move forward in what we know and do. While each reader will glean unique insights from this book, let me try to capture some of my key takeaways.

1. Personal Brand Exists

Whether we like it or not, we all have a personal brand. We have an identity that we are known for by those who know us both best and least. This personal identity sends signals about how we want to be treated and filters how others connect, interact, and deal with us. When our personal brand is implicit and unintentional we may be surprised by how we interact with others. When our personal brand is deliberate and disciplined, we can shape how we are treated. Our lives are much less complicated when we identify and act on our personal brand.

When I was leading a mission for our church, I supervised over about 500 young men and women who dedicated 18 to 24 months of their lives doing community service. During this time, they lived a very monkish existence, abstaining from the normal social and party norms of their generation. They worked to recognize and teach moral principles and they abstained from things would detract them from their mission. At the end of their service, they returned back into the "real" world where they would be tempted to succumb to more worldly patterns. One young man was very worried since on leaving his mission he would be joining the military. In our final interview, he expressed concern that he would be able to continue to

1 Our work can be found in the following books and articles:

Ulrich, Dave and Norm Smallwood. *Leadership Brand.* Boston, MA: Harvard Business Press, 2007.

Ulrich, Dave and Wayne Brockbank. *HR Value Proposition.* Boston, MA: Harvard Business Press, 2005.

Ulrich, Dave and Norm Smallwood, Aligning firm, leadership, and personal brand. *Leader to Leader,* Winter 2008 24-32

Ulrich, Dave and Norm Smallwood. Building intangible value from the outside/in *Leader to Leader,* Spring 2003, 24-30.

Ulrich, Dave and Norm Smallwood, Capitalizing on capabilities. *Harvard Business Review,* June 2004.

Jon Younger, Norm Smallwood, and Dave Ulrich, Developing your organization's brand as a talent developer. *Human Resource Planning Journal.*

live the values that he had assimilated during his mission. We talked about the four 3's. I promised him that if he would live his values without fanfare for 3 hours, 3 days, 3 weeks, and 3 months, that he would not struggle to live his values. He tested my ideas. About 6 months later we saw him and he said that he now found it easy to live his values. After 3 months of doing what he felt was right, he had developed a reputation (or personal brand) that others knew him for. His fellow troops had learned what he values and they saw that he lived those values. They honored his expectations and in fact protected him from strangers who did not know him by saying "don't invite Cody to this activity, it is not something he would be interested in."

When we are intentional about our personal brand, others will respect us and help us retain our brand. If we are not clear about our personal brand, and our behaviors vary, others will not know how to treat us and we struggle for consistency in our lives.

2. Personal Brand Can Be Created and Evolved

When I decided I wanted to be a teacher for a living, I recognized that public speaking was not my predisposition. As a strong introvert, I found it difficult to be in front of groups. Yet, I knew that if I was going to be a good presenter, I needed to replace fears with confidence. I wanted to develop a reputation as an engaging and thoughtful teacher. So, I observed some of the best professors in the world at the University of Michigan and elsewhere. I took notes less on what they said and more on how they said it. I experimented with teaching styles and approaches. I sought detailed feedback on how my efforts worked. I reflected on what I said and how I said it. I wrote notes to myself on what worked and what did not work in presentations. Over 20 years, I am still somewhat uncomfortable being in front of groups, but I have shaped my personal identity.

In a major review of the literature on nature/nurture (are you born with a set of skills or can you develop them), the Society for Industrial and Organizational Psychology found that it is about 50/50. About half of who we are (our personal brand) is strongly linked to our genealogy. As we age, we find our parents looking back at us in the mirror. And, about half is what we chose to become. With this in mind, I believe we can intentionally create the brand we want to become. The four stages Hubert lays out are a wonderful step by step approach to making out desired brand explicit. Brands evolve. They can adapt by our intentional reflection and action. While we are beholden to our past, we are not bound to it.

3. Organizations have a Brand That Becomes Its Culture

When we ask participants in workshops to fill in the blank, "our organization culture is our ______________." Most participants answer with words or phrases like: values, norms, beliefs, behaviors, expectations, or accepted ways of doing things. While we don't disagree with these accepted definitions, we think that there is a better way to define culture. All of these observations focus on the inside, what "we" are known for and do. Elsewhere, we have argued that an organization's culture can best be defined by starting from the outside in.

When we work with executive teams, we often start with, "given your strategy, what are the top 3 things you want to be known for by your best customers?" This question focuses on the outside customers. What is the identity (or brand) that you want to be known for by those who use your services. When the top team has a unity of identity, when they make this identity real to customers, and when they translate this external identity into internal management practices, they have shaped a culture that creates value and endures over time.

The four stage model that Hubert suggests proposes an explicit way to turn a desired external identity into something concrete and actionable. When the external brand becomes the internal culture, real value is created. In *Leadership Brand*, we talk about how successful leadership exists when leaders at all levels of an organization act in accordance with customer expectations. In *HR Value Proposition*, we suggest that all HR practices (staffing, training, compensation, communication, work design) can and should be aligned with customer expectations.

4. Alignment of the Firm Brand and Individual Brand Becomes a Primary Leadership Agenda

Leaders lead best when they build the next generation of leadership who does the right things right. We have argued that good leadership is not just about what the individual leader knows and does, but about how leadership becomes an organization capability that is not uniquely tied to one individual leader. A firm brand exists when it is not just a single product or service, but the reputation of the firm through many products or services. When Marriott hotel puts its name on its brand (Residence Inn, Fairfield Inn, Courtyard), consumer confidence goes up. It is not one product, but the Marriott reputation that is branded.

Likewise, leadership brand exists when leaders at all levels act to turn customer expectations into employee actions. As the outside demands of customers become the internal practices of employees, all stakeholders of a firm win. Investors increase share price because of the intangible value of the firm. Customers have confidence not only in today's product, but tomorrow's ability to maintain a stream of products and services. Employees can act on an employee value proposition and brand that connects them to the firm.

In the popular organization press, we are told lately to build on our strengths. It is very hard to disagree with this logic. Marcus Buckingham and others have argued that discovering what we do well is a first step to lasting success. Leaders whose strengths are around creativity will be more successful in innovative organizations and work environments, for example.

But building only on your strengths is not enough if those strengths do not create value for those you lead. In college, I majored in English. I developed a knack for reading novels. I could read two or three novels a week and found this easy, energizing and enjoyable. But what I have since found is that few people care about my strength of reading novels. What they really care about is my ability to analyze a situation in ways that help them reach their goals. Reading and interpreting good writing is a sustainable strength when it informs my ability to diagnose and help others work through their problems.

According to a recent movie, *The Bucket List* the Egyptians believed that the gatekeepers of heaven ask new arrivals two questions about their lives on earth: Did you find joy? Did you bring joy to others? The first question is about building on your strengths to find joy. It is necessary, but not sufficient. It is about the self, not others. The second question shifts the focus of joy to helping others find it. Put in terms of our strengths discussion, this means that we should build on our strengths that strengthen others.

Leaders may strive to acquire strengths of authenticity, judgment, emotional intelligence, credibility and other noble attributes. But unless and until they apply these strengths in ways that create value for others, they have not been totally successful. Some in the strengths movement have missed the conclusion Seligman reached in his 2004 book, *Authentic Happiness*: "The meaningful life: using your signature strengths and virtues in the service of something much larger than you are."

For leaders, this means that it is not enough to do our work well. We must also use our strengths to deliver value to others.

Conclusion

These four takeaways are not dramatic, but they shape how I think about organizations where I consult, work, and learn. They help me know that my personal reputation should be tied to the desired organization reputation. This book offers an architecture to turn these ideas into action.

Dave Ulrich
Professor, University of Michigan
Partner, the RBL Group

APPENDIX A

Personal Ambition, Personal Brand, and Personal Balanced Scorecard Forms

Authentic Personal Branding, pages 227–231

My Personal Ambition

Name: .... Date:

My Personal Vision

....

I want to fulfil my mission in the following way:

- .... (Internal perspective)
- .... (External perspective)
- .... (Knowlegde & learning perspective)
- .... (Financial perspective)

My Personal Mission

....

Key roles

In order to achieve my mission, the following key roles have top priority:

-
-
-

My Personal Brand

My Personal SWOT

My strengths:. . . . .

My weaknesses:. . . . .

Related opportunities: . . . .

Related threats:. . . . .

My Personal Brand Objectives:

- . . . . (Internal perspective)
- . . . . (External perspective)
- . . . . (Knowlegde & learning perspective)
- . . . . (Financial perspective)

My Specialization:. . . . .

My Service:. . . . .

My Dominant Attribute:. . . . .

My Domain:. . . . .

My Personal Brand Statement: . . . .

. . . .

My Personal Brand Story: . . . .

. . . .

My Personal Logo & Slogan:

My Personal Balanced Scorecard

Name: Date:

Internal

Personal Critical Success Factors	Personal Objectives	Personal Performance Measures	Personal Targets	Personal Improvement Actions	Progress	
					In Progress	Reached my Target

External

Personal Critical Success Factors	Personal Objectives	Personal Performance Measures	Personal Targets	Personal Improvement Actions	Progress	
					In Progress	Reached my Target

Knowledge & learning						
					Progress	
Personal Critical Success Factors	Personal Objectives	Personal Performance Measures	Personal Targets	Personal Improvement Actions	In Progress	Reached my Target

Financial						
					Progress	
Personal Critical Success Factors	Personal Objectives	Personal Performance Measures	Personal Targets	Personal Improvement Actions	In Progress	Reached my Target

APPENDIX B

Authentic Personal Brand Coaching Framework and the Certified Personal Brand Coach (CPBC) Certification Program

In this appendix, I introduce the Personal Branding Coaching framework and our related certification program, which is meant to be helpful for coaching you and others to build, implement, maintain, and cultivate an authentic, distinctive, relevant, consistent, concise, meaningful, crystal clear, and memorable Personal Brand, which is in harmony with your Personal Ambition and Personal Balanced Scorecard.

Authentic Personal Brand Coaching Framework

Personal Brand Coaching is based on a fifteen step framework, described in this book, see boxed text below. The emphasis here is on building, implementing, maintaining, and cultivating an authentic Personal Brand, which is in line with your Personal Ambition and Personal Balanced

Authentic Personal Branding, pages 233–249

Scorecard. The Personal Brand Coaching process involves fifteen phases with comprehensive exercises, tools, and activities associated with each phase to be used by Personal Brand coaches to coach others. The related Personal BrandSoft, described in Appendix C, will assist you to execute this process efficiently.

AUTHENTIC PERSONAL BRAND COACHING FRAMEWORK

Fifteen Steps in the Authentic Personal Brand Coaching Process

1. Look for a quiet spot and perform the breathing and silence exercise to reflect on the Personal Ambition questions. This will create an atmosphere of silence to think about yourself and to listen to your inner voice.
2. Formulate your Personal Ambition statement (personal vision, mission, and key roles). Make sure that all four perspectives (internal, external, knowledge/learning, and financial) are included. Private life and business life should be taken into account.
3. Define your strengths and weaknesses and the related external opportunities and threats, based on your personal SWOT analysis. Evaluate yourself.
4. Formulate your Personal Brand Objectives based on the SWOT analysis, related to the four BSC-perspectives.
5. Define your Specialization, Service, and Dominant Attribute.
6. Define your Domain.
7. Formulate your Personal Brand Statement.
8. Create your Personal Brand Story.
9. Design your Personal Logo & Slogan.
10. Formulate your PBSC by identifying and selecting the critical success factors within your Personal Ambition and Personal Brand statement and translate these into personal objectives with corresponding measures, targets, and improvement actions.
11. Implement your Personal Ambition, Personal Brand and PBSC according to the Plan-Deploy-Act-Challenge cycle. Get going with the continuous improvement actions with dedication and resolution and ask for feedback.
12. Learn how to cultivate and maintain your brand promise.
13. Live up to your brand promise by aligning your Personal Ambition and Personal Brand with your behavior (alignment with yourself).

14. Align your Personal Ambition/Brand with the Company Ambition/Brand, through the ambition meeting (alignment with your company).
15. Coach the manager how to coach his/her employees and to perform the ambition meeting effectively.

Become a Certified Personal Brand Coach

You can become a Certified Personal Brand Coach (CPBC) by attending the Certification Program at the Personal Branding University™. The CPBC Certification Program will make you far more effective as a Personal Brand coach and facilitator in this new and growing personal branding field, and gives you the prestige and credibility of a Personal Branding University™ endorsed certification. Here's what you'll focus on during the intensive 3-day Personal Brand Coaching workshop.

THREE-DAY WORKSHOP AUTHENTIC PERSONAL BRANDING

Day One	**Personal Ambition**
08:30–09:15	Personal Branding Code of Ethics and ICF Core Competencies
09:15–10:00	Authentic Personal Branding Model
10:00–10:30	The Personal Ambition Framework; vision, mission, key roles, and values
10:30–10:45	Coffee break
10:45–11:15	Perform the silence & breathing exercise for self-awareness
11:15–12:30	Defining and formulating your personal vision Providing individual coaching
12:30–13:30	Lunch
13:30–14:30	Defining and formulating your personal mission Providing individual coaching
15:00–15:15	Coffee Break
15:15–16:00	Defining and formulating your personal key roles roviding individual coaching
16:00–16:30	Visualizing your Personal Ambition
16:30–17:00	How to develop Personal Integrity by aligning your Personal Ambition and your behavior (alignment with yourself)

Day Two	**Personal Branding**
08:30–09:30	The Personal Branding Framework
09:30–10:30	Executing your personal SWOT analysis Providing individual coaching
10:30–10:45	Coffee Break
10:45–12:30	Defining your brand objectives, specialization, service, dominant attribute, and domain Providing individual coaching
12:30–13:30	Lunch
13:30–15:00	Formulating your Personal Brand statement/Unique Value Proposition Providing individual coaching
15:00–15:15	Coffee Break
15:15–16:00	Defining your Personal Brand story/Elevator Pitch Providing individual coaching
16:00–17:00	Designing your slogan and logo Providing individual coaching
Day Three	**Personal Balanced Scorecard**
08:30–09:30	The Personal Balanced Scorecard Framework
09:30–10:30	Defining your personal critical success factors Providing individual coaching
10:30–10:45	Coffee Break
10:45–12:30	Formulating your personal objectives Providing individual coaching
12:30–13:30	Lunch
13:30–14:30	Formulating your personal measures, targets, and improvement actions How to Use the PBSC to Create Work-Life Balance Providing individual coaching
14:30–15:00	How to implement your personal ambition, personal brand, and personal balanced scorecard effectively, according to the Plan, Deploy, Act, Challenge Cycle Providing individual coaching
15:00–15:15	Coffee Break
15:15–15:45	How to Improve Employee Engagement, by aligning Personal Ambition/Brand and Company Ambition/Brand (alignment with your company)
15:45–16:30	Coaching you to perform the ambition meeting successfully and to stimulate mutual trust
16:15–17:00	How to use the Personal BrandSoft to coach yourself and others effectively

Day one and Day three of this workshop entail the "Personal Balance Scorecard (PBSC): Linking Human Capital to Business Success" seminar which has Approved CCEU Status and has been awarded continuing coaching education approval by the International Coach Federation (ICF) in the following continuing education categories:

- 2.75 hours: ICF Core Competencies
- 1 hour: Personal Development of the Coach
- 0.5 hour: Development of Coaching Practice
- 3.25 hours: Other Skills and Tools Directly Applicable to Coaching

Who Should Attend?

This program is appropriate for coaches and other professionals responsible for life and executive coaching in both public and private organizations. It is geared towards:

- Executive & Life Coaches.
- Individuals who provide coaching within a work environment.
- Individuals who assist executives and teams implement organizational change.
- Executives and managers.
- Senior business consultants.
- Anyone who wishes to excel, to be successful in life, to develop their personal brand, personal leadership, deliver peak performance, enhance employee engagement, and enhance sustainable personal and organizational effectiveness.

Program Benefits

Personal Branding University™ recognizes practitioners who have demonstrated proficiency in using its authentic Personal Branding system in ways that are in keeping with the Personal Branding Code of Ethics. The CPBC designation is an indication that you have met the standards of our Personal Branding system as evidenced by your past work, knowledge, and Personal Brand coaching skills. It shows that you have demonstrated proficiency in the authentic Personal Branding profession. Participants who receive the CPBC designation must be re-certified every year to maintain the credential. Once you achieve the Personal Brand Coach certification your name will be listed on a registry that is available to potential clients and employers, you will be listed on the Personal Branding University™ website, and you may display the CPBC designation on your business cards, stationary, and marketing materials. You will also get the ability to set up a successful Personal Brand Coaching practice, networking opportunities with TPS International coaches from all over the world and the ability to conduct Personal Brand Coaching sessions in an international environment.

You Will Learn How To:

- Build, implement, maintain, and cultivate an authentic, distinctive, relevant, consistent, concise, meaningful, exciting, inspiring, compelling, enduring, crystal clear, persuasive and memorable Personal Brand.
- Coach others to do the same.
- Coach and facilitate improved behavior in others in a holistic way.
- Enhance your effectiveness as a coach and the effectiveness of your clients.
- Evaluate and attain your full potential and the potential of your clients.
- Coach your clients to utilize their talents effectively.
- Develop employee engagement.
- Create work-life balance.
- Bring about the best fit between employee's and company's ambition and brand, and create lasting conditions for self-guidance, commitment, passion, and happiness.

What Are the Requirements for Personal Brand Coach Certification?

The eligibility requirements to apply through the regular certification process include:

- at least two years experience as coach, consultant or trainer.
- completion of the 3-day Personal Brand Coaching workshop.
- 4 hours individual coaching to help you finalize and implement your Personal Ambition, Personal Brand and PBSC, after completion of the workshop. Participants will also talk with their instructors by phone as the coaching experience unfolds.
- a detailed description of Personal Brand coaching with at least two clients for a total of 10 hours, performed in a manner that demonstrates the use of the Personal Brand Coaching Framework with attestations from clients.

How Will Proficiency Be Assessed?

An applicant's proficiency will be assessed through a combination of a description of education, experience, testimonials by clients or employers, and a review of documents by qualified reviewers. Reviewers will be professionals from TPS International who have received training and guidelines for doing the review. The Certified Personal Brand Coach (CPBC) Certification has a validity of one calendar year and can be extended based on the results of an annual audit conducted by the local TPS International office.

PERSONAL BRANDING CODE OF ETHICS

The Personal Branding Code of Ethics is intended to promote ethical practice in the profession of authentic Personal Branding. The objective is to provide personal branding coaches with the skills, knowledge, abilities, and attitude necessary to create opportunities for achieving desired and required individual, organizational, and societal results.

The Personal Branding Code of Ethics is based on the following six principles:

1. Add Value
2. Validated Practice
3. Collaboration
4. Continuous Improvement
5. Integrity
6. Uphold Confidentiality

1. Add Value

Conduct yourself, and manage your coaching practice, in ways that add value for your clients, their customers, and the global environment.

Guidelines

- Achieve useful results that can be aligned with the Personal Brand.
- Recognize clients' training needs and address them.
- Set clear expectations about the systematic Personal Branding process you will follow and about the expected outcomes.
- Add value by serving your clients with integrity, competence, and objectivity as you apply the Personal Branding system.
- Respect and contribute to the legitimate and ethical objectives of the customer.
- Help the customer move to where it needs to be in the future.

2. Validated Practice

Make use of validated practices in Personal Branding strategies and standards.

Guidelines

- Deliver Personal Branding methods, and procedures that have positive value and worth.
- Promote good Personal Branding practices by utilizing positive reinforcement.
- Clarify personal goals and desired accomplishments.
- Detect and analyze opportunities to improve personal performance.
- Objectively evaluate the impact of interventions.

3. Collaboration

Work collaboratively with clients, functioning as a trustworthy strategic partner.

Guidelines

- Listen to the client's ideas, work closely and productively together, and build mutual trust and respect.
- Get information from your clients without making that person feel as if he or she is being interrogated.
- Integrate the client's needs, constraints, and concerns when coaching and facilitating them.
- Meet the interests of all parties involved in the Personal Brand coaching engagement, so there is a win-win outcome.
- Anticipate the client's issues; demonstrate empathy for their concerns and issues.

4. Continuous Improvement

Continually improve your proficiency in the field of authentic Personal Branding.

Guidelines

- Improve and monitor your actions and thinking continuously, make personal improvement a routine and your way of life based on the Plan-Deploy-Act-Challenge Cycle.

- Make time in your schedule to improve yourself and recognize your responsibility to improve continuously.
- Evaluate your skills and knowledge of authentic Personal Branding on a regular basis.
- Investigate new coaching methods, concepts, tools, strategies, and technologies that may be beneficial to your client.
- Ask your clients how you can improve the effectiveness of your coaching services.

5. Integrity

Be honest and truthful in representations to your client, colleagues, and others with whom you may come in contact while practicing Authentic Personal Brand Coaching. You have the moral duty to help and protect them.

Guidelines

Acknowledge any factors that may compromise your objectivity.

- Accept only coaching engagements for which you are qualified by experience and competence.
- Exhibit the highest level of professional objectivity in gathering, evaluating, and communicating information or the results achieved.
- Let clients know when you believe they are going in the wrong direction.
- Give honest feedback to your clients.
- Do not use information for any personal gain that would be contrary to ethical objectives of the client.
- Take responsibility and/or credit only for the portion of results that are clearly linked to your efforts.

6. Uphold Confidentiality

Maintain client confidentiality, not allowing for any conflict of interest that would benefit yourself or others.

Guidelines

- Respect the intellectual property of clients and others.
- Respect and value the ownership of information received.
- Do not disclose information without appropriate authority.

This Certified Personal Brand Coach (CPBC) Certification Program is Directly in Line with the Eleven ICF Coaching Core Competencies

ICF has developed eleven core coaching competencies to support greater understanding about the skills and approaches used within today's coaching profession. They will also support you in calibrating the level of alignment between the coach-specific training expected and the training you have experienced. The CPBC certification program is directly in line with these competencies. Each competency listed below has a definition and related behaviors. Behaviors are classified as either those that should always be present and visible in any coaching interaction (in regular font), or those that are called for in certain coaching situations and, therefore, not always visible in any one coaching interaction.

A. Setting the Foundation

1. **Meeting Ethical Guidelines and Professional Standards**—Understanding of coaching ethics and standards and ability to apply them appropriately in all coaching situations
   a. *Understands and exhibits in own behaviors the ICF Standards of Conduct,*
   b. *Understands and follows all ICF Ethical Guidelines,*
   c. *Clearly communicates the distinctions between coaching, consulting, psychotherapy and other support professions,*
   d. *Refers client to another support professional as needed, knowing when this is needed and the available resources.*
2. **Establishing the Coaching Agreement**—Ability to understand what is required in the specific coaching interaction and to come to agreement with the prospective and new client about the coaching process and relationship
   a. *Understands and effectively discusses with the client the guidelines and specific parameters of the coaching relationship,*
   b. *Reaches agreement about what is appropriate in the relationship and what is not, what is and is not being offered, and about the client's and coach's responsibilities,*
   c. *Determines whether there is an effective match between his/her coaching method and the needs of the prospective client.*

B. Co-Creating the Relationship

3. **Establishing Trust and Intimacy with the Client—**Ability to create a safe, supportive environment that produces ongoing mutual respect and trust
   a. Shows genuine concern for the client's welfare and future,
   b. Continuously demonstrates personal integrity, honesty and sincerity,
   c. Establishes clear agreements and keeps promises,
   d. Demonstrates respect for client's perceptions, learning style, personal being,
   e. Provides ongoing support for and champions new behaviors and actions, including those involving risk taking and fear of failure,
   f. *Asks permission to coach client in sensitive, new areas.*
4. **Coaching Presence—**Ability to be fully conscious and create spontaneous relationship with the client, employing a style that is open, flexible and confident
   a. Is present and flexible during the coaching process,
   b. Accesses own intuition and trusts one's inner knowing–"goes with the gut",
   c. Is open to not knowing and takes risks,
   d. Sees many ways to work with the client, and chooses in the moment what is most effective,
   e. Uses humor effectively to create lightness and energy,
   f. *Confidently shifts perspectives and experiments with new possibilities for own action,*
   g. *Demonstrates confidence in working with strong emotions, and can self-manage and not be overpowered or enmeshed by client's emotions.*

C. Communicating Effectively

5. **Active Listening—**Ability to focus completely on what the client is saying and is not saying, to understand the meaning of what is said in the context of the client's desires, and to support client self-expression
   a. Attends to the client and the client's agenda, and not to the coach's agenda for the client,
   b. Hears the client's concerns, goals, values and beliefs about what is and is not possible,
   c. Distinguishes between the words, the tone of voice, and the body language,

d. Summarizes, paraphrases, reiterates, mirrors back what client has said to ensure clarity and understanding,
e. Encourages, accepts, explores and reinforces the client's expression of feelings, perceptions, concerns, beliefs, suggestions, etc.,
f. Integrates and builds on client's ideas and suggestions,
g. *"Bottom-lines" or understands the essence of the client's communication and helps the client get there rather than engaging in long descriptive stories,*
h. *Allows the client to vent or "clear" the situation without judgment or attachment in order to move on to next steps.*

6. **Powerful Questioning**—Ability to ask questions that reveal the information needed for maximum benefit to the coaching relationship and the client
   a. Asks questions that reflect active listening and an understanding of the client's perspective,
   b. Asks questions that evoke discovery, insight, commitment or action (e.g., those that challenge the client's assumptions),
   c. Asks open-ended questions that create greater clarity, possibility or new learning,
   d. Asks questions that move the client towards what they desire, not questions that ask for the client to justify or look backwards.
7. **Direct Communication**—Ability to communicate effectively during coaching sessions, and to use language that has the greatest positive impact on the client
   a. Is clear, articulate and direct in sharing and providing feedback,
   b. Reframes and articulates to help the client understand from another perspective what he/she wants or is uncertain about,
   c. Clearly states coaching objectives, meeting agenda, purpose of techniques or exercises,
   d. Uses language appropriate and respectful to the client (e.g., non-sexist, non-racist, non-technical, non-jargon),
   e. *Uses metaphor and analogy to help to illustrate a point or paint a verbal picture.*

D. Facilitating Learning and Results

8. **Creating Awareness**—Ability to integrate and accurately evaluate multiple sources of information, and to make interpretations that help the client to gain awareness and thereby achieve agreed-upon results
   a. Goes beyond what is said in assessing client's concerns, not getting hooked by the client's description,
   b. Invokes inquiry for greater understanding, awareness and clarity,

c. Identifies for the client his/her underlying concerns, typical and fixed ways of perceiving himself/herself and the world, differences between the facts and the interpretation, disparities between thoughts, feelings and action,
d. Helps clients to discover for themselves the new thoughts, beliefs, perceptions, emotions, moods, etc. that strengthen their ability to take action and achieve what is important to them,
e. Communicates broader perspectives to clients and inspires commitment to shift their viewpoints and find new possibilities for action,
f. Helps clients to see the different, interrelated factors that affect them and their behaviors (e.g., thoughts, emotions, body, background),
g. Expresses insights to clients in ways that are useful and meaningful for the client,
h. *Identifies major strengths vs. major areas for learning and growth, and what is most important to address during coaching,*
i. *Asks the client to distinguish between trivial and significant issues, situational vs. recurring behaviors, when detecting a separation between what is being stated and what is being done.*

9. **Designing Actions**—Ability to create with the client opportunities for ongoing learning, during coaching and in work/life situations, and for taking new actions that will most effectively lead to agreed-upon coaching results
   a. Brainstorms and assists the client to define actions that will enable the client to demonstrate, practice and deepen new learning,
   b. Helps the client to focus on and systematically explore specific concerns and opportunities that are central to agreed-upon coaching goals,
   c. Engages the client to explore alternative ideas and solutions, to evaluate options, and to make related decisions,
   d. Promotes active experimentation and self-discovery, where the client applies what has been discussed and learned during sessions immediately afterwards in his/her work or life setting,
   e Celebrates client successes and capabilities for future growth,
   f. Challenges client's assumptions and perspectives to provoke new ideas and find new possibilities for action,
   g. *Advocates or brings forward points of view that are aligned with client goals and, without attachment, engages the client to consider them,*
   h. *Helps the client "Do It Now" during the coaching session, providing immediate support,*
   i. *Encourages stretches and challenges but also a comfortable pace of learning.*

10. **Planning and Goal Setting**—Ability to develop and maintain an effective coaching plan with the client
    a. Consolidates collected information and establishes a coaching plan and development goals with the client that address concerns and major areas for learning and development,
    b. Creates a plan with results that are attainable, measurable, specific and have target dates,
    c. Makes plan adjustments as warranted by the coaching process and by changes in the situation,
    d. *Helps the client identify and access different resources for learning (e.g., books, other professionals),*
    e. *Identifies and targets early successes that are important to the client.*
11. **Managing Progress and Accountability**—Ability to hold attention on what is important for the client, and to leave responsibility with the client to take action
    a. Clearly requests of the client actions that will move the client toward their stated goals,
    b. Demonstrates follow through by asking the client about those actions that the client committed to during the previous session(s),
    c. Acknowledges the client for what they have done, not done, learned or become aware of since the previous coaching session(s),
    d. Effectively prepares, organizes and reviews with client information obtained during sessions,
    e. *Keeps the client on track between sessions by holding attention on the coaching plan and outcomes, agreed-upon courses of action, and topics for future session(s),*
    f. *Focuses on the coaching plan but is also open to adjusting behaviors and actions based on the coaching process and shifts in direction during sessions,*
    g. *Is able to move back and forth between the big picture of where the client is heading, setting a context for what is being discussed and where the client wishes to go,*
    h. *Promotes client's self-discipline and holds the client accountable for what they say they are going to do, for the results of an intended action, or for a specific plan with related time frames,*
    i. *Develops the client's ability to make decisions, address key concerns, and develop himself/herself (to get feedback, to determine priorities and set the pace of learning, to reflect on and learn from experiences),*
    j. *Positively confronts the client with the fact that he/she did not take agreed-upon actions.*

Do You Need Additional Information?

If you are interested in learning more about our Certified Personal Brand Coach (CPBC) Program, call or write us for information on our local office closest to you.

Personal Branding University
P.O. Box 601564
North Miami Beach
Florida 33160, USA
Phone: +1-786-537-7580
Fax: +1-714-464-4498
h.rampersad@tps-international.com
www.pbuniversity.wordpress.com
www.personalbrandinguniversity.org

Personal Brand Coaching Track—What You Get

Personal Branding workshop	Certified Personal Brand Coach Certification	Re-certification
Three day Personal Branding workshop	4 hours individual coaching to help you finalize and implement your Personal Brand and support as the coaching experience unfolds	1 hour feedback with a Master Certified Personal Brand Coach on renewing your CPBC designation
A signed copy of the related coaching book, *Authentic Personal Branding: A New Blueprint for Building and Aligning a Powerful Leadership Brand* is included with the training fee.	Certified Personal Brand Coach (CPBC) designation	Updated CPBC designation
Workshop certificate of attendance, certified by the International Coaching Federation (ICF)	A one hour private meeting to introduce the Personal BrandSoftware	Every year anniversary, eligible for $1,000 award drawing from TPS International
Workshop "Personal Balance Scorecard (PBSC): Linking Human Capital to Business Success" has Approved CCEU Status and has been awarded continuing coaching education approval by the International Coach Federation (ICF) in the following continuing education categories: 2.75 hours: ICF Core Competencies 1 hour: Personal Development of the Coach 0.5 hour: Development of Coaching Practice 3.25 hours: Other Skills and Tools Directly Applicable to Coaching	1 Complete Personal Branding Training Packet at 15% off	All updated training materials available at 20% off

Personal BrandSoft at 10% off	Personal BrandSoft at 15% off
10% discount for purchases of any signed copy of the related coaching book, *Authentic Personal Branding: A New Blueprint for Building and Aligning a Powerful Leadership Brand*	15% discount for purchases of any signed copy of the related coaching book, *Authentic Personal Branding: A New Blueprint for Building and Aligning a Powerful Leadership Brand*
Once you achieve the CPBC designation your name will be listed on a registry that is available to potential clients and employers, you will be listed on www.total-performance-scorecard.com, and you may display the CPBC designation on your business cards, stationary, and marketing materials	Your name will be listed on www.total-performance-scorecard.com, and you may display the CPBC designation on your businesscards, stationary, and marketing materials
Networking opportunities with Personal Branding coaches from 100 countries and the ability to conduct authentic Personal Branding coaching sessions in an international environment	Networking opportunities with Personal Branding coaches from 100 countries and the ability to conduct authentic Personal Branding coaching sessions in an international environment.
A detailed description of Personal Branding coaching with at least two clients for a total of 10 hours, performed in a manner that demonstrates the use of the authentic Personal Branding principles with attestations from clients	

APPENDIX C

Personal BrandSoft

Personal BrandSoft is an on-line and interactive software system that will assist you with the formulation, implementation, and cultivation of your Personal Brand. It offers you the possibility to effectively build a sustainable, powerful, authentic, consistent, and memorable Personal Brand and manage and steer yourself on performance. This software system consists of the complete Personal Branding framework and the related tools discussed in this book, including measuring the progress of your brand implementation, a dashboard, alignment with yourself, alignment with your company, and Personal Branding Coaching (see Figure C.1).

The first step in this brand building process is the creation of your profile. Subsequently you formulate from every perspective, your Personal Ambition, Personal Brand, and Personal Balanced Scorecard. Options are available to make use of a predefined set of data or numerous examples in the system. Doing this, and using this possibility, you will obtain an improved understanding of yourself and have the opportunity to manage and coach yourself in an effective way. The status and progress of your improvement actions is made visible through indicators and a dashboard at

Authentic Personal Branding, pages 251–253

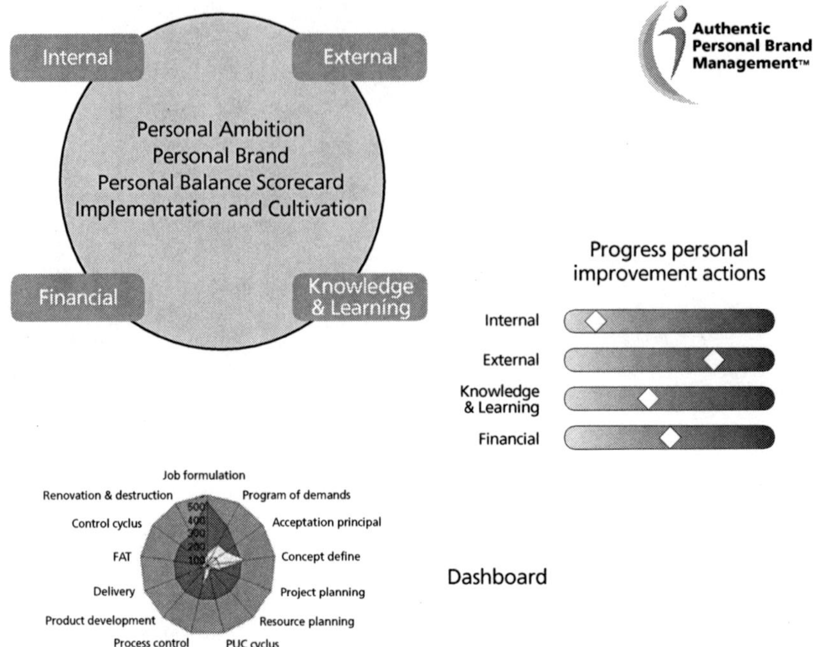

Figure C.1

any given moment. You have also the possibility to authorize others to get feedback on your actions and behaviour at any moment. Targets that have been achieved and challenges that have been taken up can also be brought up-to-date immediately.

The Personal Branding Code of Ethics is being applied here; this implies that the system respects your privacy and that no personal information can be shared with unauthorized people. Another benefit of the system is that you can benchmark yourself against any other person with the same profile. The database also contains demographic data so that the possibility exists to compare with other like-minded individuals. The system is connected to a knowledge database that gives feedback and advice to further improve oneself.

Do You Need Additional Information?

If you are interested in learning more about our Personal BrandSoft, call or write us for information on our local office closest to you.

TPS International Inc.
P.O. Box 601564
North Miami Beach
Florida 33160, USA
Phone: +1-786-537-7580
Fax: +1-714-464-4498
info@total-performance-scorecard.com
www.Total-Performance-Scorecard.com

Personal BrandingSoft
P.O. Box 601564
North Miami Beach
Florida 33160, USA
Phone: +1-786-537-7580
Fax: +1-714-464-4498
h.rampersad@tps-international.com
Info@personalbrandingsoft.com
www.personalbrandingsoft.com
www.total-performance-scorecard.com

APPENDIX D

Strategy Management System

Authentic Personal Branding, pages 255–257

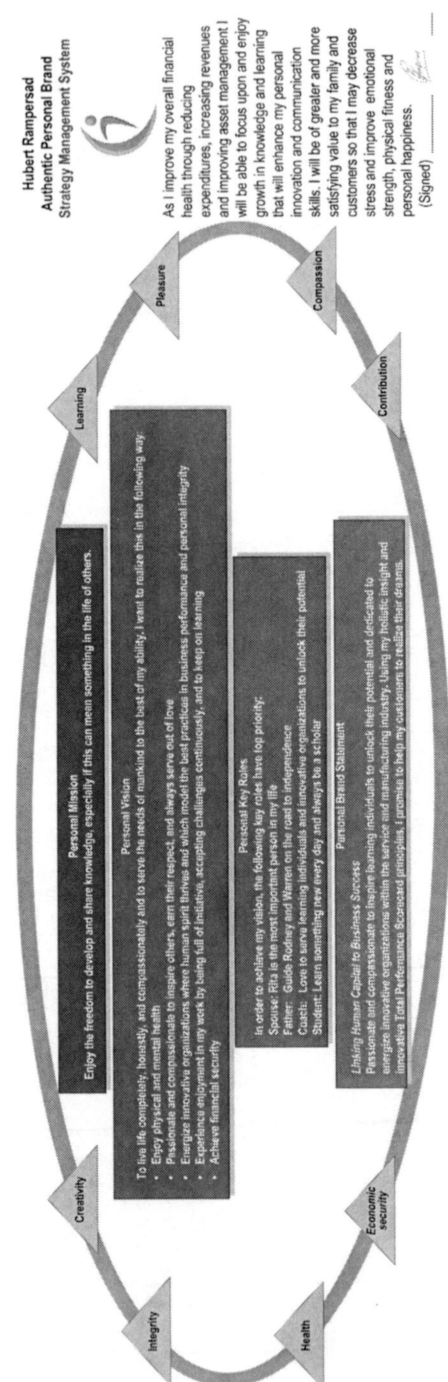
Personal Mission
Enjoy the freedom to develop and share knowledge, especially if this can mean something in the life of others.
Personal Vision
To live life completely, honestly, and compassionately and to serve the needs of mankind to the best of my ability. I want to realize this in the following way:
• Enjoy physical and mental health
• Passionate and compassionate to inspire others, earn their respect, and always serve out of love
• Energize innovative organizations where human spirit thrives and which model the best practices in business performance and personal integrity
• Experience enjoyment in my work by being full of initiative, accepting challenges continuously, and to keep on learning
• Achieve financial security
Personal Key Roles
In order to achieve my vision, the following key roles have top priority:
Spouse: Rita is the most important person in my life
Father: Guide Rodney and Warren on the road to independence
Coach: Love to serve learning individuals and innovative organizations to unlock their potential
Student: Learn something new every day and always be a scholar
Personal Brand Statement
Linking Human Capital to Business Success
Passionate and compassionate to inspire learning individuals to unlock their potential and dedicated to energize innovative organizations within the service and manufacturing industry. Using my holistic insight and innovative Total Performance Scorecard principles, I promise to help my customers to realize their dreams.
Creativity
Integrity
Health
Economic security
Learning
Pleasure
Compassion
Contribution
Hubert Rampersad
Authentic Personal Brand
Strategy Management System
As I improve my overall financial health through reducing expenditures, increasing revenues and improving asset management I will be able to focus upon and enjoy growth in knowledge and learning that will enhance my personal innovation and communication skills. I will be of greater and more satisfying value to my family and customers so that I may decrease stress and improve emotional strength, physical fitness and personal happiness.
(Signed)

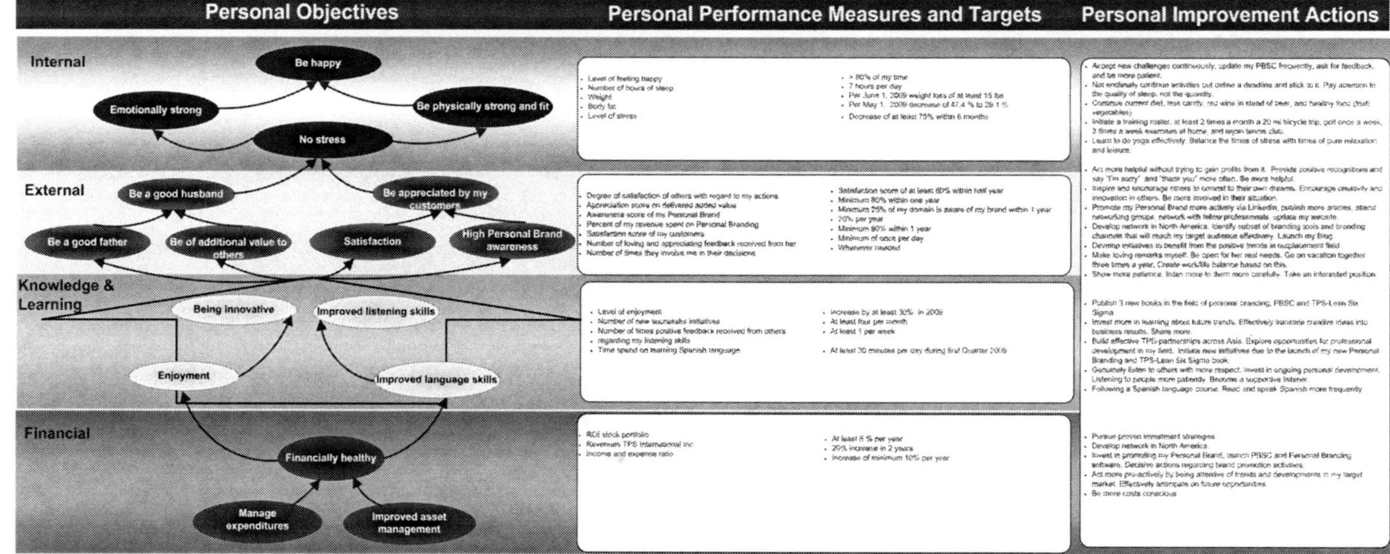
Personal Objectives
Personal Performance Measures and Targets
Personal Improvement Actions
Internal
Be happy
Emotionally strong
Be physically strong and fit
No stress
Level of feeling happy
Number of hours of sleep
Weight
Body fat
Level of stress
> 80% of my time
7 hours per day
Per June 1, 2009 weight loss of at least 15 lbs
Per May 1, 2009 decrease of 47.4 % to 29.1 %
Decrease of at least 75% within 6 months
Accept new challenges continuously, update my PBSC frequently, ask for feedback, and be more patient.
Not endlessly continue activities but define a deadline and stick to it. Pay attention to the quality of sleep, not the quantity.
Continue current diet, less candy, red wine in stead of beer, and healthy food (fruit/vegetables).
Initiate a training roster, at least 2 times a month a 20 mi bicycle trip, golf once a week, 3 times a week exercises at home, and rejoin tennis club.
Learn to do yoga effectively. Balance the times of stress with times of pure relaxation and leisure.
External
Be a good husband
Be appreciated by my customers
Be a good father
Be of additional value to others
Satisfaction
High Personal Brand awareness
Degree of satisfaction of others with regard to my actions
Appreciation score on delivered added value
Awareness score of my Personal Brand
Percent of my revenue spent on Personal Branding
Satisfaction score of my customers
Number of loving and appreciating feedback received from her
Number of times they involve me in their decisions
Satisfaction score of at least 80% within half year
Minimum 80% within one year
Minimum 25% of my domain is aware of my brand within 1 year
20% per year
Minimum 90% within 1 year
Minimum of once per day
Whenever needed
Act more helpful without trying to gain profits from it. Provide positive recognitions and say "I'm sorry" and "thank you" more often. Be more helpful.
Inspire and encourage others to commit to their own dreams. Encourage creativity and innovation in others. Be more involved in their situation.
Promote my Personal Brand more actively via LinkedIn, publish more articles, attend networking groups, network with fellow professionals, update my website.
Develop network in North America. Identify subset of branding tools and branding channels that will reach my target audience effectively. Launch my Blog.
Develop initiatives to benefit from the positive trends in outplacement field.
Make loving remarks myself. Be open for her real needs. Go on vacation together three times a year. Create work/life balance based on this.
Show more patience, listen more to them more carefully. Take an interested position.
Knowledge & Learning
Being innovative
Improved listening skills
Enjoyment
Improved language skills
Level of enjoyment
Number of new successful initiatives
Number of times positive feedback received from others regarding my listening skills
Time spend on learning Spanish language
Increase by at least 30% in 2009
At least four per month
At least 1 per week
At least 30 minutes per day during first Quarter 2009
Publish 3 new books in the field of personal branding, PBSC and TPS-Lean Six Sigma
Invest more in learning about future trends. Effectively translate creative ideas into business results. Share more.
Build effective TPS-partnerships across Asia. Explore opportunities for professional development in my field. Initiate new initiatives due to the launch of my new Personal Branding and TPS-Lean Six Sigma book.
Genuinely listen to others with more respect. Invest in ongoing personal development. Listening to people more patiently. Become a supportive listener.
Following a Spanish language course. Read and speak Spanish more frequently.
Financial
Financially healthy
Manage expenditures
Improved asset management
ROI stock portfolio
Revenues TPS International inc
Income and expense ratio
At least 8 % per year
20% increase in 2 years
Increase of minimum 10% per year
Pursue proven investment strategies
Develop network in North America.
Invest in promoting my Personal Brand, launch PBSC and Personal Branding software. Decisive actions regarding brand promotion activities.
Act more pro-actively by being attentive of trends and developments in my target market. Effectively anticipate on future opportunities.
Be more costs conscious

References and Recommended Reading

Agor, W., *Management by Consciousness* (edited by G. P. Gupta), Sri Aurobindo Institute of Research in Social Sciences, Pondicherry, India, 1998.

Arruda, W. and Dixson, K., *Career Distinction: Stand Out by Building Your Brand,* John Wiley, New York, June 2007.

Byrne, R., *The Secret.* Hillsboro, OR: Beyond Words, 2006.

Chatterejee, D., *Light the Fire in Your Heart.* New Delhi: Full Circle Publishing, 2002.

Chopra Deepak, *The Seven Spiritual Laws of Success,* Amber-Allen Publishing, San Francisco, 1995.

Covey, S.R., *The Seven Habits of Highly Effective People,* Simon & Schuster, New York, 1993.

Covey, S.R., *The 8th Habit,* Simon & Schuster, New York, 2004.

Csikszentmihalyi, Mihaly, *Flow: The Psychology of Optimal Experience,* Harper Collins Publishers, New York, 1990.

Dolan, S.L., *Stress, Self-esteem, Health, and Work,* Palgrave Macmillan, 2007.

Frost, R., Me Incorporated, http://www.brandchannel.com/, August 4, 2003

Gad, T., 4D Branding, Financial Times-Prentice Hall/Bookhouse, London/Stockholm, 2001.

Goldsmith, M. and Reiter, M., *What Got You Here Won't Get You There,* Hyperion, 2007.

Guarneri, S., *Personal Branding Revelations on Ethics,* New York.

Handy, C., *Understanding Voluntary Organizations,* Hammersworth, UK: Penguin Books, 1988.

Hansen, R.S. and Hansen, K., *Using a SWOT Analysis in Your Career Planning,* http://www.quintcareers.com/, 2007.

Authentic Personal Branding, pages 259–257

Hansen, K., *Tell Me About Yourself: Storytelling that Propels Careers*, Union Institute & University, 2007.

Jacobs, G., *Management by Consciousness* (edited by G.P. Gupta), Sri Aurobindo Institute of Research in Social Sciences, Pondicherry, India, 1998.

Kaplan, R.S. and Norton, D.P., *The Strategy-focused Organization: how balanced scorecard companies thrive in the new business environment*, Harvard Business School Press, Boston, 2000.

Kaplan, R.S. and Norton, D.P., *Strategy Maps: Converting Intangible Assets into Tangible Outcomes*, Harvard Business School Press, Boston, 2003.

Krueger Jerry and Emily Killham. At Work, Feeling Good Matters, New York: Gallup Management Journal, December 08, 2005.

Lang B., Developing a personal brand, CareerOne Pty Limited, 2007.

McCraty, R., The Scientific Role of the Heart in Learning and Performance, *HeartMath Research Center, Institute of HeartMath, Publication No. 02-030, Boulder Creek*, CA, 2002.

McANally D. and Speak, K.D., *Be your own Brand, San Francisco: Berrett-Koehler* Publishers, 2003.

Montoya, P. and Vandehey, T., *The Brand Called You*, Personal Branding Press, 2005a.

Montoya, P. and Vandehey, T., *The Personal Branding Phenomenon*, Personal Branding Press, 2005b.

Miller, W.C. and Pruzan, P., *Spiritual-based Leadership: A Matter of Faith and Confidence*, Puttaparthi: Sri Sathya Sai Institute of Higher Learning, 2003.

Peters, T., The Brand Called You, *Fast Company*, 1997.

Rampersad, H.K., *Authentic Personal Branding*, www.brandchannel.com, January 2008.

Rampersad, H.K. and El-Homsi, A., *TPS-Lean Six Sigma; Linking Human Capital to Lean Six Sigma (A New Blueprint for Creating High Performance Companies)*, Information Age Publishing, USA, 2007.

Rampersad, H.K., *The Personal Balanced Scorecard*; The Way to Individual Happiness, Personal Integrity and Organizational Effectiveness, Information Age Publishing, USA, 2006.

Rampersad, H.K., *Total Performance Scorecard; Redefining Management to Achieve Performance with Integrity*, Butterworth-Heinemann Business Books, Elsevier Science, Massachusetts, 2003.

Salary.com, Wasting time at work? You're not alone: survey, Reuters, New York, July 26, 2007.

Setty, R., Professional Branding for Technology Professionals, www.rajeshsetty.com, 2006.

Senge, P.M., *The Fifth Discipline: The Art and Practice of the Learning Organization.* New York: Doubleday, 1990.

Sharma, R.S., *The Top 200 Secrets of Success and the Pillars of Self-Mastery, http://www.robinsharma.com*, 2005.

Sri Sri Ravi Shankar, *Wisdom for the New Millennium,* Art of Living Foundation, Chicago, 1999.

Tabachnick, J., The Advantage of Personal Branding, http://www.webgrrls.com/, 2007.

Ulrich, Dave and Norm Smallwood. *Leadership Brand.* Boston, MA: Harvard Business Press, 2007.

Wise, A., *The High Performance Mind—Mastering Brainwaves for Insight, Healing, and Creativity*, Tarcher Putnam, 1995.